LEADING BEYOND RESUL
STOP MANAGING RESULTS,
START DEVELOPING PERFORMA

MARKUS DRAEGER

Note on gender-inclusive language: The form of gender designation used in this book refers simultaneously to female, male and diverse persons. Multiple designations have been omitted to enhance readability.

German Editing: Carsten Tergast, Timo Görlitz
English Editing: Craig Smith (CRS Editorial)

Cover Image: freepik
Author Portraits: Jasper Graetsch
Typesetting and Design: SWATT Books Ltd

Printing and Processing: Rudolph Druck GmbH & Co. KG, Schweinfurt

First Edition 2025

Bibliographic information from the German National Library
The German National Library records this publication in the German National Bibliography. Detailed bibliographic data accessible online at http://dnb.d-nb.de

ISBN: 978-3-9827856-0-8 (Paperback)
ISBN: 978-3-9827856-1-5 (Hardback)
ISBN: 978-3-9827856-2-2 (eBook)

Beyond Results GmbH
Lise-Meitner-Str. 2; 24941 Flensburg; Germany

beyondresults.de

MARKUS DRAEGER

LEADING BEYOND RESULTS

STOP MANAGING RESULTS
START DEVELOPING PERFORMANCE

Contents

The Game Idea

Inside the Dressing Room

The last rays of the setting sun bathed the training room of handball Bundesliga team SG Flensburg-Handewitt in warm light. A long, gruelling session was drawing to a close – a session that tested not the bodies but the minds of 'athletes' to their limits. However, instead of the smell of sweat, there was the aroma of pizza in the dressing room.

Next to two professional players were entrepreneurs, executives and scientists. Several times a year, the so-called 'Success Team' convenes experts from sport, business and science for an exchange of ideas. This event, which long since attained cult status, fosters in-depth discussions where opposing viewpoints are not only tolerated but explicitly welcomed.

We, the 'Success Team', refer to this format as 'inside the dressing room'.

Participants sit where professionals typically complete their strength training – on uncomfortable dressing-room chairs or weight benches – to sometimes reveal uncomfortable truths. The golden rule: What is discussed in the dressing room remains in the dressing room – just as it should. However, I will make an exception here.

We had already conducted several of these 'inside the dressing room' sessions, and each time the participants had been surprised by how much sport could learn from business, and vice versa. Particularly striking were the scientific findings that the business world had successfully ignored for decades. This summer evening stayed with me for some time and ultimately served as the catalyst for this book.

I was asked that evening what I thought the greatest differences were between the performance culture in sport and in business. My response surprised some participants – it was neither scientifically substantiated nor diplomatically expressed.

"I have the impression that many companies do not truly understand what performance is – let alone explain the difference between performance and results," I remarked. "While sustainably successful clubs operate in a performance-oriented manner, many companies tend to be result-driven. They do not focus on performance itself but pursue their targets without questioning the path to achieve them."

"But results are the very reason for our existence, aren't they? Isn't it the same in competitive sport?" a participant interjected. The Head of Youth Academy supported my point, noting that although results are important, they are regarded as a consequence of daily work – not as the overriding goal. He reinforced his statement by citing the successes of his young players that followed when the youth performance centre adopted this approach. Not only were more titles won, but a significantly higher number of talents advanced to the professional handball squad.

Jan Holpert, who proudly guarded the goal in 245 international fixtures for the German national handball team, added that performance cannot be 'managed' but must be continuously developed. This prompted a response from a manager from a global corporation, who had long-been perplexed as to why their sophisticated 'Performance

Management System' yielded no results and why they failed to motivate their so-called 'low performers'. The number of absence days per employee had steadily increased over the years.

A discussion took place that captivated all those present, so much so that they lost track of time and departed for home with new insights and inspiration. There was unanimous agreement on one point: outstanding performance, health and sustainability do not exclude one another but are mutually dependent.

In the end, had we discovered new answers? Perhaps a few, but more importantly, the questions we asked ourselves had changed – whether consciously or unconsciously. What does performance truly mean? What constitutes success? How do our goals influence what we ultimately achieve?

An Outdated Success Formula

The discussion left an almost unsettling impression, especially among participants from business. In a world where it seemingly only matters to achieve best times and victories, sport appears to attribute less significance to the outcome than business. In the latter, results are merely the consequence, not the ultimate objective. I am convinced that this very perspective is what makes sports psychology so effective. It assists athletes in concentrating on the critical factors that increase the likelihood of success – while their competitors remain fixated on the scoreboard.

Simultaneously, we realised that outstanding performance, health and sustainability are not mutually exclusive but rather mutually reinforcing. So simple, so evident – yet still far from the success formula that continues to be applied in many companies.

'Success = Talent + Hard Work' – this formula, written on the flipchart by a managing director during our 'inside the dressing room' event, was long regarded by many of us as the truth. However, today it leaves us helpless. It is ironic that this formula is attributed to none other than basketball legend, Michael Jordan.

Times Are Changing

While we continue to rely on this outdated success formula, the context in which it is applied has fundamentally changed. The labour market has undergone significant transformation. We emphasise to our employees that change is the only constant and that they must adapt with flexibility, while many executive teams remain remarkably inflexible – or, as it is now termed, 'resilient'. After each crisis, they revert to their original state. Although short-term measures are implemented to overcome partly self-inflicted crises, the underlying beliefs are seldom questioned or adjusted to new realities.

This is the core issue: These changes are neither temporary phenomena nor the demands of the so-called Generation Z. Instead, they reflect a deeply transforming society that prioritises human needs and values – needs and values that have long-been suppressed across generations.

A closer examination of the equation 'Success = Talent + Hard Work' reveals that not only have the conditions evolved, but the individual components of this formula are undergoing profound change.

With regards to the component 'Talent', while football still experiences an oversupply of talent, the world of business can no longer depend on the traditional 'hire and fire' model. The skilled labour shortage is pervasive, and the willingness to take on leadership responsibility is at an all-time low[1].

This is also connected to the perception of the second component of the success formula, 'Hard Work', which is often equated with endless overtime and personal sacrifices in areas such as family, health or leisure. It is a price that fewer people are willing to pay.

My predecessors, born in the 1970s and 1980s, regarded the executive levels with reverence. They diligently consulted career guides with the aspiration of one day joining the esteemed ranks of leadership. Younger individuals, however, approach these tiers with increasing scepticism. The sacrifices demanded by the traditional career path appear too big, and the cost of the presumed success too high.

Yet, rather than embrace these new values as an opportunity, we scarcely reconsider our working methods. Instead of identifying common ground between generations and using it as a solid foundation, we seek evidence that everything was better in the past. We persist in the belief that no new solutions exist for long-standing problems. The attitude is clear: 'We know how to manage crises. We just have to get through them.'

While some believe that we must work even harder than before to preserve our prosperity and competitiveness, others strive for less work – or perhaps less meaningless work.

How we address this depends on how we define success.

A Revised Definition of Success

This brings us to the third element of the equation: 'Success'.

Like many other concepts, the definition of success has evolved over time. For an increasing number of employees, results, a high salary and rapid career progression are no longer the sole measures of success. Factors such as continuous learning, a work-life balance and the meaningfulness of work have long transitioned from 'nice to have' to essential. These evolving expectations are not limited to younger generations. For those aged 50 and above, time is becoming increasingly more valuable than money – after all, there is progressively less time remaining after a professional career. Meaningful work now outweighs the importance of status and career, and lifelong learning is no longer an unfamiliar concept for many older people.

Today, a smaller proportion of people would consider themselves successful if these elements were disregarded. Nonetheless, it remains essential that companies generate profits to stay competitive and to invest in the future. The definition of success, however, has become more complex – and this is a positive development. Acknowledging this is a crucial step towards achieving sustainable success.

High Performance, Health and Sustainability are Mutually Dependent

The good news is that no one has to forgo high performance within companies. I am a strong advocate of high performance and firmly believe that it is essential to remain competitive in the global market. The new success factors do not conflict with traditional elements, but rather complement them. Holistic performance improvement can – and indeed must – be healthy and sustainable. This is already impressively demonstrated by sports psychology.

When sustainability, health and personal development become central components of our definition of success, increasingly replacing the desire for status and career, we must realign our actions accordingly. When the currency of 'time' is more valuable than 'money', burnout cases are on the rise, and both employee engagement and loyalty are declining, it is time to reconsider whether overtime truly brings us closer to our definition of success. A new approach may be necessary to achieve more with less.

There is a growing concern that performance is no longer recognised as a societal principle. The criticism is that younger generations are neither willing nor able to perform. Some 'experts' forecast the demise of the performance-oriented society.

This does not seem relevant to sport, where we still enjoy high-performing athletes and teams all over the world – spanning genders and age groups.

As humans, we remain fully capable of delivering peak performance – particularly within a team context. While conditions are changing, fundamental human needs remain unchanged. This is the desire to make an impact, to create something worthy of pride; something that is recognised by others. People continue to seek performance that brings joy and unleashes their potential, without burning them out.

Skilled Coaches are Required

It is noteworthy that successful coaches come from all age groups. All generations, from the youngest to the oldest, are represented. What distinguishes these coaches is not their age, but the attitude with which they engage their players and the motivation driving their work. The difference lies in the conditions established and the manner in which the teams are led, coached and supported.

In recent years, we have observed clubs that have operated successfully despite limited resources – and not merely in a single season, but over an extended period. Year after year, they succeed in unlocking the potential of individual players as well as the entire team, achieving maximum results from limited resources. Interestingly, they often do not train *more*, but perhaps differently.

Untapped Potential

Although mental training in sport has gained significance in recent years, it remains far from where it ought to be. It is undisputed that mental strength holds greater importance today than it did ten years ago. Athleticism, technical skills, technique and tactics have almost become hygiene factors, while the small differences between victory and defeat are often decided in the minds of athletes. Ralf Rangnick, visionary and football coach, aptly stated: "The decisive difference lies 'above the shoulders'."

This largely untapped potential is also present in business. Many jobs today require intellectual performance, but this does not necessarily mean that our thinking is purposeful or conducive to success. On the contrary, we observe increased sick leave, rising cases of burnout, declining motivation, and the frequently criticised attitude of Generation Z. In search of solutions, we make immense efforts: restructuring, large-scale employer branding campaigns, seminars on stress management and resilience, as well as the introduction of 'well-being' managers and agile teams. Fruit baskets are provided, table tennis tables installed, incentive packages assembled, and four-day workweeks introduced – all in competition for talent and skilled professionals.

The bad news is that many of these measures remain ineffective as long as fundamental conditions and deeply rooted beliefs are not critically examined.

The good news is that, often, no radical transformation is required – only small adjustments that can yield significant impact, as studies have shown[2].

In pursuit of these small yet impactful changes, I visited locations where conditions for sustainable and healthy performance improvement have already been implemented. I engaged with Olympic champions, world champions, and emerging talents. I met professional coaches, academy directors, athletic coaches, performance coaches and sleep scientists, specialising in team sports such as football, handball, hockey and basketball.

Moreover, I held discussions with my colleagues in sports psychology regarding the success factors that contribute to sustainable performance improvement. What motivates head coaches of youth teams and what profiles do they possess? What environment is necessary to unlock potential at all levels while delivering on promises? What distinguishes long-term successful coaches from their less successful counterparts? What conditions are required for coaches to fully realise their potential? What limitations does sport face, and what may have failed?

These insights led me to question which of these success factors from sport are transferable to the corporate environment. In brief: What can we learn from sport to develop our performance in a sustainable and healthy manner?

The insights of legendary coaches and thought leaders from sport, business and science were influential, as were conversations with CEOs, managing directors, Human Resources (HR) leaders and my colleagues from the field of executive coaching.

Unfortunately, throughout my research and numerous interviews, it became evident that, despite many positive examples, significant issues persist in elite sport. It is therefore all the more remarkable that some coaches and clubs have adopted a healthy and sustainable approach, achieving significant success. When I refer to 'sport' hereafter, I specifically mean the excellent examples that act as role models for businesses. I do not intend to generalise or glorify sport as a whole. There remains considerable work to be done in this area.

Personal Experience

Throughout my professional career, I have witnessed numerous changes – both successful and unsuccessful. I have not only observed these processes but have also actively shaped, supported and led them. At times, I served as a project or team leader; at others, I was a team member, a consultant, or occasionally an observer on the sidelines.

A decisive factor in the success of the change initiatives was the involvement of employees as co-thinkers and co-guides in the process. Whenever I refer to employees in this book, I include these two roles.

This dynamic participation of employees was a central aspect of my leadership experience, contributing significantly to my development as a leader over the years. Leadership philosophies of eight managers have accompanied and shaped me throughout my career. The privilege of learning from these people and their approaches profoundly influenced me and helped refine and strengthen my convictions.

This leads us to the next key term in this book – 'leader'. I have accepted this term, as even artificial intelligence does not provide satisfactory alternatives. I found synonyms such as 'superior' even less suitable. Therefore, this term remains in use, although my understanding of leadership will be thoroughly developed throughout this book.

The Outcome: New Ways of Thinking for Leaders, HR Managers and Entrepreneurs

This book is intended for leaders, HR managers and entrepreneurs, offering them new ways of thinking. It encourages a shift in perspective to examine the challenges of today's world of work through the lens of sport. As I draw on numerous examples from sport, particularly sports psychology, this book may offer greater enjoyment to readers with a sporting interest than to those with no interest in sport. Nonetheless, these readers should by no means feel excluded.

Rather than simply working harder, the book encourages focusing on sustainable and healthy performance development. It provides options for companies considering the implementation of a four-day workweek, seeking to attract both experienced professionals and young employees, and to successfully integrate them.

This book emphasises adhering to the fundamentals rather than pursuing the latest trends. It challenges traditional myths that hinder sustainable and healthy performance improvement. It challenges conservative limiting beliefs that often lead to flawed strategic decisions at the executive level. In this book, you will encounter over 100 cognitive and behavioural patterns that hinder companies from fully realising their potential. In the context of sport, I refer to these as tactical errors.

This book is not a conventional guide offering ready-made solutions. Instead, it seeks to promote new ways of thinking without prescribing universal answers. The objective is to question entrenched limiting beliefs, recognise scientific insights, and cultivate the patience required to develop new mindsets and corresponding behaviour.

I will not engage in superficial discussions about generational conflicts in this book – particularly because many studies on this subject are scientifically questionable. Instead, the essence of this book is grounded in solid commonalities. Naturally, age and life circumstances influence our attitude, but fundamental human needs have remained largely unchanged over centuries. There is scientific consensus that we all stand on a stable foundation of shared human needs.

Furthermore, I employ another unifying element – sport. Only a minority all over the world identify as 'sport-averse'. Sport often serves as an ideal entry point to a new perspective for management teams and leaders; something which may otherwise remain inaccessible due to the demands of daily business.

Regardless of the generation or gender with which you identify, I hope that while reading this book you will experience one or more 'lightbulb moments' – similar to those of the participants in our 'inside the dressing room' events. These moments of reflection and insight are the reason I became a coach and sports psychology expert, and why I wrote this book.

I encourage you to read the book from beginning to end, to fully comprehend the interdependencies of cognitive and behavioural patterns. You are equally free to start from the end and deliberately select from the 100-plus tactical errors where you particularly feel 'exposed'. For this purpose, a list of all tactical errors is provided at the end of the book, along with references to the relevant page numbers.

Limiting Beliefs

Did you know that Sepp Herberger, coach of the West German World Cup-winning football team of 1954, prohibited his players from drinking during the match? Herberger was convinced that drinking during the game diminished performance. This belief persisted among many coaches until the 1970s, when it was finally recognised that the resulting dehydration significantly weakened players. It took some time for this insight to gain acceptance and for a shift in mindset to occur among those responsible. Football has long served as an example of how deeply ingrained beliefs and cognitive biases – such as the perceptual error known as 'social proof' – influence behaviour. This effect, which compels us to act as we always have or because others do so, remains ever-present. 'We have always done it this way' – does that sound familiar?

The premise of this book is that healthy and sustainable performance development transcends generations and can deliver better results with less effort than is commonly assumed. However, to harness this potential, we must identify what has so far prevented us from realising this new definition of success. A crucial step in this process is to critically examine the entrenched limiting beliefs of business executives.

Some of these limiting beliefs resemble Herberger's drinking ban – they are deeply ingrained. Throughout the course of my research, I identified three overarching limiting beliefs, which are based on an outdated definition of success and adhere to obsolete principles.

1. We play solely for the result
"There is only one possibility: victory, draw or defeat," Franz Beckenbauer once stated, succinctly capturing the simplicity of football.

Ultimately, only the result matters in football – goals, goals, and more goals. The aesthetics of the game fade into the background once points and victories are at stake. Coaches often refer to 'result-focused play'. As spectators, we may desire a creative game, but after the final whistle, no one enquires about the 'how'. Misplaced passes, missed opportunities and a lack of creativity are quickly forgotten, so long as the victory is secured. We accept that only the measurable result matters. This mentality has become our norm. What matters is not how the victory was achieved, but that it was attained. Football is a result-driven sport.

Many companies operate in the same manner. The prevailing belief is: 'We get what we measure.' Therefore, we seek measurable success criteria. To simplify matters, we equate success with a concrete outcome, whether revenue, profit or another key metric. However, this mindset harbours a critical flaw: it renders us driven by our own target specifications. To avoid missing these targets, we often resort to panic mode or other short-term measures. This one-sided focus on result-oriented objectives causes short-term outcomes to be prioritised over sustainable success.

2. We must motivate the players

Jürgen Klopp, affectionately known as 'Kloppo' by his supporters, is undoubtedly a coaching legend. Whether at Mainz, Borussia Dortmund or Liverpool, success and titles followed 'Kloppo'. According to many football enthusiasts, he owes his renown primarily to his ability to motivate players. After all, as a footballer, he was better known for solid, dependable performances. We admire his passionate body language on the sidelines and envision how he rallies his team before every match, inspiring them to achieve peak performance. In leadership training, 'Kloppo' is often regarded as the embodiment of a motivating winner. Many believe that charismatic leaders, through emotional addresses, guide the company to success and enhance team motivation.

However, this is a limiting belief. We attempt to increase our employees' willingness to perform, rather than supporting them in optimising their ability to perform. Jürgen Klopp gained recognition not through his inspiring speeches or motivational skills, but because he maximises each player's individual abilities for the benefit of the team. When asked how he motivates his players, 'Kloppo' replied, like many other successful coaches: "I do not need to motivate my players; otherwise, they would not be here."

Under the mistaken belief that employees must be constantly motivated, we develop tools designed to drive them. We invest considerable energy in increasing willingness to perform, rather than fostering the self-efficacy and efficiency of teams and individuals. This mindset overlooks the fact that genuine motivation originates internally and that employees perform at their best when they feel effective and can leverage their strengths and abilities.

3. We must run more than our competitors

Do you watch biathlon? If so, you will be familiar with the rules: when an athlete makes a shooting error, they must complete a penalty lap for each missed shot, thereby losing valuable time compared to their competitors. This should encourage us to reflect. Why is it that we perceive overtime in business life as a symbol of high performance?

We often confuse willingness to work hard with the potential to perform. In our job advertisements, we seek employees who are willing to go the 'extra mile'. Such candidates are regarded as 'high potentials'. In many companies, employees are commended for overtime and hard work. Those who await their next holiday with tired eyes, yet still respond to emails and participate in video conferences during 'family time', receive gratitude and recognition.

In contrast, we frequently overlook expressing gratitude to those who work efficiently, critically evaluate projects and develop 'not-to-do lists' to avoid unnecessary meetings. Similarly, individuals who finish work on time to replenish their energy with family or through sport, seldom receive recognition. The volume of work completed is all too often regarded as the primary measure.

If hard work in sport inevitably resulted in titles and championships, people like Klopp would likely be unnecessary. Empathetic coaches, who show genuine interest in people and bring innovative game strategies, would remain overshadowed by the emphasis on hard work and a result-driven mindset. Instead, it is precisely these coaches who achieve long-term success. The slogan 'Try harder' is a relic of the past in professional sport and is regarded, especially when it matters most, as more of a guarantee for defeat than for sustainable success.

In contrast, we glorify going the extra mile and promote to leadership positions those who work hardest for success and prominently display their efforts. This overexertion results in equating performance with quantity rather than quality. The consequence is a dead end, where we increasingly view more work as the essential key to success, while innovative and sustainable solutions are often neglected.

A Vicious Circle

"Our heads are round so our thoughts can change direction."

With this quote, the French artist Francis Picabia defined an era in which the world lay in ruins and a young artistic movement challenged everything. The artists reconsidered their work and embarked on new paths. Although our world of work is not in ruins, we too must change our mindset. This does not require a radical 180-degree turn, but rather an adjustment of our current thinking.

The deeply rooted beliefs, as previously outlined, create a self-reinforcing vicious circle. They directly correlate with numerous tactical errors that accumulate over the course of a business year and hinder healthy, sustainable performance development. This mindset leads us to work even harder without achieving significantly better results. In the following sections, we will encounter over 100 tactical errors. While not as obvious as Sepp Herberger's ban on fluid intake, they are equally detrimental to performance. In football, the principle holds: the more tactical errors a coach makes, the lower the chances of success.

In business, myths surround leadership and motivation, perpetuated by self-proclaimed management gurus and consulting firms. Remarkably, we consistently disregard scientific evidence. According to the motto, 'what science knows, and business does', we do what we are used to doing. HR departments, in particular, jump from one trend to another, puzzled as to why all efforts fail to produce sustainable results.

New concepts, processes and instruments are prescribed to employees, though their limiting beliefs are outdated. These patterns consciously or unconsciously resist the revised definition of success. The likelihood of success is about as high as with most well-promoted diets: rather disappointing.

We must critically examine and adapt our mindset to identify opportunities for performance improvement. Only by doing so, can we break the vicious circle and achieve genuine, sustainable change.

Five Steps Towards Healthy and Sustainable Performance

Let us now explore what occurs when a newly defined success strategy is confronted with outdated beliefs, and which new avenues emerge when we recalibrate the direction of our thinking. Even more importantly: What can we learn from athletes and clubs where pressure to achieve results has been replaced by healthy and sustainable performance development? What do clubs, coaches and teams do differently when they have revised their definition of success and discarded outdated thinking patterns?

We will focus on the fundamental building blocks of healthy and sustainable performance development and progressively reveal the behavioural patterns that are consciously or unconsciously exhibited within organisations – often driven by traditional mindsets.

The journey towards healthy and sustainable performance development involves creating supportive conditions, identifying potential, developing performance, accessing it, and ultimately sustaining it. These building blocks cannot be addressed in a linear fashion; rather, they are interconnected, overlap and mutually influence one another. Implementation is complex. To make reading as pleasant as possible, we have structured the topics according to the elements outlined here:

- Establishing supportive conditions
- Identifying potential
- Accessing performance
- Developing performance
- Sustaining performance.

Establishing Supportive Conditions

In recent decades, significant efforts have been made in sport to provide athletes with conditions that allow for optimal performance development. This has occasionally resulted in excesses, as observed in certain football academies. These facilities often resemble luxurious five-star hotels, where many responsibilities are assumed on behalf of the players, allowing them to focus entirely on their performance. Critics argue that such environments have resulted in a lack of genuine characters on the playing field – individuals who assume responsibility in critical moments.

However, I do not wish to join the critics, as much has evolved in recent years, and academies cannot be generalised – the established conditions and underlying philosophies vary considerably. Nonetheless, these conditions have produced both performance-enhancing and performance-inhibiting effects, which were neither anticipated nor intended in this form.

The working environment has undergone significant change in recent years. The ongoing digitalisation, increased flexibility in working hours, and the rise of remote work opportunities have led to new work structures. For some, these changes have been a blessing; for others, they have been a challenge. While some individuals benefited and were able to enhance their performance, the new environment resulted in performance declines for others.

To better understand this phenomenon, we can refer to Kurt Lewin's field theory, a foundational concept in organisational psychology. According to Lewin's formula, an employee's behaviour can be explained by two factors: first, the individual's characteristics – including their values, motives, experiences, abilities and limiting beliefs; and second, the environment.

While we proudly announce that we have adapted to the new demands of the labour market through more flexible working hours, remote work options and initiatives such as fruit baskets and table tennis tables, we often overlook that many deeply rooted, historically established, conditions remain unaltered. These were originally created to enhance individual performance; however, we must acknowledge that, at best, they now exert only a 'placebo' effect. A closer examination reveals far-reaching consequences: these so-called 'placebos' entail significant side effects that no longer foster performance but rather impede it – similar to the academies mentioned earlier.

Let us examine these side effects in greater detail in the following section.

Sell the Sizzle, Not the Sausage

Imagine that Bayern Munich, Barcelona or Manchester City appointed a new coach, who, in his first interview, surprisingly stated: "Our goal for the forthcoming season is a single-digit league position." There is not a word about the obligation to win as many titles as possible. At the same time, SC Freiburg, typically known for its understatement, surprised with the announcement that they "aim to become German football champions".

Do you believe that the superstars in Munich, Barcelona or Manchester would be less motivated following this change of objective, and therefore would go out more frequently in the evenings? Or that the Freiburg players, inspired by their ambitious target, would demonstrate greater commitment in training, and run more, and faster? In other words: Does a change of the goal influence the way players operate?

Within the corporate environment, we are firmly convinced that it does. We are almost obsessed with goals. In many companies and corporations, written goal setting is regarded as the ultimate success guarantee. Without measurable goals, decision-makers believe nothing will be achieved.

But what about sport, where the focus is on goals, victories, championships and titles? You may be surprised that from sport we can learn that no measurable goals are necessary to achieve success. Bill Walsh, one of the most successful American football coaches worldwide, faced intense criticism at the outset of his legendary tenure with the San Francisco 49ers. He was accused of failing to establish clearly measurable goals. However, his critics were quickly silenced as the 49ers secured victory after victory. Success emerged naturally through relentless daily effort – or as Walsh famously stated: "The score takes care of itself"[3]. This attitude has long resonated with numerous teams and athletes.

In fact, goals are often overrated. They entail more undesirable side effects than most prescription medications available in today's pharmacies.

Where does this goal fetish in companies come from? It stems from our traditional thinking patterns. Without measurable goals, there is no result orientation – this is the prevailing belief. Thus, the goal paradigm in companies satisfies our deeply rooted need for measurability.

The most common guideline for goals is the SMART rule. Our goals should therefore be smart, not clever. SMART stands for **S**pecific, **M**easurable, **A**ttractive, **R**ealistic and **T**ime-bound. This rule traces back to the American company General Electric and originated in the 1960s. Over the years, the corporation has refined the concept, and as early as the 1980s, studies demonstrated a positive correlation between the SMART rule and the success of the company. However, even 'specific' was not specific enough, so the goals were expanded to 'specific **and** measurable'. The reason? We can only achieve what we can measure.

When discussing goals, the focus was no longer on the vision or the purpose. From that point forward, goals had to be measurable. This mindset has the following consequences: managers increasingly direct their attention towards short-term, result-focused objectives. Our dashboards, filled with red and green traffic lights, reinforce this. Many green indicators on the dashboard can lead to a promotion. It is commonly accepted as the ultimate indicator of performance.

To prevent managers from lowering their expectations, merely to secure green lights, the discussion around 'stretched targets' was initiated. Jack Welch introduced the concept of 'stretched goals' at General Electric. Essentially, this meant combining 'SMART' rules with ambitious objectives. Critics might argue that it remains 'SMART', but the 'A' for 'attractive' was replaced by an 'A' for 'ambitious'. The strategic goals that embody the 'purpose' are frequently overlooked. The focus on sustainable success is lost. And rightly so. Who can be certain they will still hold their position when the long-term goal is achieved?

This 'stretching' of goals primarily resulted in an effect that contradicts the ideas presented here. Goals were increasingly dictated from above or, at minimum, reviewed by higher levels. Consequently, unrealistic goals were formulated and communicated in a top-down manner. The participation of affected employees was neglected.

Frustration among most employees grew, and sarcasm became a daily occurrence in the workplace. Nonetheless, executive teams continued to communicate enthusiastically: 'If you know how to achieve the goal, the goal is not ambitious enough.' As a result, goals were often set excessively high to make employees deliver peak performance.

However, have we ever truly considered what we mean when we refer to a 'goal'? Is there a standardised definition? A review of the business world reveals that no such standardised definition exists. On the contrary, the definition of what constitutes a goal becomes increasingly complex each year. As more performance experts emerge, an increasing number of definitions enter the daily practice of leaders. For some, a goal is the ultimate objective; for others, it represents milestones along the journey; for others still, it embodies visions; and for some, goals take the form of key indicators. There are outcome and process goals, interim goals (milestones), as well as content and functional goals.

But does a person truly require a measurable goal? The answer is no. Measurable goals are not indispensable in sport or in business. Below are several reasons explaining why this is the case:

1. In a football match, both teams share the same goal: to win. However, only one team will achieve this. Alternatively, the points may be shared. Thus, the goal does not appear to be the decisive factor. Many football clubs set the objective of avoiding relegation before the season begins, yet some are relegated, nonetheless. Once again, the goal does not seem to play a decisive role. In business, our competitors often pursue similar goals to us. Yet only one business receives the order from the client. This further demonstrates that the goal alone does not determine the outcome.

2. Goals are either set too low or too high. If they are too low, it may be possible to achieve more without setting any goals. When goals are set too high, we tend to 'suboptimise'. In other words, we begin to do things we would not usually do, even if they contradict common sense or sustainability. We react instead of respond. This

makes us victims of our own goal setting. We no longer perceive results as the product of our work. Instead of driving results, we are driven by them. Thus, instead of actively shaping success, we allow ourselves to be driven by (excessively high) goals. The most problematic are goals set so high that they cannot be achieved, even with suboptimisation, which often results in cynical or frustrated employees.

3. Aligning goals across functions without conflict is nearly impossible. In an organisation with multiple functions and departments, it requires considerable effort and extensive coordination to design goal setting that is aligned with the whole company. Typically, goal conflicts arise, causing departments to work independently on their own objectives. For instance, one department is evaluated based on low inventory levels, while another prioritises rapid delivery. Project managers are evaluated based on meeting deadlines, which can negatively impact the quality by which other functions are assessed. Leaders are, among other criteria, measured by employee satisfaction, while the controller rejects all travel, events and training initiatives to avoid jeopardising the financial monthly targets. The wider perspective is lost; internal collaboration is impeded rather than facilitated. Aligning functional and departmental goals becomes an almost insurmountable task. Intended, constructive, cross-functional collaboration deteriorates into discussions where one party always wins and the other loses. This creates an ideal environment for dysfunctional organisations.

4. We live in an era of constant change, yet goal setting remains very rigid. Goals are often inflexible and no longer correspond to current conditions. Even significant changes in our environment, such as the COVID-19 pandemic or geopolitical crises, do not prompt many companies to revise goals that were established under entirely different circumstances.

Interestingly, the widely cited studies from Harvard and Yale universities, regarding the impact of goal setting, have been exposed as a myth. These studies purported that students who documented their goals in writing significantly outperformed their peers in terms of income and wealth. This conviction persisted tenaciously among many decision-makers. However, it was ultimately revealed that these frequently referenced studies never actually existed – they were 'fake'.

Experts now agree that algorithms and artificial intelligence will assume less complex tasks and decisions within companies. These tasks are referred to as algorithmic tasks. They follow a clear process to achieve a specific outcome. The other category of tasks – the so-called heuristic tasks – will continue to be performed, at least in part, by human hands and minds. It is for these tasks that our rigid goal systems prove inadequate. Goals are not the solution to the complex challenges facing today's businesses.

It is time to reconsider the fixation on goals and shift the focus towards a more flexible, value-oriented approach. The excessive focus on goals within companies results in prioritising short-term and measurable success, even during strategic deliberations. Rather than developing a vision that resonates with the emotions and thoughts of employees, we often focus on measurable criteria.

In business and in sports stadiums, there is a pertinent saying: 'Sell the sizzle, not the sausage'. This means that it is not the product itself but the excitement around it that matters. The same applies to motivation in sport; athletes are driven not by raw numbers but by the emotions that surround those numbers. The initial goal – whether a championship title or a personal best – takes on new significance once deeper motivations become clear. Motivation always stems from the 'purpose' and the associated emotions. As Jürgen Klopp once stated: "You have to show the boys the sun." Thus, it is not merely about the numbers, but about the emotions and consequences behind them. Further details will be provided as we continue.

We tend to favour what is measurable because it provides us with a sense of security. We can count the sausages, but not the sizzle. Nevertheless, we attempt to quantify the sizzle to make the intangible tangible. In most cases, this effort fails and results in the neglect of important aspects – simply because they cannot be expressed in numbers.

The annual employee appraisals represent an additional obstacle that complicates moving away from this deeply rooted belief. 'What are we supposed to evaluate if no clear, measurable goals exist?' resonates from various leadership offices.

To adequately address the challenges of today's world of work, we urgently require innovative approaches that extend beyond conventional goal setting. The time and energy devoted to developing complex goal systems could be more effectively allocated to other areas of value creation. In sport, it is acknowledged that success depends not solely on the goals themselves, but on the factors that positively influence the likelihood of success. The result is not the overarching objective, but rather the consequence of focused and consistent action. In sport, we master our goals, whereas in business we are all-too-often mastered by them. This leads many companies to react in a result-driven manner instead of responding and acting in a performance-oriented way.

This does not imply that we should simply discard all goals and set none at all. Naturally, companies require goals to communicate to their stakeholders, shareholders and the public what they aim to achieve. Similarly, clubs must inform media representatives and fans about the league position they are targeting this season, how many titles they intend to win, or why they only aim to maintain their standing. They also require key performance indicators for business planning and management. We will discuss some meaningful measures in the sections that follow. These indicators are not considered the sole criterion for success, but enable better monitoring and decision-making, positively influence our behaviour, facilitate learning, and enhance our self-efficacy.

Potential Tactical Errors

Tactical error 1: We equate success with measurable results.

Tactical error 2: We expend too much energy on goal setting and alignment.

Tactical error 3: We are driven by results, rather than driving results.

Tactical error 4: We neglect important, non-measurable success factors.

Goal Bonuses and a Coffee Set

Football fans may recall times when a win earned two points, a draw one point, and a defeat none. During the 1994 World Cup in the USA, the three-point rule (that had already existed in England since the early 1980s) was tested on the international stage. The winner was awarded three points instead of two. The trial was interpreted as being successful and, from Season 1995/96 onward, the three-point rule was implemented worldwide. It was anticipated that this would encourage a more offensive style of play and result in more goals.

However, no long-term effect ensued. On the contrary, as over the years, even fewer goals were scored in the top European leagues. Until Season 1987/88, nearly all matches featured more than three goals per game; thereafter, the number of goals steadily declined. The three-goal threshold was never surpassed again. Among the five leading European leagues in England, Italy, France, Spain and Germany, only the Bundesliga recorded an average of 2.7 goals after 2001. In all other leagues, the average was lower.

This development was generally attributed to players becoming increasingly well-trained and tactical measures growing more sophisticated and rigid. No one considered that the three-point rule itself might have contributed to this development. It was only the economists Ignacio Palacios-Huerta and Luis Garicano who revealed the damage caused by the rule change. Rather than encouraging offensive football, it had precisely the opposite effect. It became evident that fouls were committed more frequently, and warnings increased. Defensive players were brought on to the pitch more often to protect a lead. The game did indeed change, but not in the intended manner. While victory became significantly more valuable, this did not result in bolder, more open play. Instead, it fostered a tougher and more defensive attitude[4].

Being rewarded more significantly for success does not necessarily lead to an increase in our effort. Frequently, the efforts of others are undermined. This is precisely what occurred following the introduction of the three-point rule.

Another example is goal bonuses, which have largely disappeared in professional sport. Nevertheless, some semi-professional clubs still attempt to incentivise their forwards in this way. The outcome is typically as disappointing as that of the much-praised three-point regulation. The side effects of these bonuses can, at times, be toxic and seldom contribute to the success of the team. Promising game situations are squandered because the forward prefers to shoot at goal from an almost hopeless position, rather than pass the ball to a better-positioned teammate. Does this sound familiar?

The flaw in the system is evident. Bonus schemes developed with passion neither motivate the majority of players to perform better, nor lead to them scoring more goals. Instead, they cause resentment, dissatisfaction and unintended behaviours that ultimately harm the overall outcome rather than support it.

Just amateurs, we might say. We in business are professionals. Or are we?

The reality is that these 'semi-professionals' are in good company. In business, we often act in a similar way, with the consequence that entire departments are undermined by such unintended and unforeseen side effects.

The excessive deployment of one-size-fits-all bonus and incentive systems in companies originates from one of our deeply rooted beliefs in business: that we must motivate our employees. We adhere to the belief that extrinsic motivation leads to the desired success. However, experience shows that these approaches often fail to deliver the intended results and may have unintended consequences. The so-called incentive or bonus systems are designed to generally motivate employees to outstanding performance. The reality, however, is that employees focus mostly on the bonus when it is at the lower end of the scale, or when it is not being paid at all. Otherwise, the bonus is simply accepted without much enthusiasm. In good years, there is a momentary sense of satisfaction before we find ourselves back on the hamster wheel, realising that what was paid was not a bonus but compensation for hardship. Motivation: none at all.

With most incentive systems, there is a greater risk that they undermine the company's overall objectives, much like the three-point regulation in football. Frequently, they result in motivation being diminished rather than enhanced. In fact, employees cannot and should not be incentivised, just as players cannot and should not be incentivised. If we succeed in not demotivating our employees, we are already a step ahead of others. More will follow on this.

All attempts to motivate others are likely to be in vain. Companies should stop wasting time on incentive systems and instead focus their energy on preventing the harm these systems cause. Such systems foster resentment, envy and a sense of injustice. Furthermore, each employee unnecessarily spends time sustaining this system. In the worst case, as seen with the goal bonus or the three-point rule, this results in sabotage among colleagues or departments. It is well known that money can end friendships. Furthermore, it prevents companies from eliminating their complex and tangled goal systems. We require bonus systems to ensure that goals are meaningful, and we need goals to give substance to the bonus systems. It is a perfect vicious circle: everyone is occupied, yet the fundamental objective of motivation is typically missed or even forgotten.

Those who believe that such tools can sustainably motivate employees and drive them to exceptional performance are often disappointed. Those who assume that such regulations can influence employee behaviour in the long term should carefully assess whether the anticipated benefits truly outweigh the often-unintended side effects. It is of little benefit if the forward runs a few metres more but leaves teammates in promising positions, 'starving'.

These undesirable side effects are particularly noticeable in bonus systems that are paid out only after a delay of two to five years. If an employee resigns prematurely, they forfeit their entitlement to the attractive bonus. These 'golden handcuffs' often retain the wrong employees within the company – another example of a well-intentioned incentive system that impedes the sustainable performance development of an organisation.

Bonuses are just as challenging to manage as goals. Finding a fair and respectful balance is difficult. Setting bonuses too high can result in embarrassing situations – as exemplified by the Greek government following the country's unexpected victory at the 2004 European football championship. The bonus promised for winning the final was the highest ever offered to a national team at a World Cup or European Championship (one million euros per player) and was, incidentally, initially withheld. Despite this enormous sum, most players did not perceive it as a particular motivation.

Insufficient recognition can also have negative consequences. A prime example of this is the DFB (German Football Association), which presented the German women's national football team with a coffee set following their 1989 championship victory. The set comprised 41 pieces, adorned with blue, yellow and red flowers – from the 'Mariposa' collection by Villeroy & Boch. This gift became a symbol of disregard and is still cited 35+ years later as a classic example of failed recognition.

Potential Tactical Errors

Tactical error 5: We attempt to motivate employees extrinsically.

Tactical error 6: We underestimate the unintended consequences of incentive systems.

Major Transfers and Homegrown Talent

According to the football world federation, FIFA, more than 21,000 professional player transfers were completed worldwide in 2023. Total expenditure amounted to over 9 billion US dollars. The major transfers, such as Bayern Munich signing England captain Harry Kane, dominated the headlines during the close season. However, compared to the highest transfer fee ever paid – 222 million euros, which Paris Saint-Germain spent on Neymar in 2017 – these sums appear almost modest.

The media attention surrounding the transfer market often surpasses the actual events on the pitch. Football fans, ranging from young to old, are captivated by computer games and apps where the strategic buying and selling of players is crucial for success. The underlying message is clear: a prudent transfer policy is regarded as key to success. This is exemplified by cases such as Manchester City, which increased its team's market value by an impressive 840 million euros between 2014 and 2019 – 85% of which resulted from investments in new players.

There is an alternative approach to enhancing a team's value: the deliberate development and integration of homegrown talent. This aspect often remains unnoticed by fans. An impressive example is that of Liverpool, which increased the market value of its team by 830 million euros during the same period as Manchester City. Nearly 80% of this value increase was achieved through the development of existing potential and the integration of players from its youth teams.

Liverpool is not an isolated case. On average, two-thirds of the value increases among the 69 leading European clubs result from promoting their own players rather than new acquisitions[5]. Would you have expected that?

What strategy do you pursue in your company? How do you enhance the value of your team or organisation? How much 'Manchester City' is reflected in your personnel planning, and how much 'Liverpool'? In other words: How much of your effort is directed towards external talent, and how much do you invest in the further development of your existing employees?

Skilled Labour Shortage as an Opportunity

In professional football, the supply of young talent appears virtually limitless. Countless aspiring players dream of becoming professionals, which is why both external and internal strategies hold promise for clubs' success. But what if the number of talented players was to suddenly decline? We might expect that clubs, like Liverpool, would increasingly focus on developing its own players to remain competitive.

However, in the corporate environment, I frequently observe the opposite. As the skilled labour shortage becomes more tangible, companies tend to concentrate more on external solutions. They invest in employer branding, expand their recruiting departments and engage costly headhunters. Rather than enhancing people's ability to perform, companies attempt to offset the shrinking talent pool from outside.

Elaborately designed recruitment campaigns are not only costly but can also increase employee turnover. Studies indicate that more than half of those who leave a company shortly after joining cite unrealistic expectations as the primary reason[6]. Consequently, many new employees find themselves not on the anticipated 'green training fields' but rather on slippery, hard courts. The disparity between the impressive promises on career portals and the actual corporate culture is often remarkable.

An inspiring example is Spanish football club, Athletic Bilbao, which has successfully maintained its competitiveness for decades through a model that operates despite a limited talent pool.

The Success Story of Athletic Bilbao

Athletic Bilbao's club philosophy is founded on a principle that restricts the talent pool for the professional squad exclusively to players from the Basque Country. Although this self-imposed limitation might be perceived as a competitive disadvantage, the facts tell a different story. No Spanish club has produced more national players than Athletic Bilbao, and alongside Barcelona and Real Madrid, Bilbao is the only club never to have been relegated from the Spanish La Liga. During this period, the Basques have secured eight championship titles, placing them third in the all-time table of Spanish football[7].

The keys to success lie in continuity and the sustainable development of its own talent. Bilbao invests its revenues in training and likens itself to a university that ensures talent can fully realise its potential, and that its players can develop holistically as athletes and individuals. The club does not see short-term transfer success as the goal, but rather long-term development of the players. This is a matter of attitude and, as it should be, has its origin in the definition of success. Victories and titles are the consequence, not the all-determining goal. On average, a player who has made his debut in the professional squad of Athletic Bilbao spends more than seven years in this team. These players repay the trust and appreciation they have experienced over the years. They help the club to develop an identity that attracts new talent. Talent development takes precedence over scouting.

How to Become a World Champion

The euphoria after the 1990 World Cup win and the optimistic forecast by Franz Beckenbauer that German football would be unbeatable for years experienced a sharp setback after the quarter-final exit in the USA four years later. Victory at the 1996 European Championship in the 'home of football' masked a gradual development that became apparent with the 1998 World Cup quarter-final exit in France and culminated in the embarrassing performance at the 2000 European Championship in Belgium and the Netherlands – the German team was already on the short trip home after the group stage. The 2006 World Cup in their own country was approaching, and those responsible reacted with a talent development programme that had been lying dormant in the drawers of DFB bosses for two years.

In an impressive initiative, 350 centres were established across Germany, tasked with scouting and developing talent. Simultaneously, all 18 Bundesliga clubs were required, through the licensing process, to establish their own talent academies. From 2002 onwards, this requirement also became mandatory for the clubs of Bundesliga 2, in order to obtain their licence. In the first 20 years of the reform, the clubs invested nearly one billion euros in almost 60 talent academies. Naturally, not everything was flawless; errors occurred and adjustments were made, but the overall trend and the fundamental intent were sound. The reform marked the beginning of an era defined by an unwavering focus on continuous and sustainable talent identification and development – similar to Bilbao, but encompassing a significantly larger pool of talent.

This era culminated in Germany's 2014 World Cup win. While this achievement cannot be attributed solely to this country-wide transformation, it is indisputable that the initiative laid the foundation for subsequent success. Of the 23 players who secured the 1–0 victory against Argentina in the 2014 final, 21 originated from an academy. Roman Weidenfeller and Miroslav Klose were already active in professional football.

The Bundesliga saw an increase in the number of German players, while simultaneously reducing the average age of professionals by two years[8]. The reform helped usher in a golden era in German football.

Accordingly, German TV commentator Tom Bartels declared after the 2014 World Cup final, some 24 years after Franz Beckenbauer's moment of euphoria: "Germany is back in football heaven."

The Downside of Success

German football heaven soon clouded over, and in subsequent years, the team was unable to replicate its success. One reason for this was the numerous academies, where scouting became more important than the original mission: to nurture footballers' individuality and to develop them tactically, technically, athletically, mentally and socially. Rather than focusing inward, these academies, like many companies today, directed their attention outward.

Over time, scouting took precedence, and academies evolved from cost centres into profit centres. The definition of success shifted, with evaluation criteria adapting accordingly. Motivated parents and questionable player agents contributed to academies striving to secure the most promising talents as early as possible, aiming to sell them profitably. This approach was quickly established. They attracted prospects with the best chances of winning titles and an 'all-inclusive package', similar to how companies extend offers to potential candidates.

The continuous and holistic development of talent fell behind. Each year, nearly 30% of talent was replaced, and the likelihood of remaining in the academy after three years was only 33%. After five years, this figure dropped further to 20%.

A Vicious Circle

In youth teams, the focus increasingly shifted towards titles, with emphasis placed on results. Championship titles enhanced the likelihood of attracting the best talent to the region. The definition of success had gradually evolved, and the coaches aligned themselves accordingly. In some academies, the German championship title became more a guarantee of promotion than the sustainable and individualised development of talent.

The revised definition of 'talent' centred on short-term success and championship titles. This set a vicious circle in motion that proved difficult to halt. Those who dropped out were deemed 'losers', while those who persisted at least had the opportunity for financial success. A player transfer could cover the costs of the academy for several years.

The true 'losers' in this game were the talents and, subsequently, German football. Continuous and individualised talent development was sacrificed for the pressure of short-term results, with scouting prevailing over talent development. Does this sound familiar?

'Project Future'

Meanwhile, other nations ascended to football prominence – unsurprisingly, those that invested in continuous, individualised and holistic talent development, as German football did on its path to the World Cup in 2014, before abandoning this virtuous course. As is often the case, success is not the outcome of short-term actions or the efforts of individuals, whether players or coaches. Continuity, a well-considered philosophy and effective supportive conditions are the true enablers of success in sport. These achievements stem from focused and sustained work beneath the surface, and result from the sustainable enhancement of performance at both individual and collective level. In sport, the foundation for this is invariably through talent development.

In German football, this understanding ultimately led those responsible to initiate 'Project Future' in 2018, aiming to restore German football to the world's elite and secure its lasting position there. To achieve this, the young players and their optimal development again became the centre of all considerations. The beginning had arrived, but this required years of lobbying by experts, scientists, system critics and visionaries who were not deterred from their path, even by personal attacks from powerful decision-makers in German football. It remains to be seen when and if these efforts will bear fruit, and whether we will once again witness the next wave of enthusiasm from a German sports reporter or national coach.

Although business does not deal with multi-million transfer fees, I observe many companies that, similar to German football, lose their focus. Topics such as recruiting and employer branding dominate, while the continuous and targeted development of employees is neglected. How is the situation in your organisation? Have recruitment and employer branding pushed internal talent development into the background?

The development in German youth football serves as a metaphor for a widespread issue. Too often, we lose sight of the fundamental 'why' when pressure for quick results prevails. Attention is disproportionately focused on the visible, shining successes above the surface, while the essential foundations for future success, hidden beneath, are overlooked. There are additional factors that prevent us from operating as consistently as Athletic Bilbao. We fall prey to the allure of enticing, prestigious major transfers.

A Major Transfer Phenomenon

When Cristiano Ronaldo announced his return from Juventus to Manchester United, the sale of his jersey with the number 7 generated approximately 38 million euros in revenue within just 12 hours. Although the club receives only a fraction of this revenue, this exemplifies the immense impact of such major transfers in sport.

Frequently, it is not the clubs themselves but executives or player agents who benefit from such stars when they commit to 'their' club. A major transfer instantly elevates not only the market value and appeal of the entire team, but also the egos of ambitious club executives.

If you believe that such tactics are reserved exclusively for egocentric club bosses, consider the corporate world. Here, the hiring leader enhances their own market value overnight by recruiting a 'top-tier talent'. The ability to attract and convince high performers to join the team underlines their personal persuasiveness and management ambitions. A major transfer serves as a personal 'career booster'. In contrast, continuous coaching and the targeted development of internal talent often happens behind the scenes, without significant public recognition, and it usually goes unnoticed by superiors. However, if you aim to pursue a long-term successful strategy like that of Liverpool, you should consider the leadership skills and initiatives you intend to value, going forward.

Unfortunately, as long as it remains advantageous for career progression and easier to hire costly new employees, effective and sustainable talent management will rarely be prioritised within companies.

I am not criticising the hiring of talented new employees. It is, of course, prudent to integrate external expertise to expand the workforce and address specific gaps. What I criticise is the excessive glorification of this practice. Scouting and talent development should coexist. Internal talent development must be at the centre of every organisation.

A leader who neglects this essential task in a challenging labour market and, instead, seeks costly reinforcements, deserves no promotion – just like a youth coach who, by focusing solely on short-term success, allows talent to deteriorate.

Unfair Comparison

Another tactical error in the category 'Scouting versus Talent Development' is closely linked to the previously mentioned behaviour. We tend to underestimate the risk of a transfer failure, compared to the risk that our internal talent might 'fail'. Why is this the case? Quite simply, because the comparison is unfair.

The less time and investment we dedicate to the development of our talent, the lower the level of trust that they can replace the departed person. When players are consistently placed on the bench, there is a lack of confidence in their ability to succeed at a higher level. Instead of giving internal candidates the opportunity to develop in new roles, we search the transfer market for a potentially better, already 'fully developed' candidate. This provides a sense of security and simplifies management's decision-making. The classic argument, 'But he has no leadership experience', becomes a vicious circle that is difficult to break.

The absurdity of the idea that external new hires can fill the gap more quickly and effectively becomes evident when examining how new employees are typically recruited within companies. Whereas in sport, regular observations or trial sessions are feasible, in business, we often rely on limited impressions from a few interviews; at best supplemented by a psychometric test. Assessment centres are becoming increasingly obsolete. The reliability of these limited impressions is questionable, particularly when hiring managers are left to make decisions independently.

Moreover, apples are compared to pears. The detailed heroic achievements of the external candidate are contrasted with the more balanced data points of the internal candidate. An uneven competition, in which the internal candidate is often at a disadvantage. Here, once again, the fact that negative experiences or anecdotes carry more weight than positive aspects work against us.

Rapid Disillusionment in Sport and Business

Disappointment and unhappiness can occur quickly in sport and business. In sport, where transparency is near absolute, new acquisitions do not always make an immediate impact like Harry Kane did following his high-profile transfer to Bayern Munich. In the 2023/24 season, the five major European leagues spent over six billion euros on transfer fees[9]. Panic purchases, such as Barcelona's payment of a substantial 105 million euros plus potential bonuses to Borussia Dortmund in the summer of 2017 to fill the void left by Neymar's departure, are not uncommon. According to media reports, the expensive 'stopgap' Ousmane Dembélé reportedly spent more time playing video games than proving himself on the pitch. The French international, now at Paris Saint-Germain and considerably reformed, is in distinguished company. The list of costly transfer flops across various sports is extensive.

Naturally, we do not deal with such sums in business, but you will undoubtedly recall some eagerly anticipated new acquisitions within your professional environment. The initial enthusiasm waned once it became clear that this individual was, after all, only human. Some move on before anyone notices; others remain and are passed around within the company before ultimately leaving. In business, we sometimes wish for a consultants' guild, akin to that in sport, which would broker 'transfer flops' (failed new acquisitions) on behalf of the company to the highest bidder.

We Expect Top Performance from Day One

In the fields of recruitment and scouting, professionalism is essential. People in these departments are highly qualified experts who have increasingly received attention and development in recent years – both in business and in sport.

The careful selection of new team members is the primary focus. New team members should not only demonstrate professional competence, but optimally complement the existing team with their personal skills. Expectations are high, and rightfully so; much is expected from these promising newcomers.

However, the question arises: Is it too much, or perhaps excessive? Often, companies and clubs fall prey to premature accolades without considering that personnel rotation involves people, not interchangeable pieces. It is not the pieces themselves that make the difference in forming a high-performing team, but the cohesion that holds the pieces together. In many cases, the issue is not the player or employee, but rather that the expectations placed upon them are simply excessive.

Sports history demonstrates that transferring successes from previous seasons to new environments does not always work. A notable example is Harry Maguire, who, after a couple of successful years with Leicester City, transferred to Manchester United in the summer of 2019 for £80 million. Despite his prior achievements, it became evident that performance depends not only on skill and attitude, but also on context.

Maguire's contribution to the 'Red Devils' has been subject to critical scrutiny, and his errors have resulted in significant attention on social media. Whether this effectively helps to limit transfer loss remains questionable. To clarify: I am less critical of the highly regarded players who all-too-often succumb to external pressure. What concerns me more are those who permit these unrealistic expectations and communicate without considering the consequences.

The misconception that players or employees can immediately deliver peak performance is widespread, not only in sport but also in business. Expectations must be realistic. Companies should recognise that an individual's performance depends not only on their abilities but also on their interaction with the team.

In this context, it should be emphasised that a player transferring to a new club cannot simply replicate their previous performances. Every club represents a unique environment. Adaptation requires time. Studies indicate that, on average, it takes three years for a player to regain their original performance peak following a club change, if they do so at all. Some players never return to their former level after a transfer, through no fault of their own[10].

This principle translates directly to the corporate environment. Effective onboarding – that is, the purposeful integration of new employees – is essential for the success of a new team member. Nonetheless, studies reveal that nearly 80% of companies are dissatisfied with their onboarding processes[11]. More than just colourful PowerPoint presentations are required. Regular communication, alignment of expectations and, above all, patience, are indispensable. We expect first-class performance from day one, even without professional and sustainable onboarding. In many cases, the initial enthusiasm surrounding a major transfer gives way to the realisation that the costs incurred, until the new addition fully meets expectations, are significantly higher than anticipated.

Individual superstars can only perform as well as the team allows. Therefore, my criticism is particularly aimed at those who believe that a high-performing team can be assembled like a jigsaw puzzle that is missing its edges. Coaching legend Arsène Wenger aptly stated: "There is always a need for new players, but new is just new." Many club officials must come to terms, year after year, with the fact that their team does not function as a cohesive unit but rather as a collection of individual players lacking clear structure – and this was certainly not 'planned'.

Continuity as a Response to Ongoing Change

We return here to our example of Athletic Bilbao. As you may recall, a player who debuts in Bilbao's professional squad spends, on average, more than seven years with the team. This provides Bilbao with an advantage that many other clubs lack – low turnover. Consequently, hierarchies can develop, and the players' sense of belonging is exceptionally strong. They behave less like employees and more like owners – an attitude rarely found in many other clubs and companies. High salaries and sophisticated incentive systems cannot substitute for this attitude. Players reciprocate the trust placed in them and the appreciation they have experienced over the years. They contribute to establishing an identity for the club, which in turn attracts new talent.

Consciously and continuously investing in the development of talent fosters trust in our ability to take the next step. We become familiar with the talented individuals and develop a sound understanding of their abilities, strengths and developmental potential. Temptation to engage in the transfer market for costly new acquisitions gives way to the commitment and determination to realise the potential of our talent.

In an era where constant change is considered the 'new normal', we emphasise resilience and agility. Yet, the solution to many of our fundamental challenges lies in continuity. Although this may appear somewhat unremarkable and does not satisfy the impulse for activity or the ego of ambitious managers, it enables proactive action rather than reaction. This approach avoids the typical 'stop and go' mechanisms frequently observed in many companies. It is characterised not by activity, but by focus and consistency. This attitude is – as we might expect – reinforced by a revised definition of success, which measures success not by immediate results but understands them as the outcome of sustainable thinking and action. It is time to refocus on our employees and provide them with the necessary conditions and development opportunities to pre-empt discussions about major transfers.

Potential Tactical Errors

> **Tactical error 7:** We prioritise 'talent scouting' over 'talent development'.

> **Tactical error 8:** We underestimate the 'total costs' of new acquisitions.

> **Tactical error 9:** We expect top performance from day one.

> **Tactical error 10:** We are blinded by previous heroic deeds.

The 'Too Much Talent' Effect

Are you familiar with the 'too much talent' effect? This effect describes a widespread misconception in sport and in business. The effect is based on the assumption that the relationship between talent and performance in team sports is linear. Under the motto, 'More is better', we aim to recruit the best talent, integrate them into a team, and are then surprised when results fail to meet expectations.

In 2014, researchers published a study called 'The Too Much Talent Effect'[12]. The researchers conducted experiments across various team sports and demonstrated that beyond a certain concentration on top talent, negative impacts on team performance may arise. This is particularly the case when team members are highly interdependent, as is typical in team sports. The concentration on top talent frequently undermined internal collaboration and team cohesion. These talents do not necessarily have to be high performers; often, self-perception is sufficient.

This misconception – that an abundance of talent inevitably leads to success – was expressed by French national football coach Didier Deschamps, who stated: "I have players who compete in Ligue 1, and others in major clubs participating in the Champions League. The more I have, the better"[13]. Nevertheless, between 2008 and 2014, the World Cup and European Championships ended prematurely for 'Les Bleus' each time, either in the group stage or the quarter-finals, accompanied by significant scandals within 'L'Equipe Tricolore'.

Similar star-studded teams in previous years often failed to unite into a unit greater than the sum of its individual players. These teams frequently resulted from an unstructured procurement policy, enabled only through external financial backing. Real Madrid and Manchester City went through this painful learning curve before winning the Champions League. And even Paris Saint-Germain learned the lesson and won the Champions League in 2025. Compared to previous years, the new head coach, Luis Enrique, was more involved in the planning of the new team. And he formed exactly that – a team – rather than a collection of individuals. Even the biggest critics were positively surprised how players like Ousmane Dembélé worked for the team like never before. You may wish to speculate if team spirit did increase after superstars like Kylian Mbappé had left. In many matches before, the 'one-man teams' contributed less on the field than the sum of their individual parts. All these teams have learned from their mistakes and increasingly focused on the compatibility of their players – both in terms of skill and character.

What Franz Beckenbauer observed after the frustrating group-stage exit of the West German football team at the 1984 European Championship remains true for some clubs: "They are all good footballers. The only problem is, they cannot play football."

The 'Super Chicken' Experiment

A highly illustrative experiment on this subject is the 'super chicken' experiment conducted by the biologist, William Muir. This study, carried out with chickens, clearly demonstrates that a team of 'average chickens', assessed by the number of eggs laid, is often more effective than a team of 'super chickens'. Muir observed the chicken groups over six generations, yielding a remarkable outcome: the team of 'average chickens' prospered. They were well-nourished, well-feathered and their productivity increased significantly over time. In contrast, only three 'super chickens' remained alive from the other team. The rest had turned on each other and pecked each other to death. Companies operating according to the 'super chicken' model – that is, believing that assembling the supposedly best individuals and granting them control will succeed – often encounter outcomes similar to those described by Muir: aggression, dysfunction and inefficiency[14].

Frequently, the key actors operate under the principle of 'me over we'. The focus is on being the best within the team rather than the best for the team. However, for a team to function effectively, this mindset must be reversed: it must be 'we over me'. The team takes precedence over the individual; the emphasis is on the shared goal and the wider perspective. The aim is to be the best for the team, not merely the best in the team.

Applying this principle demands not only exceptional sensitivity but also meticulous orchestration and leadership of the team. Without this, there is a risk that the configuration will collapse due to individual interests, leading to internal conflict. This phenomenon has been observed repeatedly in major football tournaments, particularly with the English and French national teams, which were composed of lone fighters and 'one-man teams' – a clear manifestation of 'me over we'.

Legends, Mercenaries and Wanderers

Football professional and Arsenal legend Tony Adams once offered the advice: "Play for the badge on the front of your jersey and people will remember the name on the back." At first glance, this memorable saying may appear to be a romantic idealisation, achievable only in rare instances. Adams himself embodied this philosophy like few others: he spent his entire 19-year career wearing the jersey of Arsenal. Thomas Müller, who in 2024 entered the record books as the sole record holder of Bayern Munich with over 710 appearances, is also an example of this type of club loyalty. However, not everyone can or wishes to follow this path.

Nevertheless, we should regard this attitude as an opportunity to critically examine our thinking patterns. Frequently, we tend to interpret a high readiness to change as an indicator of increased motivation and ambition. However, the examples of Adams and Müller demonstrate that loyalty should not be equated with a lack of willingness to learn or insufficient ambition. On the contrary, it can result in consistently high performance and sustainable success. This does not imply that leaving our comfort zone is not sometimes advisable. The essential question is: Ambition – for what purpose?

There are players – or, more broadly, professionals in their careers – who negotiate increasingly lucrative contracts year after year through strategic changes. This often occurs even when their performance declines over time. Naturally, it is important to be aware of our market value; however, this must not come at the expense of the team or the company. If it becomes apparent within the first few weeks that a new player or employee is merely a temporary solution, this rarely enables the team to realise its full potential. Instead, such individuals are frequently more focused on their forthcoming contract negotiations than on delivering their best performance, here and now. Exceptions, of course, confirm the rule.

Particular caution is warranted with colleagues who, from the outset, regard the company or position solely as a stepping stone. While this strategy may succeed in isolated cases, it is generally destined to fail. These individuals are distinguished by their capacity for self-presentation; their guiding maxim is: 'See and be seen.' Their actual contribution to team or company success often remains questionable. Or, to continue the sports analogy: they focus not on the badge on the front, but on the name on the back of their jersey. In many cases, it is preferable for the company if these people move on after two years – time that primarily serves their own career – before they cause further harm. Yet, paradoxically, they often manage to ascend the career ladder precisely because of this. We will later explore, in more detail, why this is the case.

These individuals differ markedly from the 'wanderers' such as Lutz Pfannenstiel. The former goalkeeper played for professional football clubs in six European associations, as well as other clubs around the world. It is neither quick money nor rapid career advancement that motivates these wanderers, but rather curiosity, a spirit of adventure, and an interest in other cultures and perspectives. These wanderers often integrate swiftly and make valuable contributions to the team before moving on. They differ fundamentally from their colleagues described earlier.

The wanderers have a distinct assignment: they fill gaps, inspire, and serve as vital elements within the team structure and dynamics. Long-term planning with them is uncommon, yet a significant contribution is expected during the period of collaboration, without any expectation of lifelong loyalty. In this way, the wanderers differ markedly from the 'mercenaries' or 'job-hoppers' frequently criticised in sport.

Increased readiness to change should not be perceived as a flaw. Naturally, this can reflect a healthy curiosity and flexibility – qualities that are increasingly demanded across industries today. It may also indicate that players or employees are continuously striving to enhance their skills to become the best in their field and to compete with high performers.

However, this can result in them never fully realising their potential, as their focus remains on the next step rather than on making the greatest possible contribution in the here and now. High salary and fame transform from being natural consequences of performance into the primary goals to which everything else is subordinated. This marks the beginning of the end. No club should contract such players, and every company should carefully evaluate whether a gap in the team should truly be filled with such a profile.

Given the current shortage of skilled and leadership personnel, it will be particularly challenging to limit the number of 'mercenaries' within an organisation to ensure sustainable performance improvement. In this regard, companies may benefit from the fact that young people entering the labour market have little affinity for the concept of 'career', which will likely lead to a decrease in the number of 'mercenaries'. Conversely, the number of 'wanderers' is expected to increase over time. It is advisable for companies to distinguish clearly between mercenaries and wanderers. The contributions to sustainable and healthy performance development are very different.

Mercenaries consistently focus on their next career move (the next organisation). It is essential to understand how these individuals define personal success. Do they possess the intention to contribute to team success, as many do, or do they aspire to make a genuine difference? Although it may seem like a subtle distinction, in team sports it makes a significant difference whether players are simply present with good intentions or are true team players who are genuinely eager to make a meaningful contribution to team success. This can be observed on match day – particularly when the presumed underdog knocks the overwhelming favourite out of the cup.

High Salaries versus High Performance

The most reliable way to avoid this tactical error is to offer salaries that are fair but not excessively high. Disproportionately high salaries often result in an excessive number of mercenaries. Players and agents are well-aware of where they can earn the most.

In some companies, competitive salaries are still combined with deferred bonus payments, providing mercenaries with little incentive to continue exploring opportunities in the labour market. This is why, in certain cases, it is not advisable to scrutinise every euro – specifically regarding dismissals and contract terminations, which in some countries involve severance payments. If employees, despite the efforts of management, do not make a meaningful contribution to the company's success or are not expected to do so in the future, the parting of ways should be immediate. Everyone is familiar with the image of the bad apple that spoils the entire basket. It is a risk, as many sports clubs have found out, to carry expensive 'benchwarmers' for years without any significant performance improvement.

To specifically highlight this performance aspect and avoid attracting talents solely interested in quick financial gain, Liverpool, for example, employs a clear salary strategy. The remuneration of their 17-year-old 'stars' in their first professional year is capped at a level closer to the average salary of a regular employee than to the excessive amounts typically associated with highly paid professional players[15]. This philosophy cannot always be directly applied in the corporate environment; however, one important rule remains: Do not underpay. Compensate fairly, but never excessively. Excessive salaries not only strain the balance sheet, but can diminish willingness to perform.

Naturally, there are exceptions, particularly within certain expert groups, where paying high salaries is unavoidable. Nevertheless, even for these experts, it is essential to remain within the salary range and avoid exorbitant salaries.

Team Cohesion as a Success Factor

The significant cost that clubs and companies incur when they mistakenly equate high readiness to change with increased motivation, fail to adequately recognise loyal 'average performers', and neglect to distinguish between mercenaries and wanderers, is substantial. Rather than continuously developing teams and fostering sustainable team cohesion, they rely on groups of high-performance players and short-term-contracted mercenaries, hoping for rapid success – an approach that fails in most cases.

An impressive counterexample was demonstrated by the German basketball world champions. Upon his appointment, coach Gordon Herbert required a three-year commitment from each player, with the vision of winning three medals within this timeframe – an ambitious goal that many journalists found astonishing. This mutual commitment united the team as if bound by an invisible thread[16]. Although they did not achieve three medals, the success of this approach was evident with a bronze medal at the 2022 European Championship and a fourth-place finish at the 2024 Olympic Games. The pinnacle was reached in 2023, when the team were crowned world champions following an epic semi-final victory against the USA and a final win against Serbia. This example demonstrates that long-term commitment and team cohesion enable far more sustainable success than short-term, purchased peak performances ever could.

Team cohesion was also perfectly demonstrated by the Greek national football team in 2004, when, despite a lack of individual stars and spectacular football skills, it won the European Championship title. Step by step, the team worked together, supported one another, and ultimately achieved the significant common goal. The coach, Otto Rehhagel, aptly summarised it: "In the past, everyone did what they liked. Now, everyone does what they are capable of."

Leicester City, who won the Premier League in 2016, is another prime example of the magic impact of team cohesion. While the Manchester clubs struggled with coaches approaching the end of their tenures, Chelsea was in free fall under José Mourinho, and Jürgen Klopp only joined Liverpool after the season had begun, Leicester's cohesion surpassed that of all other teams throughout the season. Sometimes, football is that straightforward.

There are numerous instances in which the team with the best individual players did not achieve victory. Frequently, this was due to the favoured teams lacking the necessary degree of team cohesion. It holds true that it is not the individual 'stones' that determine the outcome, but rather the substance between the stones that binds them together.

Potential Tactical Errors

Tactical error 11: We mistakenly equate increased readiness to change with higher ambition.

Tactical error 12: We overpay.

Tactical error 13: We build teams rather than develop them continuously.

Tactical error 14: We underestimate the importance of team cohesion.

Identifying Potential

The identification of potential plays a vital role in the economic success of elite sports clubs. This applies both to the identification of external talent and the development of internal youth players. Consequently, the scouting departments and academies of many professional clubs have gained considerable importance. The failure to recognise potential has both direct and indirect economic consequences. Such short-sightedness often results in the premature end of a talent's dream of a professional career. In most cases, this goes unnoticed: the young player returns to their boyhood club with shattered dreams or, in the worst case, permanently retires from football.

The consequences can be even greater if another club signs the overlooked talent and develops them into a professional, or even a superstar. If this occurs too many times, the scout or youth coach may lose their job. Consider what might have happened if Bayern Munich scout Jan Pienta had sent the lanky and unorthodox Thomas Müller back to his boyhood club. That would have been a fatal mistake for German football.

Overlooking potential can not only ruin careers in professional sport but can result in financial losses amounting to millions. In business, it is essential to identify and develop potential – albeit with a crucial difference. Just as the young footballer returning to his boyhood club often goes unnoticed, so does unused potential within companies. The reason is clear: the costs do not manifest as a single, overlooked talent, but accumulate over time. Consider how costly it becomes if you fail to utilise just 10% of your employees' potential. Even in medium-sized enterprises, these costs can quickly reach millions.

So, what prevents us in business from taking this 'discipline' more seriously?

Low Performers and Self-promoted Heroes

Monday is *kicker* (German football magazine) day. For me, as for many football fans in the pre-digital era, it was a ritual: going to the kiosk, buying the new *kicker*, and immediately checking the editorial ratings for the weekend performances of the players.

By the way, did you know that German football legend Lothar Matthäus shared this passion with me and, during his time in Mönchengladbach, reportedly went from the disco to the train station on Saturday nights because the *Bild am Sonntag* was sold there earlier than anywhere else[17]? Presumably, to have his heroic deeds confirmed once again. Well, I read *kicker*, Lothar Matthäus read the *Bild* newspaper. Yet both of us eagerly awaited the judgement of the 'specialist press' – albeit for different reasons.

These grades were, for me and many other football enthusiasts, fascinating – they were tangible and concrete. A judgement printed on paper yet seemingly carved in stone. Nevertheless, I found these evaluations highly questionable and, at times, unjust.

Spectacular aerial saves by goalkeepers appeared to be valued more than them anticipating situations and coordinating their defence. Sound positioning by defenders was regarded as less valuable than the 'full-blooded tackle', which only became necessary due to a prior positional error. Players who consistently provided assists did not often receive good marks, simply because their teammate – the forward – squandered the opportunities. The culture of heroism was pervasive. Without remarkable heroic deeds, the highest grade attainable was a 3 – at best influenced by a candid interview with the player that sold well.

While Lothar Matthäus devised strategies to steadily improve his ratings in *Bild* and *kicker*, I continued to run every Monday morning to the local magazine kiosk to purchase *kicker*, to check the ratings, to be astonished, and increasingly frustrated. Consequently, one day I decided to stop buying *kicker*. Approximately around the time Lothar Matthäus ended his career.

Performance Management in Business – Much Like at *Kicker*

We might assume that business does not operate like *kicker* or the *Bild* newspaper. After all, we have sophisticated systems designed to assess employees objectively and fairly. However, the reality often differs. Many assessment systems within companies employ a logic similar to that used by *kicker* or the *Bild* newspaper for over 50 years.

While football players have taken legal action against evaluations, in business we still encounter a readiness to judge and condemn. Leaders need not go as far as *Bild*, which assigned former Hamburg professional Valdas Ivanauskas a rating of 7 after a poor performance, accompanied by the comment: "Even *Bild* lacks the words for this."[18]. In business, the number 7 is unnecessary. In many companies, any rating below an average of 3 (on a scale from 1 to 5) aligns closely with the assessment of *Bild*: "Does not deserve the money."

When visualising the Gaussian distribution (also known as a normal distribution) in the context of a company's workforce, the 'low performers' appear far to the left of the curve. These 'unstable candidates' are somehow carried along. They resemble players who concede goals and entangle themselves. Or those who are so inconspicuous that their jersey could be returned to the kitbag, unwashed.

Wasted Potential

To the right of the 'low performers' lies the large middle section, the three-candidate system. The average (or should we say, the 'average chickens') – solid, reliable, but not exceptional. They play without standing out – no heroic deeds. These employees make up the majority but receive less attention than those at either end of the curve.

At the far right, at the end of the sharply declining curve, we find the 'high performers' – those who deliver consistently, match day after match day. This group also includes those who score goals in quick succession because the ball was expertly set up for them. Or those who resort to full-blooded tackles, which became necessary due to earlier failures in their positioning. Or those who pull off spectacular saves, even though they could have caught the ball. With a grade above average, these people advance within companies to the higher echelons. This brings increased attention, occasional development opportunities, and even salary adjustments.

We therefore 'attend to' the few 'low performers' and actively seek out the conspicuous 'high performers' who stand apart from the average. Meanwhile, mediocrity is signalled to the majority of our employees – with devastating consequences. Scientific studies demonstrate that labelling employees as average often results in a decline in work performance[19]. Or as former professional footballer Erik Meijer stated: "Nothing is worse than being second."

The number of employees this relates to is considerable. Consultants and managers should be aware of, and somewhat uneasy about, the unrecognised potential they leave untapped every day. It is astonishing that we let this happen.

The player ratings from *kicker* and the *Bild* newspaper are a brilliant invention – at least for their own circulation and thus for the publishers and readers. However, they do not assist players in making meaningful comparisons or in realising their potential. That is the role of coaches. Apart from football coach Hans Meyer, who reportedly issued a report card to every player after each training session, only a few successful coaches use ratings, and only when they pertain to clearly defined competencies.

But what, then, is the purpose of evaluations within companies? They reinforce our deeply ingrained beliefs.

Firstly: They satisfy our need for measurability. The belief that performance must be managed results in performance being quantified. "You get what you measure." We simply operate in a 'result-focused' manner.

Secondly: They serve as evidence of ambitious expectations. In some companies, 10% of the 'low performers' are dismissed to reinforce the performance culture. It still feels appropriate and important to maintain a group that does not meet our high standards. 'Controlled failure rates' uphold the level of ambition.

Thirdly: We believe that the solid candidates with an average score will exert greater effort to become 'high performers' in the forthcoming year. Here, as well, one of our thinking patterns is at play. We are convinced that we must motivate our people. We either anticipate an evaluation above average or, to use sporting parlance, face the relegation zone as one of the bottom three.

This is particularly counterproductive for our solid, average performers. They do not modify their behaviour to make a more valuable contribution to the company. Instead, they focus on being noticed. They tackle (or foul) rather than foreseeing a situation in which they don't need to tackle. They fly through the air instead of directing with confidence. They shoot instead of passing to the better-positioned teammate. In the worst case, they strive to be the best in the team rather than the best for the team, which can mark the beginning of the end for a well-functioning collective.

The meaning and purpose of evaluations in companies are sometimes seen as absurd. They do not contribute to sustainable performance development for the employee or the organisation.

And what about the leaders? Under the pressure of grading, they consistently feel responsible for engaging more thoroughly with the employee and their performance. However, they often feel more coerced than genuinely responsible. It cannot be said that the managers fail to prepare themselves. Yet, this preparation is driven less by a desire to support the employee and more by the fear of having to justify the assigned grade. Meticulous preparation is undertaken for the low performers – followed by the average performers with a distorted self-image, from the leader's perspective. For the high performers, little resistance is expected; rather, grateful acceptance. Consequently, the leaders feature among the 'losers'. Instead of engaging in a genuinely inquisitive conversation aimed at identifying the factors that hinder or promote the employee's ability and willingness to perform, they are occupied with justifying the assigned 'grade' and retrospectively supporting it with arguments.

As a result, much of the evaluation process becomes a regrettable exercise, with no winner. It serves as an appendix to the painstakingly implemented goal and bonus systems. In most cases, these systems do not effectively enhance the employee's willingness to perform, nor their ability to perform.

If there is any doubt that assessment practices cause more harm than good, it should be noted that assigning grades – and the manner in which this is done – is questionable.

Certainly, the situation is not as severe as a former professional football player and national team member discovered. For instance, the *kicker* ratings for evening matches were often determined before kick-off to ensure they could be included in the print edition. Unlike the assessment systems commonly used in some companies, the *kicker* ratings for weekend matches remain relatively fact-based and objective. In this way, the observations made during a 90-minute game are distilled into an absolute rating. Attentive journalists rarely overlook the key moments upon which such evaluations are based. In companies, the manager is often coincidentally present precisely when a moment of brilliance occurs. In the best case, a strong performance shortly before the evaluation can overshadow an entire season. This moment is impactful and lingers with the manager. However, to avoid leaving this to chance, selected employees develop their own self-promotion strategies. Consequently, we can observe in meetings or later at the hotel bar how these employees – without the assistance of player agents – seek opportunities to showcase their knowledge or recount their past heroic deeds. Their goal is to become a 'high performer'.

Naturally, many companies strive to make this evaluation process as objective as possible. However, despite the transparency of the established criteria and all company-wide calibration efforts, the manager's bias continues to play a significant role.

It is difficult to deny that a good relationship with the manager positively influences evaluations, much like Lothar Matthäus' relationship with the press during his active career. Consequently, we foster conformist 'yes-men' who – if they were athletes – would talk a great deal but say very little (which regularly frustrates us fans). In everyday company life, however, this is silently accepted. Such behaviour is counterproductive when seeking sustainable performance improvement.

In most cases, this system ultimately undermines itself – specifically when companies reach the inevitable conclusion that a 'low performer' is, in fact, a collective product of both an employee who is neither capable nor willing and their manager. The latter has likely failed to fulfil their primary responsibility, which is to establish performance-enhancing conditions for their employees and to ensure that the team is more than the sum of its individual parts.

The reality is that this game nearly always produces 'losers' – unless someone learns to remain in the manager's good books and makes their heroic deeds visible. This increases the likelihood of progression into a 'valuable' player, come the next performance evaluation cycle. Most other players remain in the 'grey' zone and don't receive the recognition they deserve, let alone realise their full potential. At every level, we squander potential by comparing heroic deeds, high visibility and willingness to perform – combined with a degree of conformity – with actual performance. As if this isn't enough, we extrapolate future potential solely from current performance. This issue is addressed in the following section.

Potential Tactical Errors

Tactical error 15: We judge instead of support and challenge.

Tactical error 16: We manage performance rather than develop it.

Tactical error 17: We try to measure what cannot be measured.

Tactical error 18: We classify 90% of our employees as average.

Tactical error 19: We devote too much time to the so-called 'low and high performers'.

Tactical error 20: We reward self-promoting heroism and compliance.

Green Bananas and 'Baby Faces'

"You are not selected" – this statement from my youth coach hit hard. My boldest and most secret dreams of a professional football career were shattered. I was eliminated from the regional selection squad. As a goalkeeper, I was about a foot too short. I looked like I was 12, not 14. The world seemed to have lost its mind. What had changed? My jumping ability was excellent; I was a team player, demonstrated great reflexes on the line, and possessed an excellent overview of the game. Motivation and reliability? In the past year, I had not missed a single training session. Yet, that was not sufficient. Overnight, I lost my talent status, despite having the same skills, motivation and strengths the day before. I was the same character, goalkeeper and team player. I was still talented, but I was not branded as 'talent' any longer.

Yes, this is my personal story, but many other 'talents' face similar experiences. They fall through the scouting net. This is a common reality in sport and somewhat inevitable. Within a maximum of ten years, talents must be developed to succeed as professionals. Therefore, early and consistent selection is essential, even if capable athletes remain confined to lower levels. In Germany, only about 1–2% of football players training in reputable academies succeed in reaching the Bundesliga. This represents a rigorous selection process.

The focus is placed on talent with the highest likelihood of breakthrough. In an industry with a revenue exceeding 11 billion euros and more than 125,000 full-time employees in Germany, there is no time to invest in unsuitable players.

Nonetheless, gifted players with significant potential are overlooked by this selection process. One reason is the assumption that current performance predicts future potential – an expensive fallacy, as prominent examples demonstrate. Lionel Messi nearly failed to achieve an unprecedented career because, in his youth, he was as small and frail as the young goalkeeper mentioned above. Pep Guardiola was first discovered and nurtured by Johan Cruyff in Barcelona's B team. Thomas Müller was also excluded by the standard criteria established for future professionals due to his long, slender legs. Miroslav Klose, the record goalscorer of the German national team at the time of writing, had never played for a representative team before Otto Rehhagel discovered and supported him at Kaiserslautern. Ljubomir Vranjes, considered too small, was removed from the Swedish youth national team at the age of 15 before rising to become one of the most successful handball players worldwide. Even the arguably greatest quarterback of all time, seven-time Super Bowl champion Tom Brady, was advised in high school to switch sports. Numerous examples demonstrate that players often develop into elite athletes only after a delay. This phenomenon has a name: it is known as the 'relative age effect'.

What Do You Do with Green Bananas?

In football, the 'relative age effect' has long-been a well-known phenomenon. Studies indicate that players born in the first quarter of the year are four times more likely to be selected for the German national team than their peers born in the other quarters. This trend persists across all ages and teams up to the youth national team, where approximately 50% of players are born within the first three months of the year. The reason? Athletic, conditioning and cognitive abilities are generally more developed in older players.

A selective focus on current performance levels often prevents the systematic identification and development of potential. The sports sector has recognised this dilemma and is actively working to address it.

An increasing number of clubs no longer prioritise demonstrated performance alone. Instead, they seek young, ambitious players who are eager to continuously improve, who are curious, and who are open to learn. Particular attention is given to those who, in their youth, struggled to keep pace in the shadow of physically more developed teammates[20].

This model is especially adopted by clubs that must compete with limited budgets and pursue long-term strategies against financially stronger rivals. Potential is valued over past achievements – a principle introduced by football legend Johan Cruyff at Ajax and later at Barcelona. In both instances, sustainable success validated his approach.

Not only clubs but entire nations have revolutionised their development concepts, with groundbreaking results. Belgium, for instance, ensures that so-called 'late developers' are not prematurely discarded. Kris Van Der Haegen, who facilitated the transformation of Belgian football and was responsible for coach training, compares these players to green bananas: "You do not discard them; rather, you wait until they are ripe"[21]. Five of the 11 players in the starting lineup during the semi-final of the 2018 World Cup were among these 'late maturing players', including Kevin De Bruyne. Although the match was lost 1–0 to France, the success was the result of a shift in mindset, particularly among the coaches. Rather than sacrificing their 'baby faces', as they affectionately called these players, due to short-term performance setbacks, they patiently continued to develop their potential. This approach was acknowledged by the decision-makers, who refrained from prematurely pulling the plug in the face of unmet success. The result: In 2018, after more than a decade of focused development efforts, Belgium reached first place in the FIFA World Ranking – a remarkable ascent from 66th place in 2009. The path was long, yet sustainable and rewarding.

Perhaps it is our lack of patience and the prevalent fixation on results that prevent companies from undertaking a similar journey. Perhaps it is also our 'old mindset' that causes us to overlook future potential. For instance, we tend to infer leadership potential from presence, convincing communication skills and self-confidence.

This misunderstanding is further reinforced by the assumption that long working hours equate to outstanding performance. This notion persists, though quotes like this one from Theodor Fontane highlight other contributing factors: "Talents are often not so unequal; the differences lie in diligence and character."

We assess current performance and willingness to perform, and judge from a superior position whether potential exists. It is hoped this potential will eventually lead to success for 'high performers' at the executive level. This completes the cycle. Working days at this level are typically long. To succeed, we must be prepared to go the extra mile. In this way, we cultivate the next generation of leaders who will replicate our mistakes and engage in similarly misguided talent selection.

Within companies' 'talent pools', we find almost exclusively 'high performers'. But what does this mean? Driven by limiting beliefs, it is not their potential that is selected, but rather their effort and ability to market themselves. I doubt that the German footballers would have won the 2014 World Cup, or that the Belgian players would have reached the top of the FIFA World Ranking, with this type of talent selection.

The Diversity Inhibitor
In companies, 'high performers' are often evaluated using uniform criteria, which facilitates comparability but hinders the identification of complementary skills, potential and motivational drivers. This approach fails to create a cohesive unit of unique employees who could collectively make a difference. Instead, we act as if we could win the championship with a team of 11 forwards or 11 'one-man teams', only to be surprised when the ball ends up in our net.

Returning to Fontane: "Talents are often not so unequal; the differences lie in diligence and character." While diligence is easy to recognise and appreciate, how do we evaluate character? Here, the wisdom of American football coach Bill Belichick is relevant: "Talent sets the floor, character sets the ceiling." But how can character be measured?

In sport, there is an increasing emphasis on qualities that are not immediately visible. These character traits include loyalty, personal responsibility, self-motivation, decision-making, honesty, openness to criticism, team spirit, willingness to learn, and empathy. The German national football coach Julian Nagelsmann describes many of these abilities as 'talent-free' factors, as they can be developed and trained independently of innate talent or technical skill.

The quick judgement, "you are a talent", is increasingly being replaced in sport. The focus lies on identifying, nurturing and effectively deploying the top competencies of each player, whether it is their instinct in front of goal, their spatial awareness, their speed of action, or their leadership qualities.

However, in business, we face difficulties because we cannot adequately measure all these qualities. Therefore, we continue to rely on hard and diligent work as the criteria. After all, the great Cristiano Ronaldo once said: "Talent without hard work is nothing," and the equally great Michael Jordan observed: "Everybody has talent, but ability takes hard work."

While experts advocate for diversity and companies implement diversity criteria, and job descriptions are crafted to avoid excluding any candidate, our thinking patterns in scouting often remain unchallenged. It is precisely these patterns that shape the appearance of our executive level. The concept of 'going the extra mile' as a benchmark for high-performance capacity is the primary inhibitor of diversity. This selection criterion inevitably results in career advancement being reserved for those willing to make the greatest compromises concerning family, health and other personal interests.

The 'Talent' Label Dilemma

In the academy of German handball Champions League winners SG Flensburg-Handewitt, the label 'talent' is deliberately avoided. The reason for this is that it results in the loss of crucial percentages in performance development. The focus is not on selecting talent. Instead, top competencies are identified, individually nurtured, and thereby the potential fully developed.

Thomas Tuchel offers a similar perspective, emphasising that the pursuit of the next career step often prevents young coaches, reputed to be coaching talents, from dedicating themselves with full commitment and passion to their current responsibilities. Throughout my 20-year corporate career, I have witnessed numerous 'eternal talents' – highly regarded, well compensated, yet never truly integrated. The desire for career advancement often outweighed the drive to make a valuable contribution to the company and the team – fuelled by the conviction that they are a talent with the potential to reach the very top. Here, we lose energy that would be better invested in the sustainable performance improvement of our teams.

Language plays a crucial role in this context. Whether we say someone 'is a talent' or 'has talent' exposes the fundamental dilemma of talent management in business. Defining clear criteria for the former leaves little room for nuanced evaluation – just as Markus, who was too short, discovered that he was no longer considered a talent.

Our tendency towards black-and-white thinking means we lack the necessary subtlety required to enhance performance in a holistic manner. This hinders us from identifying and nurturing genuine top competencies and results in confident, diligent employees focusing more on their careers than on creating sustainable, added value for the company.

Some will be remembered in the company's history as perpetual talents. Meanwhile, those deemed 'untalented' continue working rather than engaging in development. Here, we lose significant ground on the path towards company-wide sustainable performance improvement. It is time that, when selecting leaders, we move beyond rewarding past achievements and instead learn to anticipate their future contributions.

Potential Tactical Errors

Tactical error 21: We deduce future potential based on current performance and visibility.

Tactical error 22: We think in black and white. You are either a talent, or you are not.

Premature Talent Selection and Short Career Windows

In January 2007, our daughter was born – undoubtedly the most emotional moment of my life. Holding this little 'being' in my arms, I experienced overwhelming love and growing pride, alongside a profound respect for the responsibility that rested upon us from that moment forward. From this point, we committed ourselves to ensuring her happiness and well-being. Believing that our lives would now revolve entirely around our baby, I managed to check off one item on my 'bucket list' in the year preceding her birth: I ran my first – and last – marathon in Berlin. I had already ended my active football career, as the dual demands of work and sport were significantly impacting my health, and my global work schedule was scarcely compatible with intensive performance training.

However, I never pursued the idea of reducing my professional commitment. My newly established family had two weeks of holiday before I returned to the 'hamster wheel', spending approximately half of my working time on business trips – mostly across different time zones.

It was neither financial constraints, a motivation to be with my family, nor an enthusiasm for business travel that prevented me from scaling back. Rather, it was my limiting beliefs. Like many of my peers, I was conditioned to believe that the decisive phase of our careers was imminent. 'The next ten years will determine whether you succeed in your career and how much you will earn later,' was the prevailing sentiment. While some of my friends made extensive use of parental leave, I was guided by the belief that this would be impossible for me.

In retrospect, I do not fault my advisors at the time, as they were, in a certain respect, correct. During this period, I indeed laid the foundation for my professional career and steadily increased financial security. It may seem ironic: by working even more during a phase when a part-time job would have been the most sensible option for all involved, I created the freedom to work part-time, later on. However, this additional work was only possible because my wife reduced her working hours following the birth of our daughter.

Today, approximately 20 years later, much has changed – although not sufficiently. The majority of new professionals would find little affinity with my convictions at that time. Even lecturers today tend to be more cautious when offering advice of this nature. While applicants' mindsets have evolved, corporate practices have remained largely unchanged.

Career trajectories are still frequently determined within the first quarter of our professional lives, which for many coincides precisely with the period of starting a family. Selection occurs early and remains elitist. Our talent development programmes continue to be founded on the assumption that careers follow a linear path. Large corporations, in particular, establish elite groups and invest in specialised programmes for the so-called 'high potentials'. These individuals are expected to assume leadership positions in the future. They often possess both the willingness and the opportunity to dedicate themselves fully to their careers during this life phase – as I did at the time, graciously supported by my family.

We operate similarly to professional football: we invest early in a few exceptional talents and gradually filter out others. The prevailing view is that anyone without leadership experience by the age of 40 either does not want it or is unable to attain it. This is not always due to a lack of motivation, but often results from individual life circumstances. Some employees may decline promotion opportunities for years because they believe that career advancement inevitably entails longer working hours – a perception frequently reinforced by their environment.

This practice disadvantages those who, in the early stages of their career, neither have the opportunity nor the desire to invest excessively in their work. A significant potential is lost, particularly regarding diversity.

To Succeed at the Top, You Must Develop Breadth

What lessons can we draw from talent selection in sport? In competitive sport, most experts agree today that premature and elitist selection impedes the development of young talent, rather than fostering it. Successful careers – whether in sport or professional life – seldom follow a straightforward path. Many Olympic, world and European champions have not followed a direct route to becoming professional athletes. "To succeed at the top, you must develop breadth," emphasises Berthold Bisselik, who has been successful for decades as a coach and youth coordinator in professional sport – in basketball, hockey and football alike[22].

In my discussions with coaches from sports such as basketball, handball and hockey, it became evident how creatively and passionately they strive to develop potential. Each player is regarded as valuable and is developed individually – similar to the approach of the Belgians in football. With approximately 500,000 active football players, Belgium has significantly fewer talents than a city like Paris. This limited resource necessitates longer-term player development and discourages premature exclusion. As a result, fewer talents are lost. In contrast, many football nations and companies indulge in the questionable luxury of focusing their attention on an elite minority, while numerous other talents are left behind.

In light of the growing skilled labour shortage and the declining interest in leadership positions, the question arises: Can we truly afford to continue acting like we do in football? Or should we instead adopt the mindset of those involved in so-called 'fringe sports'? Elite development programmes convey a clear message: Most employees lack the potential to reach the executive level, 'late starters' fall through the cracks, and hidden talents remain undiscovered.

Would it not be more prudent to approach every employee with curiosity and openness? This would allow top competencies and potential to be identified and nurtured regardless of age, tenure or career stage – at every phase of professional life.

Learning at an Advanced Age

In sport, an athlete generally has between ten and a maximum of twenty years to develop, whereas a professional career typically spans between thirty and forty years. Therefore, in professional life, we theoretically have two to three times as much time to continue developing and to contribute our experiences and skills for the benefit of the team. Unfortunately, many individuals do not fully utilise this time – partly due to their own responsibility, but also as a result of prevailing company practices.

A football player usually reaches their peak between the ages of 25 and 28, roughly at the midpoint of their career. Nonetheless, some players experience a second peak in their later years, as they can support the team with their experience. They simply assume a different role and apply their strengths and experiences.

Take the footballer Claudio Pizarro as an example. Even at the age of 40, he was still scoring goals in the Bundesliga – netting in an impressive 21 consecutive seasons. It was not only his goals but also his presence, attitude and composure that made him invaluable, despite reduced playing time.

An examination of the Brazilian Serie A demonstrates that players can continue to make valuable contributions in the latter stages of their careers. At 38 years old, defender Rafinha, who played 266 matches for Bayern Munich, contests the fewest duels among defenders. Instead, he manages many situations intuitively and boasts one of the highest pass completion rates in the league. He is regarded as a key factor in his team's success.

In the coaching profession, age does not prevent anyone from continuous improvement. World champion coach Gordon Herbert reports that, for him, everything came together only upon assuming the role of head coach of the German national basketball team. He explains that he was able to leave behind the 'Gordie' who often raised his voice to demand something, thereby creating space for a new 'Gordie' – one who enjoyed working with the players and was inspired by a new guiding principle: "The burden of the journey must never, in the long term, outweigh the joy of the journey"[23].

What holds true for national coaches and players equally applies to other employees who, like fine wine, increase in value with age. Calmness, as exemplified by Claudio Pizarro, and a strengthened, realistic mindset, as seen in Gordon Herbert, are qualities that do not necessarily disadvantage leaders in business. Under certain circumstances, individuals expend less energy on confrontations and instead act with discernment and the necessary foresight, as exemplified by Rafinha. This applies not only to those who assumed leadership responsibility early, but particularly to those who develop an interest in new responsibilities during the second half or even the final third of their career.

In many cases, however, the reality is different: we invest during the first third of our careers and then reap the benefits. The belief that the course is set during the initial years of our careers is deeply ingrained. For those who have held a leadership position for some time, it is crucial not to reveal too many weaknesses. From a certain age, individuals are regarded as 'trained' and ready to present themselves.

For those who, for various reasons, decided against a leadership position during the critical phase, the career window often remains closed, even if life circumstances change. There is seldom a second chance; the opportunity appears to have gone. Older employees, in particular, are ideally suited to experiment with leadership, as they have typically had the opportunity to learn from various managers. Over the years, they often develop a strong intuition for leadership, but no longer receive opportunities to apply it in practice. This is a critical error that particularly costs female leaders, who are lost due to prevailing practices.

It is neither wise nor fair to allow, promote or require individuals to pursue or abandon their careers during the period when women bear children and young families care for their offspring. Equally unethical is the failure to develop all employees to realise their potential.

By widening the scope within which a 'career boost' may and should be initiated, we increase the likelihood that, in the future, a more diverse range of individuals – irrespective of gender or age – will assume leadership positions. In doing so, we would almost imperceptibly counteract not only the expectation of going the extra mile but also another diversity inhibitor, thereby making a significant contribution to healthy and sustainable performance development within organisations.

Potential Tactical Errors

Tactical error 23: Our development programmes are too elitist.

Tactical error 24: We select our 'high potentials' too early.

Accessing Performance

'Choking under pressure' is a well-known term in sports psychology that describes how an athlete fails under pressure – at the decisive moment of competition – and does not deliver the required performance. Coaches often do not expect athletes to perform at their best in such situations. In fact, only about 20% of athletes manage to deliver outstanding performance under pressure. Sports psychologists focus intensively on how this rate can be increased and how the likelihood can be improved that their young players achieve peak performance even in stressful situations.

Bill Shankly, the legendary coach of Liverpool in the 1960s and 1970s, famously stated: "There are people who think football is a matter of life and death. I do not share that view. I can assure you, it is far more serious than that." In many companies, there is a sense that work is conducted with a similarly unreasonable urgency. But how much potential is lost when individuals are expected to 'deliver' under constant pressure?

There is no reason to believe that our capacity to achieve outstanding performance under pressure exceeds that of renowned elite athletes. If the same holds true for companies as it does for athletes, then there exists a vast reservoir of untapped potential. To access this potential, we must examine more closely the dynamics of performance and pressure.

Dressing Room Speeches and Company Cars

When Jürgen Klopp left Borussia Dortmund in the summer of 2015, he had not only coached the most matches in the club's history, with 318 games, but had also achieved an impressive average of 1.90 points per game. Under Klopp, the club secured numerous titles and was long regarded as one of the teams playing the most attractive football in Germany. To illustrate the coach's popularity among the Dortmund supporters, Mario Basler once remarked: "They cheer in the South Stand simply when he cleans his glasses on the bench without incident." At his subsequent role in Liverpool, Jürgen Klopp continued to shine with similar brilliance.

Klopp is reputed to be an exceptional motivator. It appears that under his leadership, his players run faster, pass more precisely, shoot with greater power, and play with superior tactical intelligence compared to most others. His ability to motivate is regarded as outstanding. These reflections occur to me as I attend a leadership seminar hosted by a large medium-sized enterprise. The founder and managing director is trying to communicate his credo for the coming years to those present: "We need more motivation specialists like Jürgen Klopp within our ranks!" resonates from the stage. He portrays the passionate and emotional dressing room speech delivered before a decisive match, which inspires the players to achieve peak performance.

The medium-sized enterprise, like many others in its position, looks enviously at successful football coaches, but overlooks a crucial point. The difference between Coach Klopp and Sales Manager Ms. Adams does not necessarily lie in Klopp being a better motivator or his motivational appeals being more effective. As previously stated, the renowned football coach does not need to motivate anyone – in fact, he cannot. If his players were not motivated, they would have stayed in bed and not made the effort to attend training. Klopp understands that it is not his responsibility to motivate his players.

Individual Motivation Drivers

Successful coaches recognise that the objective is not to motivate individuals directly, but to establish conditions that enable the potential of both individual players and the team to be realised. Motivation is assumed to be inherent. Therefore, motivation is not considered an independent objective, and little time is devoted to enhancing it. Successful coaches and sports psychologists have recognised that eliciting outstanding performance is a highly individual and personal endeavour.

The football coach and FIFA Men's Coach of the Year 2021, Thomas Tuchel, identifies three types of player.

The first type comprises those who are determined to be the best. Their goals are often personal in nature: they take pride in appearing on front pages or receiving individual awards. We are all familiar with these players. When a coach effectively channels their motivation, these players can be extremely valuable to the team. However, if the ego exerts excessive control, it can adversely impact the team's performance.

The second category comprises players who define themselves through strong relationships. They seek to be an integral part of the team, work towards shared success, and prefer to remain in the background. These team players are also well known to us. Although some of them – based on measurable output – may be considered 'average players', they often contribute significantly to the team's cohesion. When you consider your management team or your sports team, you will undoubtedly recognise several of these team players.

Finally, there is the third type of player: those who strive for continuous self-development. They are curious and wish to understand the level of their skills and how far their talent can take them. These players consistently strive to embrace new challenges[24]. They are often referred to as players with a 'growth mindset', a concept we will explore further. For them, the emphasis lies less on the outcome and more on the continuous process of improvement. They think and act in a process-oriented manner. Had the racing legend Ayrton Senna become a footballer, Tuchel would likely have placed him in this third category. When asked what truly motivates him, Senna responded: "I always want to improve. That brings me happiness. Whenever I sense that my learning process is slowing and my learning curve is flattening, I become less satisfied."

In scientific research, a three-factor model is often employed to explain human behaviour. The self-determination theory, which categorises factors into autonomy, competence and connectedness, is particularly prominent in sports psychology. These fundamental needs are remarkably uncontested, even among experts.

Connectedness refers to the importance that others hold for us and that we hold for others – that is, how closely we feel connected to others. Autonomy is about the need to make and act on decisions independently and with self-determination. Competence describes the extent to which an individual feels effective – that is, how competent and efficacious they perceive their actions to be.

In recent years, additional concepts and theories have been introduced. Although not all are as scientifically robust as the self-determination theory developed by Edward Deci and Richard Ryan, two of these approaches will nonetheless be highlighted here.

Daniel Pink, author of the bestseller *Drive*[25], expands the model by introducing an additional driver, which he terms 'purpose'. This concept is best translated as 'meaning' or 'mission'. Emma Hayes, FIFA Women's Coach of the Year 2021 and Olympic gold medallist, highlighted the purpose and deeper significance of her actions as a crucial motivator for her players – or, as she expressed it, 'loyalty to the mission'. This mission can manifest in a variety of ways. In certain successful football nations, players initially strive to provide for their families through their football talent, as Rasmus Ankersen aptly illustrates in his book, *The Gold Mine Effect*[26]. A highly significant assignment.

Pelé, arguably the most legendary football player of all time, came from very humble beginnings and had to earn money by shining shoes as a child to support his family. Zlatan Ibrahimović learned to assert himself in Rosengård, a suburb of Malmö known as a social hotspot. Cristiano Ronaldo also grew up in impoverished conditions on Madeira, as did Lionel Messi, who spent his childhood in the working-class neighbourhood of La Bajada in Rosario. Kylian Mbappé grew up in Bondy, a suburb of Paris, in social housing.

There is considerable debate as to whether it was this significant purpose that drove these elite football players – the desire for continuous improvement – or, alternatively, the pursuit of social recognition (status). This driver is identified, among others, in the SCARF model.

During my part-time studies at Oxford, I had the opportunity to listen to David Rock. Among his many achievements, Rock is founder and director of the NeuroLeadership Institute. His ability to structure and simplify complex concepts inspired me, and continues to do so. David Rock's SCARF model[27] draws upon the following motivators; the initial letters of which form the acronym of the model:

S – Status
C – Certainty
A – Autonomy
R – Relatedness
F – Fairness.

Thomas Tuchel will recognise himself within this model. The category 'Status' largely corresponds to the first player type described – the player who strives for fame and recognition. The category 'Relatedness' reflects the second player type – the one who feels a strong connection to the team and finds fulfilment in being part of a collective. In addition to these two dimensions, 'Autonomy', 'Certainty' and 'Fairness' also play a central role.

One player performs better when provided with a clear match plan (certainty), whereas another realises their full potential only when granted maximum freedom or allowed to act intuitively, as exemplified by Thomas Müller or Zlatan Ibrahimović (autonomy). Another player soon requires a clear and understandable explanation as to why they are repeatedly benched (fairness). In very few cases do players require a sophisticated bonus system or goal agreements to realise their potential on the field. It is individual approaches that motivate players to achieve peak performance.

This diversity is reflected within companies. Some people work to provide for their families – a fundamental, highly relevant and honourable motivation. Others pursue perceived status. Studies indicate that personal growth, meaningfulness and, especially, autonomy have become increasingly important in some parts of the world.

Fairness is increasingly recognised as a fundamental prerequisite, supported by initiatives promoting diversity, equity and inclusion. The strategy of motivating the majority of young employees with high salaries, company cars and prestigious titles (status) to pursue the challenging career path will, however, become progressively more difficult to enforce at the executive level.

All these models bear strong similarities and represent simplifications of reality. For those who prefer a more nuanced approach, the so-called Reiss Profile or its German adaptation – the Luxx Profile, which was notably employed during the successful 'Project Gold' of the German national handball team in 2007 – may be utilised. Additionally, Klaus Grawe's consistency theory and the work of Professor Julius Kuhl offer frameworks that can assist leaders in better understanding human behaviour.

Regardless of the approach taken, the objective is not to differentiate between 'right' and 'wrong' or 'good' and 'bad' motivators. For athletes, it is demonstrably healthier and more sustainable to focus on continuous improvement rather than to base their well-being on recognition and applause (status). Nonetheless, both types of motivation can lead to exceptional performance, as they stimulate the drive for ongoing development.

What matters is not to painstakingly identify which drive is predominant – and even less to confine individuals to rigid categories. Rather, it involves recognising the diversity of motivation drivers and fostering dialogue around them. This can not only prevent considerable frustration during change processes within companies but also, much like successful coaches, assist in better unlocking a team's potential.

Motivation is highly individual both in sport and within organisations. Perhaps this is why many leaders do not dedicate sufficient time to it. It is often more tangible to apply measurable approaches, such as ambitious goal setting, to enhance motivation. In business life, we tend to overlook the diversity of individual drivers that cause outstanding performance.

Many companies continue to base their fundamental assumptions about motivation on behaviourism, rooted in the theories of Pavlov and Skinner. This principle, founded on simple stimulus-response relationships, was originally developed through laboratory experiments with animals. Although some employees may feel as if they are running on a hamster wheel in their professional daily lives, it is important to recognise that humans differ from laboratory animals through their emotional and social values – values that were not accounted for in such experiments. Consequently, global 'one-size-fits-all' incentive systems that presume all individuals are motivated by the same factors are often ineffective.

Such systems, which operate on the 'carrot or stick' principle, undermine one of the most fundamental psychological needs – the need for autonomy and self-determination.

Motivation is not created; it is either revealed or obstructed. People are naturally motivated, though shaped very differently and individually. The focus is not on increasing motivation or glorifying motivational speeches, but on avoiding demotivation of players. It is essential to identify what hinders motivation. For this purpose, the concept of self-determination theory offers valuable insight. We constantly exist within the realm of our three fundamental psychological needs: the need for autonomy or control, the desire for connectedness, and the need to feel effective – that is, to be able to contribute (competence).

The Motivation of Sales Teams

During my time as head of an in-house consulting group for sales and marketing, I led the global implementation of a Customer Relationship

Management (CRM) system. This system was designed to enhance customer service as well as sales effectiveness and efficiency, by providing greater transparency. The key to success was in understanding that autonomy, in particular, was a significant motivator for many sales employees. It was one of the reasons they chose a career in sales. It became apparent that the CRM system would not be seen as an investment for the future, with significant customer benefits, but rather as a control mechanism that would potentially restrict the autonomy of sales employees. We therefore implemented a sales coaching programme. Within this framework, we demonstrated to the sales employees how the factual basis and transparency provided by the CRM system enhanced their decision-making, saved time, and significantly increased their chances of securing orders. The employees experienced these benefits firsthand and no longer perceived their valued autonomy as being at risk. The previously critical discussions evolved, and the system largely populated itself with relevant data. These new processes were supported over several years by a globally distributed network of sales coaches. Patience, focus and continuity proved rewarding. Today, the CRM system is an integral and indispensable component of all sales and marketing activities.

In transformation projects, it is common to face the challenge that employees do not support the change. Rather than judging from a top-down perspective, we should ask what motivates employees to resist change. Behind this resistance is a motivation that must be understood. Understanding individual motivators is key to transforming resistance into acceptance.

Naturally, in cross-organisational projects, it is not feasible to consider every single employee and their drivers. However, should we not invest a little more time in this? Let us take marketing as an example.

Even in poorly managed product launches, so-called 'personas' are created, and product features and communication are individually tailored. Every detail is thoughtfully considered to address the various drivers of the target audience. For each driver, there is an appropriate product, accompanied by a fitting core message. To achieve this, market research is conducted, and client segments are precisely defined. However, in internal projects, the diversity of employees often appears to be reduced to a binary distinction – those who are willing and those who are not.

This brings us back to Jürgen Klopp. His success is not founded on generic motivational phrases, but the fact he recognises each of his players as unique individuals. In a world filled with shades of grey, he treats people individually, with positive curiosity and genuine interest. In numerous interviews, it is evident that he likes them and strives to understand them, including their drivers and their individual 'purpose'. He appears to create the conditions for maximum willingness to perform. It is evident that 'Kloppo' takes pleasure in winning, but equally in unlocking the potential of each player[28].

A significant and necessary step would be for companies to critically review their existing motivation systems and fundamentally realign them. The time currently spent filling these rigid systems with content could be far more effectively invested in dialogue concerning individual drivers and fundamental psychological needs. This very exchange brings us closer to the goal of achieving healthy and sustainable performance improvement. However, this shift in thinking requires curiosity, empathy and, above all, time – time deliberately invested in personal conversations with each individual employee. However, this investment is worthwhile. Please give it a try.

Potential Tactical Errors

> **Tactical error 25:** We categorise employees as either 'motivated' or 'unmotivated'.

> **Tactical error 26:** We have an insufficient understanding of our employees' basic needs.

> **Tactical error 27:** We unintentionally demotivate our employees.

Panic Mode and The Extra Mile

"If you want to lose, look at the scoreboard." This statement was made by Paul Assaiante, a two-time Olympic Coach of the Year and author of *Run to the Roar*[29]. In both sport and business, much depends on the results achieved. Any romanticised notion of 'new work' that suggests otherwise presents a significant risk to ambitious, performance-oriented companies, whether they are corporations, medium-sized enterprises or start-ups.

The truth, however, is more nuanced: delivering performance and thereby achieving results should bring as much satisfaction as it does for long-term successful elite athletes and success teams. Yet, an unconditional focus on the measurable outcome – the 'what' – often results in the opposite effect, causing not only the loss of joy but also of valuable potential despite all efforts.

Some successful coaches have already institutionalised this approach. A prime example is seen at German football club SC Freiburg, which consistently manages to better harness potential than its competitors, year after year. They do not succumb to activity when things do not proceed as planned. Rather than measuring themselves solely by results, they concentrate on the 'how'. Their belief in the collective capabilities, success and the chosen match plan enables continuous development.

The decisive factor is not measuring the 'what' but focusing on the 'how' – day by day, week by week. In sport and business, what is not easily measurable makes the true difference. From these intangible or difficult-to-measure elements arise competitive advantages that are scarcely replicable – now and in the future[30].

Let us examine the tactical errors that these coaches, athletes and clubs typically avoid.

Panic Mode

In the 85th minute of a cup match, the home team is trailing 1–0. Despite creating numerous chances, the opposing team's goalkeeper has saved all attempts at goal. It is time to go 'all-out-attack'. All tactical instructions are abandoned. Instead of confidently and optimistically adhering to the match plan until the end, fear of defeat has taken over. The players send the ball high into the opponent's penalty area, hoping it will somehow reach their forwards. The chances of turning the game around in this manner are minimal. Rising panic inhibits clear thinking. This fear is a poor guide to success.

You may be wondering why teams resort to such a measure. As a leader of a company, would you handle it differently?

Parallels can be drawn to business life. Within companies, we often observe similar actions reminiscent of the 'scrappy football' played during time added on. In times of crisis, panic mode can ensue. The outcome is what matters, and short-term suboptimisations are implemented to achieve measurable goals. Inventories are rapidly depleted, long-standing suppliers replaced, price adjustments made, hiring freezes imposed, travel budgets slashed, and people development programmes suspended. Everything is aimed at not missing the established, measurable goal. A never-ending vicious circle: a stop-and-go dynamic that hinders any form of continuous and sustainable performance development. These short-term suboptimisations create an illusion of control but are, in fact, the clearest evidence of its loss. The fear of defeat results in actions that contradict the company's vision and corporate values, yet these are displayed as glossy posters along office corridors. The 'diesel scandal' involving the Volkswagen Group was arguably one of the most significant panic modes the German industry has ever encountered. Similarly, in sport, it requires little effort to uncover the next doping scandal, thanks to our goal fetish.

Such an approach often results in those responsible within companies being celebrated and promoted. Pure result orientation is the prevailing credo. However, this way of working is superficial and temporary, and merely covers wounds like a bandage. The underlying cause is seldom identified and addressed. Our fixation on measurable figures – the 'all or nothing', winning or losing – comes at the expense of sustainable and healthy performance improvement.

Another month passes, and employees wonder why their company no longer has regular season games, only knockout matches. The outcome is an influx of excellent result managers who are not necessarily effective leaders, and even fewer success coaches who ensure sustainable performance improvement. The focus is on the 'what' rather than the 'how'. We focus solely on the immediate result, on the here and now, the next game, without understanding which parameters would ensure sustainable success.

The example of Danish football club FC Midtjylland demonstrates that it can be done differently. The two founding clubs, Herning Fremad and Ikast FS, whose teams formed FC Midtjylland's first team in 1999, continue to exist and maintain their own youth teams. This perpetuates a concept particularly practised in Denmark, designed to enable smaller clubs to establish themselves economically and athletically in the top league on a lasting basis. Moreover, they win games in the final minutes without nervous hesitation. Their confidence in themselves and in their match plan makes the difference. The match plan, and even the club's transfer policy, are based on mathematical calculations that incorporate probabilities – and do not allow panic to ensue in search of a solution. An exceptionally compelling topic that could warrant an entire book. The sustainable outcome: FC Midtjylland had, at the time of writing, celebrated four championships, two cup victories and had become a regular competitor in European tournaments. During the 2023/2024 Bundesliga season, we observed another impressive example of a team that, irrespective of the scoreline, relied on its strengths and match strategy. German football club Bayer Leverkusen secured victory in six matches during time added on – doing so without haste or a lack of planning. Rather than resorting to brute force, they exhibited patience and trust in their game strategy, which ultimately proved successful.

The Principle of Hope

While clubs and companies that operate forcefully cannot be accused of doing nothing (they simply do not know any better), the situation differs for those clubs and companies that have committed themselves to the principle of hope. In this context, the strategy aims to maintain hope that the next month or year will be better. Perhaps circumstances will change: a competitor faces delivery difficulties, raises prices, or a major customer grants the company an unplanned assignment. The prospect of success is, at best, fifty-fifty.

This recalls the superstition observed among some athletes, particularly in football. In 2018, sports journalist Christoph Biermann noted that football players, coaches and managers are more superstitious than most other professional groups[31].

I have yet to meet a salesperson who, after successful business transactions, keeps the blue lucky sweater on as long as Udo Lattek did in his role as sports director of Bundesliga football club Cologne during the 1987/1988 season, until they lost for the first time on the 15th match day in Bremen.

Nor have I encountered a colleague who enters their office first with the right foot, as many athletes do when stepping on to the field. I would be even less inclined to consider wearing a colleague's underwear when entering difficult negotiations. This was reportedly done by Gerrie

Mühren, the legendary football player of Ajax, who always wore the 'underpants' of his teammate Sjaak Swart during matches.

In business life, the irrational belief persists that things will improve without genuinely taking action, thanks to hope. Over time, this transforms an 'unrelegatable' into an 'unpromotable', whether in sport or business. Those familiar with German football will likely think of Hamburg, to whom this applies.

The 'Extra Mile'

The 'extra mile' is arguably the most popular concept, esteemed at the executive level. It closely resembles the principle of hope but presents itself in a different form. In the long term, this concept is no more effective than the principle of hope, yet it aligns better with our convictions. The extra mile, like the 'all-out-attack' philosophy, creates the impression of doing everything possible for success. If it fails, everyone is expected to make an even greater effort.

In sport, it may be effective when a team is reduced in number and mobilises all efforts in the final 30 minutes to compensate for the deficit. However, no sensible club would play an entire season with only ten players, as this would clearly overwhelm every individual player.

This very principle, however, has become entrenched in many companies in recent years and is euphemistically referred to as 'going the extra mile'. The cause of the performance deviation is addressed by signalling to employees that they must increase their efforts to be at least on par with the competition.

Within companies, those willing to work longer hours are often regarded as 'high performers' – though not necessarily more focused. This is not about concentration, discipline or making a sustainable contribution, but simply about relentless running. The goal is to run longer and faster than the competition – a pattern deeply embedded in our traditional thinking.

In sport, it has long-been recognised that success does not depend on running as much as possible, but on selecting the correct paths to run at critical moments. A compelling example of this is the Dutch football club AZ Alkmaar, which consistently challenges the major teams in continental football, despite comparatively modest resources. For this club, the term '**FEAR**' is significant. Many players, under pressure, make the mistake of panicking and running aimlessly. For them, 'FEAR' stands for 'Forget Everything And Run'.

AZ Alkmaar trains its players to reinterpret these four letters as 'Face Everything And Respond'. Players are encouraged to define their own meaning of 'FEAR' and to actively engage with challenges[32].

Many companies could benefit from adopting this attitude, as they often tend to choose the less considered option under pressure. They lose sight of their original plans. While they do not literally flee, they succumb to frantic activity – more than ever before. The fatigue that manifests at the end of the day as dark circles under the eyes is regarded as an indicator of hard work. Especially in my home country, Germany, work is often most valued when it causes at least some discomfort or even pain.

In many companies, going the extra mile is rewarded with a promotion. This is a reward for not having achieved the targeted goals on the first attempt. Inevitably, I think of the penalty round in biathlon. Here, there is more honesty, and it is plainly called a 'penalty round' because not all shots hit the target. But how would that sound? No – it is better to say, 'going the extra mile'. Now, players are needed who roll up their sleeves and withstand adverse conditions.

The problem is that many companies must not only go the extra mile or endure a brief period of being outnumbered. What was intended as a sprint quietly turns into a marathon, at the end of which employees can be playing at a numerical disadvantage.

The 'Blame Game'

When the 'all-out-attack' approach fails to achieve success, football fans witness two distinct responses.

Some coaches take responsibility: 'We failed to implement our match plan, lacked strength in duels, lost our composure and made incorrect decisions in front of goal. My player substitutions also failed to produce the desired effect. We will learn from this experience and approach our next challenge with renewed strength.'

A discerning observer recognises that the coach is focusing on factors within his and his team's control. No blame, no panicked justifications – only the commitment to learn from mistakes. In sport, this is referred to as 'control the controllables'.

Other managers, coaches and players, however, tend to engage in the 'blame game', seeking fault beyond their sphere of influence – whether it be the uneven pitch or the official in charge. Stefan Reuter, during his time as Borussia Dortmund team manager, stated: "I do not want to comment on the referee's performance, but what was called was outrageous." Ewald Lienen, whilst coach of Cologne, made this sardonic remark about the referee: "He does not laugh himself to death when we make a bad pass."

When neither the referee nor the circumstances provide a valid excuse, when coaches appear helpless or the pressure becomes overwhelming, we observe yet another manifestation of the 'blame game'. According to a 2011 study, 65% of coaches are dismissed due to lack of success, with an average tenure of less than 14 months. This short-term result orientation has profound effects on the players, as demonstrated by the example of Hamburg. As a native of Hamburg, it pains me to witness the years of desperate attempts to maintain the label 'unrelegatable'. In 2018, this effort failed, and the club's stay in the Bundesliga was over after 54 years, 261 days, 35 minutes and 10 seconds.

Since then, Hamburg have been striving to return to the top division, which they managed in May 2025. Before opting for greater patience and consistency in the 2021/2022 season, 13 coaches attempted in just ten years to lead Hamburg back to the big time. Short-term interim solutions, such as firefighter Horst Hrubesch, are not even accounted for in this calculation.

The 'blame game' results from the human tendency to construct a simple narrative and offer an explanation – even when it does not reflect reality. This behaviour is also known as 'story bias'.

This 'story bias', which many of us criticise in professional football, is encountered daily within our organisations. The same business leaders who critique these clubs in casual conversations at the coffee machine are themselves confined by a framework they have custom-made.

CEOs are not dismissed as swiftly as coaches. Their tenure is approximately five times longer than that of a coach – even though they cannot attribute blame to the officials or an unplayable pitch. For managers worldwide, it is advantageous that companies operate as cross-functional team sports. When the general market situation cannot be invoked to explain missed goals, there is a habitual tendency to shift the blame on to another function. In cases of success, however, these very departments are typically excluded from the commonly recounted success narrative. The 'self-serving bias' causes individuals to attribute their successes to their own abilities, while blaming failures on external factors. Similar patterns are evident in sales analyses, where lost orders are attributed to missing product specifications or excessively high prices, whereas won orders are credited to personal negotiation skills and long-term relationship management.

Destructive friction between different company functions is pervasive, whether between sales and marketing, production and procurement, or quality and development. It is a recurring dynamic that typically produces no winners, only losers – and is exacerbated by the fixation on goals.

Changing the System

Returning to sport, when neither the use of 'all-out-attack' nor 'running more than the opponent' achieves the desired effect, the new head coach fails to deliver, and no funds are available to acquire new players to strengthen the team, a new game system is often adopted. These changes are primarily intended to be visible – to demonstrate that active countermeasures are in place and that control has not been lost.

In football, for example, a 'false 9' is employed instead of a traditional centre forward. 'False 9'? Yes, you heard correctly – it is a technical term from football. While the traditional number nine positions themselves centrally and occupies the central defenders, the 'false 9' disengages from their markers and moves out to the wings. This strategy aims to disrupt the compact defensive block while the player simultaneously engages in combination play in midfield. Scoring goals remains their responsibility, nonetheless.

In other words, the player no longer solely fulfils the original role – scoring goals, for which he was hired – but also undertakes tasks that typically belong to other departments. In football, 11 players remain on the field during such a system change. In business, however, similar changes often aim to distribute the same workload to fewer people. This is frequently presented under creatively named projects, accompanied by the assertion that change is the only constant. This offers little support to employees who suddenly must perform many tasks without mastering any, much like the 'striker' of former times.

When even partial mergers of departments or similar organisational manoeuvres fail to bring improvement, the final measure is implemented: the system is completely overhauled. For example, the head coach might switch from a 4-4-2 formation to a 4-3-3, or from 4-3-2-1 to 4-4-1-1. There are no limits to imagination. These numbers represent the individuals of the team – defenders, defensive and attacking midfielders, as well as the attackers. You will notice one constant: the goalkeeper's position always remains unchanged. The rules require it – one cannot play with two goalkeepers nor without one. In the corporate environment, this inviolable position typically represents the executive management. Even when surrounding structures are altered, its role remains untouched – this rule is unwritten but widely accepted.

While such tactical adjustments in football take effect relatively quickly with the right personnel, commitment and perseverance, yielding success after a few games, comparable changes in large organisations often result in prolonged stagnation. This is followed by months, sometimes years, of unlearning and relearning. These processes are usually costly, especially when opportunity costs are considered.

Naturally, there are situations in which restructuring is appropriate – for instance, when companies grow and must prepare for future challenges. However, such measures are often precisely what the executive level is reluctant to admit: a sign of losing control. There is a tendency to cling to the belief that the problem lies not in how we work, but in how we were organised, which made us inefficient. This leads us back to our 'story bias' – the narrative may not be entirely true, but it is easily comprehensible. Costly consultants frequently reinforce this.

This belief provides comfort, as it partially absolves us of responsibility. Even better, such restructuring can be implemented swiftly – at least on paper. It aligns perfectly with our belief that problems can be 'patched up', much like a leaking gutter at home. In this context, we embody the motto, 'Can we fix it? Yes, we can!', as enthusiastically declared by Bob the Builder.

The time is now for HR departments. They can demonstrate their expertise by creating detailed organisational charts and assisting overwhelmed managers in filling the empty boxes with the appropriate names. A form of 'paint by numbers' for advanced practitioners. Typically, the previously carefully maintained succession plans are overlooked, as crisis mode prevails. Only what is immediately required matters. What does not fit is made to fit – a concept that is also familiar with Bob the Builder. However, in this context, it concerns people rather than machines.

Honestly, how often have you observed a colleague's behaviour change drastically, simply because they now occupy a different box within the organisational chart? How often has everything suddenly become easier and more efficient following a restructure? It is similar to football – there are winners and losers. Some colleagues embrace the new structure, while others reject it. Over recent years, we have experimented extensively, yet the sobering insight remains: organisational forms are only as effective as the people who create them. The success of a system depends fundamentally on the mindset and actions of its employees. Naturally, restrictive processes and structures must be identified and optimised; however, in most cases, restructures do not offer a genuine solution to the challenges of the modern world of work.

The End Justifies the Means

All these tactical errors arise from deeply ingrained thinking patterns. They stem from a distorted definition of success that compels us to manage results rather than cultivate sustainable performance. The focus is on the glittering peaks of the iceberg, while the foundation beneath the waterline is neglected.

For many result managers in companies, a month in which financial targets are not met is, by definition, a bad month. It does not matter whether talented employees were recruited, a comprehensive company strategy was developed, or innovative projects were initiated. Conversely, everything is deemed acceptable if targets are exceeded, even when other success indicators are in the red. If the outcome is favourable, the end justifies the means. We simply prefer a win at all costs over a draw or a defeat. Once again, many of our leaders are trained to manage results rather than to cultivate sustainable performance.

Christian Streich, who successfully coached German football club SC Freiburg for more than a decade, is dedicated to sustainable performance development. After some of the team's defeats, he told journalists, out of respect for their critical questions and in line with his own belief: "The result is not satisfactory, but the way my team played makes me proud and gives me a positive outlook for the challenges ahead."

In sport, numerous cases have shown that a consistent focus on the 'how' can lead to a turnaround, rather than succumbing to the tactical errors already described under the pressure of lacking victories.

Regrettably, we seldom hear similar statements from CEOs. Employees might respond more positively if their managing directors openly acknowledged: "Our second quarter was not satisfactory, but the development of our team and our organisation fills me with great confidence. We will sooner or later reap the results of this sowing." How this can be achieved is explained in the next section.

Potential Tactical Errors

Tactical error 28: We look at the scoreboard too frequently.

Tactical error 29: We resort to panic mode to achieve results.

Tactical error 30: We demand going the extra mile to achieve results.

Tactical error 31: We engage in the blame game.

Tactical error 32: We change our (game) system too often.

Success Factors and Expected Goals

Another pioneer of this philosophy, who regards the result as a consequence, and therefore does not operate in a result-driven manner, is the former German national hockey coach and three-time Olympic champion Markus Weise. It is unsurprising that he referred to himself as a 'performance coach' – his focus is consistently on performance. He is not misled by the results, neither positively nor negatively. Moreover, when analysing victory or defeat, these coaches avoid the mistake of seeking overly simplistic explanations, as is sometimes the case in business. Do you recall? When a month goes well, success is attributed to the high-performing leadership team. When it goes poorly, difficult market conditions are cited as the decisive factor. A lost assignment is blamed on the price, while a won one is credited to negotiation skills.

This mindset, which shifts responsibility situationally, often prevents companies from gaining genuine insights.

In sport, we frequently observe conspicuous explanation attempts. How often do we hear, after victory, who the key success factors were. Sometimes it is the goalkeeper who saved the penalty kick in the final minute, sometimes the goalscorer who scored a hat-trick, and other times the defender who cleared the ball off the line, preventing a goal. In our search for explanations, we tend to think in simple cause-and-effect terms – a process known in psychology as 'attribution'. We attribute victory to a specific cause, and because this is conveniently simple and easily marketable, we single out the individual who presumably decided the game and label them the ultimate 'success factor'. There are always games in which a few key moments involving individual players determine victory or defeat. However, even in such moments, the secret to success does not rest solely on a successful goal or a saved penalty kick.

To foster a healthy and sustainable performance culture, we must refine our understanding of the so-called success factors. Success factors are elements deemed essential for achieving positive outcomes. In other words, these factors increase the likelihood of success. However, in very few cases are individuals or events solely responsible for sustainable success. Neither the goal nor the decisive shot in the final minute are the primary causes of sustainable success. It wasn't NBA star Dennis Schröder who made Germany basketball world champions. Likewise, the England women's football team, affectionately known as The Lionesses, did not win the 2025 European Championship solely because of the spectacular saves of goalkeeper Hannah Hampton, the winning penalty of Chloe Kelly, or the tactics of head coach Sarina Wiegman.

These acts of heroism would have been insignificant had the entire team not acted collectively. The team exhibited the trained behavioural patterns to which they committed during their preparation for the tournament. The spectators could sense each player's eagerness to support their teammates – both on the field and from the sidelines. The players were genuinely anticipating the moments when they could assist one another or compensate for each other's mistakes. The belief in victory outweighed the fear of defeat. This mindset is the outcome of numerous discussions, exercises and repetitions – both tactical and mental. It does not emerge from the formulation of measurable goals, but from investing in factors that enhance the likelihood of success.

As we have established, sustainable success for teams and athletes cannot necessarily be measured solely by goals or outcomes. For them, results are rather the logical consequence of their daily actions – whether in training or competition. The true objective of their daily efforts lies in these success factors, which they know in detail and pursue consistently. Performance primarily emerges where it remains invisible to others, beneath the surface. The true success factors are often unremarkable, embedded in everyday life – yet they constitute the key to long-term success.

Success factors increase the likelihood that visions and dreams will become reality. They have a significant impact on success and form the foundation for sustainable and healthy performance. They must be carefully developed and maintained to be accessible under stress; that is, in competitive situations. These are often behavioural patterns, routines and attitudes that become ingrained over time – comparable to brushing our teeth in the morning. Such automatisms may relate to the shooting posture in football or manifest in interpersonal respect, effective communication, handling defeat or setbacks, positive body language, or maintaining focus despite distractions.

Principles of Action

The success factors are not necessarily complex transformations but rather simple behavioural patterns that, when accumulated, can make a decisive difference. These are so firmly ingrained that we do not revert to old, destructive patterns under stress. They are actions taken to increase the likelihood of 'winning'. It is as straightforward as that.

These success factors vary in measurability, with some being entirely immeasurable. These factors will distinguish, in future, between good and excellent; static and dynamic; and arrogant and inquisitive companies. They will be the difference between companies that can select their talent and employees, and those that lament a skilled labour shortage and must invest heavily in employer branding and external recruitment. The difference lies in the fact that some companies merely discuss corporate values, whereas others translate them into concrete, easily understandable and actionable behavioural patterns.

A notable example is Netflix. Nearly two decades ago, then Chief Talent Officer Patty McCord and CEO Reed Hastings began systematically reviewing and continuously evolving the company's internal culture. This process gave rise to the 'Netflix Culture Deck', a presentation that has shaped collaboration at Netflix for decades. This document extended well beyond the conventional value pyramids. Over 125 pages, it detailed which behavioural patterns are valued at Netflix and which character traits and attitudes are encouraged – or not tolerated[33].

The focus was on principles of action that provided guidance rather than imposing rigid rules. Employees were given a clear framework within which they could freely develop. Similarly, the success coaches featured in this book firmly embed their playing philosophy in the minds and hearts of their players through simple principles. They think in a multifaceted manner, yet their communication remains clear and concise – never complicated, nor banal.

For example, Pep Guardiola required his players at Barcelona to recover the ball within four seconds of losing it. Why? Because during this brief phase, the likelihood of success is at its highest. Subsequently, a withdrawal occurs. This clear guiding principle enabled the players to make appropriate decisions based on the situation, thereby responding effectively to the increasing complexity and rapid pace of the game. Such behaviour is difficult to quantify but clearly observable. It allows little room for individual interpretation and is significantly more impactful than value posters displayed in dressing rooms or clubhouses.

The same applies to the deliberate avoidance of certain actions, such as unnecessary disputes over referee decisions. Here, as well, demonstrated respect and focused behaviour are evident, often reflected in the fairness rankings.

There are other measurable success factors from the world of sport, exemplified by none other than the multiple World Footballer of the Year, Cristiano Ronaldo.

The Ronaldo Principle
The British consulting firm 21st Club Limited analysed nearly 1,500 shots by Cristiano Ronaldo between 2010 and 2017 while wearing the Real Madrid jersey in league matches. Excluding penalty kicks, Ronaldo averaged an impressive near seven shots per game. He shot significantly more often at the opposing goal than other forwards. Even

more importantly, he usually took these shots from optimal positions that offered an exceptionally high probability of success.

A similar pattern is evident among other top forwards. They shoot frequently and predominantly from promising positions. This clearly demonstrates that success results from the interplay of multiple factors. It is counterproductive to increasingly take shots from hopeless positions, or to have a good position but fail to direct the ball on target. Therefore, it is ill-advised to focus solely on one of these factors and to designate it as a key indicator, which in the worst case may be mistaken for the ultimate goal. This is a tactical error that is unfortunately widespread in companies and can cause considerable harm.

The Emergence of Expected Goals

In 2012, the concept of 'expected goals' was introduced for the first time – a model that quantifies the probability of scoring a goal. During the first half of the 2017/2018 season, renowned coach Pep Guardiola demonstrated with his Manchester City team how this concept can be effectively applied in practice. Every goal scored by his team was from within the penalty area. It was evident that Guardiola had worked intensively with his players to achieve this. The numerous goals were ultimately the logical outcome of this remarkable performance.

I personally witnessed how such a concept can be applied to the business world. We were in the process of implementing the aforementioned Customer Relationship Management (CRM) system for an international sales team of approximately 4,000 employees. To ensure this initiative was meaningful for sales, we launched a global coaching programme for our sales teams alongside the system implementation. The objective was to equip the sales managers with the fundamentals of effective coaching. The coaching dialogues established the foundation for leveraging the data available in the CRM and focusing our energy on potential client orders with the highest likelihood of success. Our 'expected goals' were 'expected wins', referring to the anticipated client orders.

Other teams, not yet included in the roll-out, continued to compete by expanding the size of their pipeline – yet without achieving significant success in the desired outcomes. They operated like a forward who shoots as frequently as possible but seldom from advantageous positions.

In contrast, the trained teams adhered to the Ronaldo principle. They sought to position themselves advantageously with the support of their colleagues and concentrated their energy on orders with a realistic chance of success. They focused on the success factors that enhance the likelihood of winning.

Patience and Focus in Business

"Champions behave like champions long before they become champions," NFL legend Bill Walsh once remarked. They are patient and focused. They understand that their efforts will bear fruit because they accumulate – day by day, week by week, year by year. Their focus is not on the outcomes but on the actions that increase the probability of success. A lack of focus on essential behaviours or habits generally indicates that sustainable, long-term success is unlikely. Why should we believe that this differs in business?

The focus should be on the elements beneath the surface, which are often overlooked – here we find the true success factors. Success is not the primary goal but rather the consequence of consistent behavioural patterns and other underlying factors. Setting seemingly clever SMART goals or presenting golden behavioural rules on colourful charts at the executive level and communicating them downward is insufficient.

What could we achieve in business if we demonstrated the same patience as clubs that steadily advance through persistent focus on their success factors, season after season, without drastic course changes or scandals? From an external perspective, this may seem unspectacular, particularly in the sports entertainment industry, where rapid success and spectacular highlights often take centre stage. However, this is precisely where the distinction lies: Developing successful behavioural patterns and attitudes requires time and patience – resources that not all organisations are able or willing to invest.

This is not about head coaches who lack the desire to win. They are ambitious and driven. Performance coaches utilise measurable and observable factors to assess the team's progress. Nevertheless, they avoid the mistake of treating these data points as goals. These data points remain indicators that require continuous evaluation. This signifies our shift from success factors to success indicators.

When a Measure Becomes a Target

The saying, "When a measure becomes a target, it ceases to be a good measure", coined by Marilyn Strathern in 1997, aptly illustrates that a metric loses its validity as a measure once it becomes a target. This phenomenon is known as Goodhart's Law. At the time, the British anthropologist intended to criticise the monetary policy of the Thatcher government. Numerous economists and behavioural scientists agree that any metric used as a target loses its original significance. This occurs because individuals focus on achieving the target itself, rather than the intended outcome of the target. Incentives amplify this effect.

In business, this insight is often overlooked by many decision-makers. Key Performance Indicators (KPIs) are frequently designated as bonus-relevant targets. Rather than focusing on success factors, a goal is pursued blindly. The consequences of this pursuit of measurable goals and the constant focus on the scoreboard have already been described.

When indicators are not used as criteria to verify whether the correct path has been taken, but are instead declared as goals, goal attainment becomes an end in itself, and is politicised. Results are negotiated, manipulated and suboptimised. Energy is wasted on precisely hitting the target, instead of focusing on the success factors. Overachieving carries the unfortunate implication that a more ambitious goal will be pursued the following year.

A pertinent example of the misuse of success metrics is frequently observed in sales teams. Often, the 'pipeline' and the 'win rate' are directly tied to the bonus system. The pipeline represents the potential revenue from all orders that could be secured within the current year, whereas the win rate denotes the percentage of orders actually won. Since both metrics can be easily manipulated individually, many sales leaders rely on a combination of these indicators. Consequently, some sales employees adopt rather peculiar strategies, focusing their energy on 'optimising' these metrics to maximise their bonuses.

The problem does not lie with the indicators themselves – which are indeed meaningful – but with their misuse on both sides. Success indicators, originally designed to encourage behavioural change and long-term performance development, have been transformed into immediate targets. This vicious circle must be broken to establish a sustainable performance culture.

Rather than allowing meaningful success indicators to deteriorate into target specifications, we should empower sales employees to make well-informed decisions, concentrate on the right business opportunities, and collaborate across teams. The focus must remain on what is essential: optimally utilising the available time to achieve shared success. It is essential to foster the hidden success factors beneath the surface, rather than pursue superficial goals.

During the aforementioned CRM implementation, dialogues between managers and employees were aligned, so they were fact-based, forward-looking and focused on profitable growth. The three 'Fs' (fact-based, forward-looking, focused on growth) were easy to remember, and with each conversation, we could immediately assess whether the appropriate behavioural patterns for sustainable success were demonstrated. Consequently, success was not long in coming.

The CRM system – and the data and indicators managed within it – remained precisely what it was intended to be – a means to an end. It facilitated more targeted conversations involving appropriate team members, to engage and harness energy for clients and business opportunities that aligned with our individual understanding of success. This understanding of success could take many forms: from acquiring new clients and developing existing ones to creating innovative solutions with niche providers.

The sales teams ultimately operated like Pep Guardiola's Manchester City in the first half of the 2017/2018 season, when all goals were scored from within the penalty area. They positioned themselves strategically to maximise the likelihood of a successful outcome. They did so, not because ambitious target specifications were imposed upon them and used to judge or condemn them, but because it made sense and success brings satisfaction. All employees understood that the likelihood of success increased when they positioned themselves in the most advantageous spot for a shot on goal, even if this was not part of their compensation criteria.

Potential Tactical Errors

Tactical error 33: We do not know our true success factors.

Tactical error 34: We lack concrete principles of action.

Tactical error 35: We select inappropriate success indicators to evaluate our performance.

Tactical error 36: We consider success indicators in isolation.

Tactical error 37: We convert well-chosen success indicators into goals.

The Mother of All Defeats and Penalty Misses

On the 26th May 1999, I was sitting comfortably with a few friends in front of the television, like millions of other football fans worldwide. It was the Champions League final between Bayern Munich and Manchester United.

22:30:31: Bayern are leading 1-0. Defender Michael 'Tanne' Tarnat asks referee Pierluigi Collina how much time remains. The referee signals 'one last action'. At the sideline, preparations are underway for the grand 'Mia san mia' celebration. Staff members bring champagne and a box full of caps bearing the inscription 'Champions League Winner 1999 – Bayern Munich'. UEFA officials are already adorning the trophy with red and white Bayern ribbons. Journalists are about to dispatch their reports on Bayern's dominant performance. We too are already embracing each other with joy and increased beer consumption – the victory appears certain.

22:30:35: While we find ourselves in football's seventh heaven, David Beckham is preparing a corner kick at Camp Nou in Barcelona, nearly 1,600 kilometres away. Seconds later, the score is 1–1 as Teddy Sheringham scores. The offside protests from Mehmet Scholl and Oliver Kahn go unheard. Referee Collina restarts the game. Not only are the Bayern players stunned, but we sink disappointedly into the sofa.

22:32:16: Another corner kick for Manchester United. Beckham takes it again, and one second later the ball hits the back of the Bayern goal for the second time. Within 102 seconds, the dream of the title has been shattered. The substitute Ole Gunnar Solskjaer scored and plunged Bayern, my friends and me into a profound valley of tears. Solskjaer, known in England as the 'baby-faced assassin', fully lived up to his nickname[34].

This match went down in history as the 'mother of all defeats'. In particular, the last-minute equaliser suggests that some Bayern players may no longer have been fully focused – a reaction that is both understandable and profoundly human.

Explanatory Attempts

For many years since, myths have surrounded this memorable match. Many experts, unwilling to accept the phrase, 'That's football', have sought further explanation. Football is complex, even though we often simplify it in discussions on a regular basis. There are even studies on the 'mother of all defeats'[35].

They demonstrate that following the substitutions, the hierarchy and role distribution at Bayern Munich became disrupted. While team cohesion at Manchester United strengthened in the final minutes, it deteriorated for Bayern, particularly after the self-initiated substitution of Lothar Matthäus ten minutes before the end of the match. Mehmet Scholl later remarked that Matthäus "always bails out when it gets tight". Such thoughts are as unhelpful in decisive moments as premature considerations of the trophy presentation. They deplete mental capacity that would have been essential for the here and now.

Although we may never conclusively determine whether such thoughts were decisive in the defeat, sports psychologists and other experts agree – unproductive thoughts hinder us from acting appropriately at critical moments. It is not about concentrating, but about focusing on what is essential.

We should not attempt to suppress thoughts, but rather learn how to manage them. Thoughts will inevitably arise – that is certain. The skill lies not in controlling them, but in preventing them from controlling us. The critical question, therefore, is how to handle these thoughts, how much attention to allocate to them, and whether we can maintain focus on what truly matters; on what truly counts.

Sports psychologists equip players with strategies and techniques to bring them back to the here and now. Destructive self-talk or thoughts that do not support the goal hinder individual players or entire teams from overcoming challenging situations. It is difficult to say if the inability to 'refocus' caused the mother of all defeats. Nevertheless, it is indisputable that this is a cause of numerous significant career setbacks, lost games and disrupted seasons.

But what enables us, as humans, to remain focused? Let us first acknowledge that players remain focused even during a decisive defeat – unfortunately, not on the correct elements. In very few cases are individuals truly unfocused. Regrettably, we often fail to concentrate on what is genuinely effective. Instead, we allow ourselves to be distracted by random thoughts that pass through our minds. Our minds are constantly active, yet most of the thoughts that arise are of little benefit. On average, individuals experience over 6,000 thoughts per day, of which only a small fraction – approximately 3% – are considered positive. Negative thoughts prevail with a ratio of 8:1[36]. Under pressure, these negative thoughts often become more pronounced. This tendency is inherent in human nature – we are inclined to focus on threats. This phenomenon is no different for athletes under performance pressure, particularly when they are striving in a Champions League final to prevent an imminent defeat. Unless they have trained themselves to consciously observe and regulate their thoughts.

For athletes, thoughts during a game are obstructive if they do not relate to the here and now. This applies both to past situations, such as the aforementioned substitution of Lothar Matthäus, and to thoughts about the future; for example, the forthcoming cup presentation accompanied by the boisterous 'beer showers' that are tradition at Bayern Munich. Successful athletes master the art of focusing. The crucial difference lies in their ability to concentrate on the here and now at decisive moments – both on and off the field. This focus can be the subtle difference in sport between missing opportunities and emerging as a top scorer.

A fitting slogan that shaped the German national basketball team into a focused and high-performing unit was: 'Be where your feet are.' This phrase underscores the importance of the present moment and helped the team perform exceptionally well, especially under pressure. The slogan comes from the eponymous book by Scott O'Neil, one of the most successful sports entrepreneurs and former CEO of the Philadelphia 76ers[37].

The key to success lies in focusing on the present task. Rather than dwelling on the past or future, the player and the team should direct their energy and mental capacity towards performing at their best, here and now. Only in this way can tactical instructions be executed precisely, and individual abilities be utilised for the benefit of the team.

Stimuli in Everyday Business Life

In business life, there is no need for late equalisers to divert us from our course. A slight 'cough' from the executive board, a disappointing monthly result, or a new initiative from corporate headquarters is enough to make us lose our focus. In these moments, we may allocate our limited capacity to activities that do not contribute to the original definition of success – thus, they may not be supportive. Multitasking is often regarded as a talent. The truth is, multitasking is neither a talent nor truly feasible. On the contrary, in the vast majority of cases, it hinders us from achieving our goals. More on this later.

Sometimes, an enticing project idea to which we find it difficult to say "no" is enough to be perceived as 'hungry'. Alternatively, the manager introduces a new impulse that is immediately converted into a non-negotiable initiative. Rarely does another project yield; instead, the new initiative is simply executed 'on top' of existing commitments. We can be as certain of the manager's recognition, as of the opportunity to be regarded as a 'high performer', thanks to the outdated definition of performance. Although focus may be lost, a high level of activity often appears to be beneficial. Focus is more often interpreted as a lack of openness to new ideas, rigidity or even stubbornness, rather than as a demonstration of consistency, continuity and, above all, discipline.

It is no secret that many departments work with particular focus when the manager is attending a conference or is on holiday. A similar situation arises when the corporate headquarters is closed for company-wide holidays. During these weeks, many employees consciously forgo taking holiday to avoid being continuously subjected to new demands, brainstorming sessions, workshops or initiatives. This is not a time for 'not working', but rather for focused work. 'While the cat's away, the mice will play' is not applicable here, despite what some managers might think.

It is essential to emphasise that new impulses and project ideas are fundamentally important. It is vital to remain open to these and not rigidly adhere to the predetermined plan. However, a significant distinction lies in whether there exists an effective process to evaluate if a new idea or project is more purposeful than the ongoing activities. Just as athletes assess in the final minutes of a game whether an emerging thought is beneficial, we can apply the same approach in business, provided we clearly understand our definition of success.

It should not matter who proposes the new project. In some companies, even the manager clearing their throat can trigger a significant upheaval. New initiatives from the executive level are seldom questioned, although ongoing activities often need to be halted to allocate the necessary attention to the new project.

It does not always require the manager to complicate the project portfolio without prior consultation. Sometimes, it is the employees themselves who work passionately on 'their' project. However, it is essential to assess whether these activities serve only the individual or genuinely benefit the collective. It is remarkable how team members and team leaders spend their time. Even more remarkable is when they document or review their week.

Regardless of the source of new impulses, companies often exhibit a high activity level. We repeatedly mistake movement for progress. Upon examining how many of these activities genuinely contribute to success, we find numerous elements that do not belong on this list. This represents a form of ineffective multitasking – ultimately, nothing more than a manifestation of cognitive laziness[38]. Such cognitive laziness results in limited available capacities being squandered on tasks that neither directly nor indirectly contribute to the collectively defined success.

This returns us to an example from sport. The principle in sports psychology is straightforward: an athlete possesses a limited mental capacity. Sports psychologists endeavour to assist athletes in optimising the use of this capacity. Distractions that prevent athletes from optimally applying their abilities in the here and now represent wasted mental capacity. Such thoughts will inevitably arise. They cannot be prevented or suppressed, but we can decide how much attention and time to allocate to them and how to manage them.

Identifying and Categorising Impulses

For employees, the numerous impulses encountered in everyday company life are similar to the thoughts athletes experience on the playing field. While successful athletes can distinguish between supportive and non-supportive thoughts, it is more challenging for teams operating in the fast-paced business environment to make this distinction. Whereas successful athletes have learned to prevent non-supportive thoughts from controlling them, the opposite often occurs in companies. Constantly reacting to impulses results in those impulses controlling actions, causing the original game plan to be quickly forgotten.

It is therefore essential for organisations to establish mechanisms that enable teams to distinguish between supportive and non-supportive impulses, and to categorise them both effectively and efficiently. One of the most successful basketball coaches worldwide, Phil Jackson, succinctly stated: "Being aware is more important than being smart," meaning that attentiveness outweighs cleverness.

Responding Instead of Reacting

In sport, a powerful technique known as 'thought stopping' is employed. In this process, the athlete deliberately applies a 'stop signal' as soon as they recognise that a thought might disrupt their focus. They consciously choose not to grant any further attention to this distracting thought. Rather than being distracted by looming interruptions, the athlete refocuses on what can be influenced in the here and now.

Regrettably, many teams within companies overlook this mechanism. Instead of proactively responding, they react to daily stimuli. The lack of clarity on what success looks like further complicates the evaluation of whether new ideas or projects are truly purposeful. Although complex decision-making models exist, none match the effectiveness of a clearly defined definition of success.

As a result, many teams feel externally controlled and individuals lose their sense of self-efficacy. In both business and sport, professionals adhere to their plans, whereas amateurs are easily distracted by external factors. Or, as the Swiss psychiatrist and founder of analytical psychology, Carl Jung, stated: "The world will ask you who you are. If you do not know, the world will tell you." This applies equally to individuals, teams and entire organisations. Professionals understand their success factors and work diligently on them, whereas amateurs are often diverted from their course by urgent matters. Over time, they lose control and desperately attempt to counteract – a vicious circle that must be consciously broken to enhance performance in a healthy and sustainable manner.

Within a company, decisions and prioritisations are often more complex than the clear thoughts of an athlete before or during competition. The corporate context is more nuanced and less binary, with numerous shades of grey between 'supportive' and 'non-supportive'. Despite this complexity, there is a fundamental parallel: the ongoing challenge of managing more ideas and projects than resources available.

Doing Less, Achieving More

A company that is able to deliberately say "no" demonstrates focus and a clear orientation towards those activities that contribute most significantly to success. A well-known principle applied here is the 80:20 rule. In the realm of leadership, this rule states that 20% of activities account for 80% of success. This principle is often successfully employed in product management when prioritising product features that offer the greatest benefit to clients. Surprisingly, this efficient mindset is frequently neglected in everyday business life.

In an era where artificial intelligence, decision-making models and business plans dominate, simple and proven methods often fade into the background. The art of prioritisation lies in applying simple yet effective principles, rather than being overwhelmed by the perceived necessity of complex models. Such models typically prove to be old wine in new bottles.

Prioritisation demands the courage to say "no" and a clear identification of the essential elements that yield the greatest success. Within an entrepreneurial context, this does not indicate a lack of resources but demonstrates focus and foresight. It involves excluding everything that is non-supportive and does not significantly contribute to our definition of success. Although parting with favourite projects can be painful, it is crucial on the path to healthy and sustainable performance development, and thus to long-term success.

Sports professionals demonstrate that renunciation is a virtue; they understand what to avoid. Frequently, it is precisely what they choose not to do that ultimately leads to their success. In this way, they adhere to the timeless wisdom of management guru Michael Porter: "Decide what you will not do." I have personally witnessed the energy and capacity unleashed when we focus solely on the essentials. The strategy behind this company-wide transformation was named 'Core & Clear', and the name was indicative of its purpose.

Letting go of old habits, parting with valued projects or entire business units can unleash new energy. Similarly, it can be liberating for teams to be granted the permission to say "no", to actively decide to halt a project, to refrain from starting one, or to skip certain meetings.

Just as an athlete can consciously choose whether to devote their limited mental capacity to a particular thought, a team can deliberately decide whether to allocate its limited resources to continuously incoming impulses. This presupposes a high level of consciousness regarding the definition of success. It may sound ironic, but the key is to do less to achieve more. Successful athletes provide us with a clear example.

Unfiltered

The question remains: Why is it so difficult to break this vicious circle and reduce activity? Some teams lack a clear understanding of success and its parameters. There is an absence of consciousness and a filter to distinguish truly important activities from those less purposeful. In many companies, the manager or department head assumes this filtering role, which may lead to quick but not always meaningful decisions for sustainable success.

There is an additional factor that accelerates the vicious circle – or, in this case, the hamster wheel. It is well established that perseverance and continuity lead to sustainable success, rather than activity. This principle becomes evident when considering New Year's resolutions – whether it is the morning yoga routine, evening strength exercises or that diet. Success manifests only when we remain committed.

Most good intentions are abandoned within the first few weeks of the new year. This results in disappointed expectations and the conclusion that the changes supposedly yield no benefits. Fitness studios capitalise on this with costly annual memberships, and many individuals move from one diet to another, emotionally driven by hope and impatience.

Hope and impatience are also constant companions of leaders. The cause once again lies in our thinking patterns. Consistency and perseverance are difficult to discern. It is easier to initiate new projects under the motto, 'We run more than our opponents', hoping that these efforts will be recognised 'at the top' and that one of the many initiatives will succeed. In many companies, activity is still valued more highly than continuous, persistent work beneath the surface.

Continuous improvements are less visible than spectacular actions.

When firefighting, costly new acquisitions and company value posters are more recognised than continuous work on success factors that goes on beneath the surface. Sustainable and focused work is rarely experienced – it is that simple. This is about showmanship rather than sustainable performance development. Ultimately, we receive not only what we measure but, above all, what we truly focus on.

Complexity and speed cloud our clear perspective on what is essential. It is expected not only that our employees remain constantly accessible, akin to an emergency call centre, but that they respond to emails with remarkable speed. Any response exceeding the 60-minute threshold rigorously tests managers' patience. While colleagues' resilience may vary in nature and duration, there is consensus that the sender of the initial email determines the urgency and importance, not the recipient. Another principle applies here: the higher the sender's hierarchical position and importance, the more significant the request. Although this appears logical, it becomes inefficient when hierarchy dictates not only importance but also urgency.

You may be familiar with the Eisenhower Matrix, which is a simple yet effective method. It is so straightforward that it may seem almost redundant to revisit it. However, its value lies precisely in its simplicity, much like Pep Guardiola's four-second rule. The matrix offers a solution by providing a clear structure with equally explicit courses of action. With its two axes – importance and urgency – it serves as a practical tool for prioritisation. It assists in determining whether and when a task should be completed[39]. Yet, as with the importance axis, the urgency axis requires a clear definition. This is one reason why employees may be familiar with this decision matrix but often struggle with its application. The problem? There is no universally accepted definition of 'urgent'.

Changing Perspective

Did you know that England international football players took an average of only 0.28 seconds to react to the referee's whistle during penalty shootouts between 1976 and 2008? They immediately ran forward and often hit the ball over the bar, wide, or directly into the goalkeeper's arms. By comparison, Usain Bolt reacted only slightly faster during his world record in Berlin in 2009, with a reaction time of 0.15 seconds. This remarkable reaction speed of the English players was significantly below the average of other nations. However, as we know, this did not benefit them. According to penalty kick expert Geir Jordet, their hasty reaction to the whistle was a decisive factor in why England were unable to win a penalty shootout at European Championships or World Cups for decades[40].

Parallels can be drawn in business, although our response times to emails are generally longer. Nevertheless, it often takes only a brief moment before we read the manager's email and feel compelled to respond immediately. Just as football players interpret the referee's whistle as a signal for immediate action, we instinctively classify emails as extremely important and urgent.

The consequences are noticeable here as well, though less dramatic than a missed penalty kick in the home of football. The recipient of an email typically involves additional employees to ensure the response is accurate. The email is forwarded, colleagues are copied in Cc, or, in the worst case, in Bcc. Responses are quickly given in a pragmatic and straightforward manner to demonstrate to the manager that everything is under control. However, all the internal research, necessary emails, meetings and phone calls remain unseen. This domino effect permeates the entire organisation, tying up resources that could have been utilised more effectively elsewhere.

A well-intentioned request from the manager can unknowingly consume significant capacity without the email's author realising it. Just as it is not the referee's role to prevent the English football players from hastily taking the penalty kick, it is not the manager's responsibility to shield the employee from premature activity. Rather, it is the responsibility of the recipient to pause, take a deep breath, and only then act. This attitude requires a new mindset on both sides. It must be accepted that it is important first to calibrate ourselves and focus on the essentials, regardless of who initiated the impulse to act.

Interestingly, English penalty kick takers have trained this 'calibration' in recent years, achieving significant success. The goal was to restore the players' control over the situation. They modelled their approach on successful penalty takers such as Harry Kane and Robert Lewandowski, who do not interpret the referee's whistle as a signal to start running immediately, but rather as the starting cue for their carefully rehearsed ritual. On average, these players take three to four seconds before commencing their run-up. They do not react impulsively to the whistle but deliberately manage the process.

This example highlights the significance of reframing our thinking, as commonly applied in traditional coaching. Whereas earlier English coaches often viewed the penalty shootout as a form of lottery, Gareth Southgate transformed this perspective. He communicated to his players that, although they cannot control the final outcome, they can decisively influence the process. This mindset enhanced the players' sense of autonomy and self-efficacy – two of the three fundamental psychological needs essential for peak performance, which we have addressed previously.

How does this manifest in your company? What thought processes or rituals do you engage in when you receive an urgent task from your manager, or an email you consider important arrives in your inbox? Which principles assist you in calibrating yourself, maintaining focus and responding rather than reacting? Or does such an email feel more like a referee's whistle, compelling you to start running immediately, much like the English football players of earlier times?

In an era when we can order cars overnight and download books within seconds, a delayed email response often appears inexplicable and nearly inexcusable to many. The heightened expectation for rapid responses leads to assumptions that a colleague working from home might be ironing their shirts or attending to personal errands instead of addressing the email. Alternatively, the colleague may generally lack the 'sense of urgency'.

It is often overlooked that the employee may be focused on another task and does not allow themselves to be distracted by their inbox. While the possibility that the email is responded to with lower priority due to its insignificance is not excluded, it is by no means accepted.

In organisations where constant availability and rapid response times are regarded as performance indicators, efforts are made to meet these expectations. We may indeed have a definition of 'urgent', but it is simply the wrong one. Consequently, multitasking is glorified as a performance indicator contrary to scientific evidence – a continuation of what science knows, and business does.

Multitasking

Can you imagine sports stars like Thomas Müller bringing their mobile phones on to the training field to respond to fan enquiries or manage their social media channels? Probably not. Yet, this occurs in meeting rooms. Excessive expectations regarding availability and response times lead meeting participants to unabashedly answer emails or engage in internal chats while a valued colleague delivers a meticulously prepared presentation.

In school, dreamers sat at the back of the room were occasionally embarrassed by teachers who unexpectedly directed questions at them. The resulting awkward silence often lingered. This practice is rarely employed in meeting rooms. On the contrary, the principle of 'more is more' frequently prevails. Being 'busy' is deemed to be OK. Moreover, respect is accorded to these people for apparently being capable of multitasking.

As on the training field, the principle should apply here: 'all or nothing'. Athletes on the training field give 100% in every aspect – physically and mentally. Everyone contributes with dedication and focus to ensure an effective training session. Beyond being prepared for the meeting, it is essential to remain focused during the meeting, blocking out potential distractions – just like an athlete who has learned not to fall foul of destructive thoughts. This is how we become a valuable contributor to the meeting, rather than merely a name on the attendance list.

This type of multitasking is not only disrespectful but also highly unproductive and costly. Fast response times are undoubtedly critical in customer service and are often regarded as a success factor. However, within a company, rapid reaction times can indicate a loss of focus. Rather than demonstrating high performance, this behaviour prevents us from performing at the highest level.

Why? Because, in most cases, it is not genuine multitasking. Humans are simply incapable of managing two tasks simultaneously that demand full concentration. What we can practise is so-called 'background tasking', where we perform a task that requires minimal mental capacity while focusing on another. An example would be walking during a conversation – walking operates automatically on 'autopilot', allowing us to focus on the discussion. A similar situation occurs when washing dishes during a phone call. Experienced 'dish washers' will not suffer significant losses in productivity or quality.

What we predominantly engage in is the so-called 'switch-tasking'. In this process, we constantly switch between different tasks, creating the impression that we are accomplishing multiple things simultaneously. In reality, however, this mode of working has been demonstrably ineffective and inefficient. If you are sceptical, consider trying the experiment conducted by psychologist Megan Johnson from the University of California, Berkeley. The exercise involves three simple steps: first, count from one to ten as quickly as possible. Simple, isn't it? Now, please recite the alphabet from A to J. This should not pose a significant challenge. To simulate switch-tasking, alternate between numbers and letters – for example, 'one, A, two, B', and so on. How did you experience that? Was it as easy and quick as the previous tasks?

Constantly switching between the two sequences considerably complicates the exercise. Similarly, in everyday work, frequent switching between different tasks makes our lives more difficult. Instead of working more efficiently, we lose both effectiveness and efficiency.

In the pursuit of sustainable performance, it appears counterproductive when leaders follow up with employees half an hour after sending an email, to ask whether it has been read.

Regardless of which principles of action are established, they should enable employees to work with focus without having to meet unrealistic expectations concerning availability and response times. Otherwise, employees risk being very busy but ineffective. Constantly having to refocus consumes time and energy, and does not contribute to healthy and sustainable performance development.

The Fair-weather Footballer

To complete the spectrum of possible distractions, it should be noted that deviating from the planned course does not always require an email or a phone call. Let us again visit the sports field. In sport, we do not begin only when the referee starts the game. Preparation, both physical and mental, begins hours or even days in advance. Numerous factors can be influenced to ensure players are in the desired condition at kick-off.

Some players need to calm themselves before the game and may engage in breathing exercises. Others prefer a colleague to give them a slap to get into the right mindset. Everyone has their own method. However, in sport, there are also uncontrollable factors.

It's 2pm, and the team bus of the current league leaders arrives punctually, 90 minutes before kick-off, outside their opponent's stadium. Marcel, the fair-weather footballer, glances from the corner of his eye at the lush green pitch. For a club threatened by relegation, it is not so bad, he thinks. We call him Marcel, inspired by Marcelinho, the Brazilian footballer who, in the first decade of this millennium, was known for his skill as well as extreme performance fluctuations while playing for Hertha Berlin and Wolfsburg in the German Bundesliga. Critics argued that his level of play was heavily dependent on the weather, which is why he was labelled a 'fair-weather footballer'.

Marcel sees himself scoring a goal, but only minutes later his illusions are shattered. Shortly after arriving in the dressing room, the assistant coach announces that the game will be held not in the stadium but on the adjacent field due to heavy rainfall over the past few days. Marcel searches in vain for the lush green turf. For him, this is reason enough to complain about the opposing club and the referee. He had accepted playing football on this lush pitch. This situation favours the opposition's tough footballers, while as a delicate technician, he is deprived of the opportunity to showcase his football talent.

In this mental state, it will be difficult for Marcel to realise his full potential on the field. Unless he succeeds in focusing on the factors within his control. To summarise: He will not succeed in this match. After 45 dismal minutes, Marcel's workday is already over. As the team is influenced by their leadership player Marcel and directs their frustration towards the referee, they not only lose the match but also their defensive captain, who is sent off after receiving an early red card. This is how games that appeared certain victories on paper are lost. They return home without the three points, enduring one of those frustrating journeys best forgotten.

Fair-weather footballers perform to their best when conditions align with their expectations. In such circumstances, they adhere to agreements, operate within their element, and realise their potential. However, when it rains or is stormy, good intentions are forgotten. Excuses and the 'yes, but' syndrome take control. Attention shifts to numerous distractions that impede performance. Regrettably, most of these causes lie beyond our control or sphere of influence. We become a victim, losing sight of our strengths, and redirect focus outward. The longer we search, the more reasons we uncover for why things are not working.

Peripheral Issues

Does this sound familiar to you? Rather than focusing on factors we can genuinely influence, we often become entangled in so-called peripheral issues – a tendency that, regrettably, is increasingly prevalent within companies. There is ongoing debate about the insufficiently sized fruit basket, the seemingly unfair company car policy, the home office regulations perceived as unjust, inflation, supply chain disruptions, sales, procurement, the marketing department, product development, or the new manager's lack of industry experience. The list appears to be endless.

At the forefront of these discussions is the structure of the organisation. At times, the hierarchy is considered too rigid; at others, the structure is deemed too flat, the matrix too complex, sometimes too regional, and at other times too global. I firmly believe that the organisational structure can make a significant contribution to the company's success. Equally, I am convinced that it is more beneficial not to constantly question or frequently change this structure, but rather to embody it.

As long as the organisational structure remains a constant topic of discussion, we experience friction losses. Employees may use the structure as an excuse for not delivering their optimal performance, much like the footballer Marcel does in adverse weather. In terms of organisational structure, our goal should be to empower employees to perform at their maximum capacity under all circumstances – a principle endorsed by sports psychologists.

We tend to focus excessively on matters beyond our control – on background noise that captures our attention without genuinely contributing to collective success. After all, it is enjoyable to complain without assuming responsibility – much like the millions of national coaches who emerge from their hiding places during every major sporting event.

I would like to clarify that this is not about uncritically accepting all conditions. Rather, it involves carefully considering which factors are within our control and which we might reasonably influence and should therefore seek to influence. These deserve our attention. Ultimately, we must be clear about which conditions we have to accept because we can neither control nor influence them. Energy expended on these constitute wasted resources and prevent us from fully realising our potential.

These background noises often begin gradually, much like the destructive thoughts experienced by an athlete. The more attention they receive, the more dominant they become. In team sports, as is common in most companies, these dynamics tend to reinforce themselves – unfortunately, often in a negative way. Within organisations, the focus is not solely on 'leadership' but also on 'followership' – a subject that has been largely overlooked in recent decades – despite the fact that nearly every leader is also a follower, having a superior. Even the CEO typically reports to the supervisory board.

The principle remains: We become what we focus our attention on. This insight, derived from neuroscience, is now regarded as indisputable. If we devote excessive attention to matters beyond our control or influence, we forfeit considerable potential. Such disruptive factors should be avoided or addressed promptly when sustainable performance development is the objective.

Reflections On the Future

We have discussed the importance of remaining present and concentrating on what truly matters. We have also identified several disruptive factors that can hinder this focus. A particularly evident reason is that we frequently become preoccupied with future concerns instead of concentrating on the here and now. This was exemplified by the Bayern Munich players in their Champions League final defeat to Manchester United in 1999, when their future-oriented thoughts impeded the delivery of outstanding performance at that time.

The complexity and duration of planning processes in companies are exacerbated not only by sophisticated goal systems and bonus schemes but by the early commencement of planning for the following year, often immediately after the summer break. This extends until the end of the first quarter, leaving only three months to dedicate full attention to current matters. This timeframe can be likened to the quarter of a match during which a football team is fully engaged out of a total of 90 minutes – insufficient to win a game and insufficient to reach peak performance.

I am far from asserting that companies should avoid engaging with the future. Naturally, we should. However, while we communicate to the world how rapidly it turns and that change is the only constant, we become entangled in meticulous planning of budgets and goal agreements for forthcoming periods spanning several months. We expend excessive time planning and forecasting the future instead of actively creating it.

The conditions continue to evolve, even within this planning period. Meanwhile, in these uncertain times, we yearn for security. Valuable resources are allocated to planning, which detracts attention from the here and now. While we engage in intensive discussions about which outcomes should shine above the surface next year, we lack the time to focus on the foundational elements that make these outstanding results possible. We either work in the present, justify past actions and results, or plan for our future.

Having learned over the years that 'top-down' goals do not enhance employee motivation (as we have discussed), we initiate processes to actively involve employees. Although these goals are initially welcomed, many employees do not feel genuinely involved as time goes by. The planning process consumes resources at all levels, yet the outcome barely differs from management presenting an 'ambitious seasonal goal' to the press – it is the case of a wolf in sheep's clothing. Consequently, they prefer to emulate Bayern Munich, which annually declares that anything less than the treble would be a disappointment. At least we know where we stand, both as a fan and as a player.

When considering the energy middle-management must invest in these coordination meetings – often yielding frustrating results – it quickly becomes evident that a significant potential remains untapped, which could be better leveraged elsewhere on the path towards healthy and sustainable performance development.

It is not only the definitions of success and performance that require reassessment, but also our understanding of motivation. You have been introduced to the three essential components of motivation: intensity, direction and persistence of effort. Undoubtedly, we have already mastered the assessment and demand of intensity. But how often do we regularly review our direction, and to what extent do our efforts truly contribute to our definition of success – assuming we have one? Do we work with discipline and consistency on the established success factors, or do we allow ourselves to be distracted by seemingly urgent tasks and non-productive thoughts?

Potential Tactical Errors

Tactical error 38: We lack a clear definition of success.

Tactical error 39: We do not have a consistent definition of what is important and urgent.

Tactical error 40: We fail to focus on what is essential.

Tactical error 41: We expend too much energy on things we cannot influence.

Tactical error 42: We allow ourselves to be driven by impulses.

Tactical error 43: We react instead of respond.

Tactical error 44: We are unaware of our disruptive factors.

Tactical error 45: We spend too little time in the here and now.

Tactical error 46: We spend too much time justifying the past.

Tactical error 47: We spend too much time planning and forecasting the future.

Passion, Emotions and a Chimp

We have explored the significant costs incurred when we follow impulses that are not checked, whether they stem from our own thoughts or external stimuli. Uncontrolled behaviour results in a loss of focus, which subsequently diminishes both effectiveness and efficiency. Although we work more, results often do not improve. This not only leads to frustration but also to exhaustion and, in the worst cases, to prolonged illness. The addiction to activity and multitasking has numerous side effects that impede sustainable and healthy performance development at all levels.

There are additional unintended consequences if we do not learn how to consciously manage our impulses. Football fans often witness how players and coaches waste their energy by continuously arguing with the referee. Coaches frequently assert, with conviction, that they employ this as a strategic tool by standing protectively in front of their players and attempting to influence the referee through authoritative gestures. I do not believe in it; however, I lack the scientific foundation to substantiate my perspective with facts.

Be that as it may, in football it is almost socially acceptable to criticise the referee. Week after week, verbal attacks are directed at an individual whose sole responsibility is to protect the players and ensure fair competition. Why? Clearly, we are unable to police this ourselves. New regulations at football's 2024 European Championship represented at least a first step towards more respectful treatment of referees.

The 2024 European Men's Handball Championship in Germany featured exciting matches in sold-out arenas. Every two to three days, the modern 'warriors' took to the court, subjecting themselves to constant tests of endurance. Every inch is fiercely contested. Referees do not have an easy task. Where one official sees a foul by a forward, another awards a penalty. Despite their passion and determination to win, players respect the referee's decisions. They applaud each other, and help each other to their feet. There is no complaining about the referee, only respectful acceptance of their rulings. Retaliation or group confrontations, common in other sports, are absent. Disrespectful gestures towards the referee are rare or non-existent.

Naturally, it cannot be denied that a penalty kick or a red card in football has a greater impact on the outcome than in handball. Nevertheless, despite the emotions involved, it is notable that complaints about referees are generally absent in handball.

It could be argued that handball players are potentially more intelligent and, therefore, better equipped to manage their emotions. However, I was unable to find any scientific evidence supporting this hypothesis. On the contrary, the era of mindless statements in football appears to have come to an end. Contemporary national players communicate with deliberation, and the proportion of high school graduates and university students within professional football has risen. Academies now place greater emphasis on comprehensive academic education alongside football training. Consequently, Andreas Möller would likely understand today that he could only achieve his goal of playing in Italy from 1992 to 1994 while in Turin at Juventus – and that Real Madrid, who had previously shown interest in the skilful midfielder, is not in fact part of Europe's 'boot'.

What, then, motivates football players to become upset with the neutral official? Are football players simply more passionate about the game? Emotions are widely regarded as the clearest indicator of dedication. However, a closer examination of competing handball players reveals that passion and the will to win are not exclusive to football. Regardless of the division in which they compete, handball players demonstrate remarkable dedication, and it appears that the world of handball has not yet been infiltrated by the destructive influence of money. While football players in the third tier sometimes earn salaries exceeding 100,000 euros per year, third-division handball players often receive monthly expenses in the lower three-digit range – even experienced players. This clearly shows that a lack of passion is not the reason for the absence of referee criticism.

A common misconception is that being passionate necessarily involves displaying emotions, and vice versa.

However, the words of NBA coach Pat Riley challenge this assumption: "Sport teaches us to live with passion and to master our emotions."

Thus, passion and emotions are not inherently linked. Here is a brief explanation of the difference: Passion is sustained enthusiasm, whereas emotions are transient expressions of feelings such as anger, frustration, joy or fear.

Passion requires active engagement and a connection to a vision, while emotions tend to be reactive in nature and are typically triggered by specific moments.

This distinction separates those who simply follow and react to their emotions from those who become aware of their emotions, pause briefly, and then respond purposefully and in a manner that serves the team.

Viktor Frankl, a survivor of the concentration camps during the Second World War, described this choice as the space between stimulus and response.

Both passion and emotions can have positive effects when we learn to manage them intentionally, without suppressing them.

In business, the boundary between passion and emotions often becomes blurred. Emotions are simplified and perceived as indicators of passion. However, not every emotional reaction is an expression of dedication.

Meetings can become intense. Individuals may feel insulted, aggressive, frustrated, pressured or misunderstood. As an immediate consequence of this emotional mix, interruptions occur, team members attack one another, personal criticism is expressed, accusations are made, or the competence of colleagues is questioned. Within the corporate context, a minimum standard of decency and respect is often still upheld. After all, we must continue working together for some time and must not completely alienate our colleagues. Not to mention the consequences if our tone of voice slips. Unlike with abusive footballers, conflicts tend to be more subtle. We show our frustration, cross our arms, and signal to everyone that there is disagreement, which includes verbal retaliation at the right time.

The crucial difference? In the corporate environment, there is no video replay or neutral referee. Leaders are required to engage in constructive discussions and make informed decisions. A neutral observer would likely share the frustration that well-paid and trained leaders repeatedly struggle to act objectively. An impartial facilitator could improve certain meetings, as sad as this may be.

Just as persistent tardiness and inadequate preparation for meetings are tolerated, so too is the acceptance that colleagues are driven by emotions and respond impulsively to stimuli. The consequences include not only friction losses during and after meetings, but decisions that often lack logic and rationality. These questionable decisions must then be presented to the workforce based on numbers, data and facts, representing yet another obstacle to sustainable and healthy performance development. This costs companies time, energy and money.

This raises the question of how passionate employees can be guided to make rational and logical decisions. But is this truly the goal? After all, we do not want emotionless machines in meetings. This remains one of the last domains where artificial intelligence cannot replace us.

It remains true that every decision, whether we like it or not, is an emotional decision. Emotions are our driving force. Studies show that individuals with damage to the emotional centre of their brain can identify many rational reasons for their actions, but still fail to act. The emotional driving force is absent.

Therefore, the goal is not to suppress emotions and revert to the 'Homo economicus'. This would be impossible, as needs and feelings invariably precede behaviour. In other words: We can only act rationally after experiencing emotions. The objective is not to avoid emotions, but to become aware of them and manage them effectively.

While passion is explicitly encouraged, emotions should be controlled – as Pat Riley stated – in a manner that neither limits our potential development nor leads to actions that contradict our definition of success. To learn how to manage these emotions effectively, we must understand how emotions influence our behaviour.

The ABC Model

The ABC model, developed by Albert Ellis[41] in the mid-twentieth century, provides a straightforward explanation for the origin of emotions and behavioural patterns. It is founded on the understanding that it is not the events themselves that disturb us, but our interpretation of those events.

In a football match, for instance, it is not the event itself that generates an emotion, but rather the interpretation of the situation. How else can we explain that one fan bites his fingernails, while another jubilantly takes another sip of his drink? Both spectators watch the same match and see the identical result on the scoreboard. Yet, their emotions could not be more different.

Ellis recognised that feelings or actions are not caused solely by an external or internal stimulus. He observed that the sequence, 'event leads to feeling', is overly simplistic, and that a critically important intermediary step exists: the evaluation. This is precisely what he described in the ABC model:

Activating experiences – internal or external perception of
   activating experiences
Beliefs – assumptions, interpretations and evaluations
Consequences – consequences, behaviour and feelings.

If an event directly caused a feeling, we would have little control over it. However, between the event and the feeling lies an evaluation. This is where sports psychologists and coaches find an effective point of intervention. Viktor Frankl highlighted the space between stimulus and response, recognising that our power lies in choosing our response. Our development and freedom reside in this response. Therefore, the goal is not to suppress emotions but to regulate our response to them.

The Two Systems of Our Brain
The understanding that our brain operates with two systems is not new and was popularised by Daniel Kahneman's bestseller, *Thinking, Fast and Slow*[42]. The primary mode is feeling, while the secondary mode is devoted to thinking. Although this concept simplifies our complex cognitive processes, awareness of it can significantly aid self-regulation.

System One, our fast and unconscious brain, is optimised for feeling and anticipation. This automatic reaction was crucial for survival in the past, enabling threats to be detected and responded to within milliseconds. The 'fight or flight' response triggers the release of the stress hormone cortisol in such situations. Athletes understand how to harness these feelings before a competition, whereas managers often attempt to fight or suppress their emotions, which yields limited success. Very often, suppressing emotions intensifies their influence.

The limbic system and the amygdala, also referred to as the 'fear centre', govern these processes. While System One proves valuable in certain situations, it may fail within complex human societies.

System Two, the conscious brain, assumes responsibility for analytical thinking. It enables advanced planning and complex calculations, thereby underpinning 'mature' behavioural patterns. The prefrontal cortex, a lobe located directly behind the forehead and unique to humans, regulates this system and plays a pivotal role in emotion regulation. Viktor Frankl's concept of the space between stimulus and response becomes tangible here – serving as the key to emotional intelligence and the capacity to manage our impulses.

Both systems offer distinct advantages; however, the feeling arises first (System One), with rationality engaging thereafter (System Two). This interplay generally functions well, but can result in illogical thinking when the systems are not properly aligned.

Particularly under pressure, our fast brain, which governs 'fight or flight' responses, tends to override our slow brain, responsible for logical reasoning. This leads to impulsive and emotional actions rather than a deliberate and thoughtful approach.

Comprehending our functional mechanisms and the capacity to regulate our behaviour are critical topics for athletes, and are equally relevant within business. The recognition that the interpretation of a situation generates emotions constitutes a fundamental principle in sports psychology and professional business coaching. Both athletes and employees can enhance or reverse their emotion regulation through increased consciousness and addressing their biases.

The Chimp Paradox

Another renowned psychiatrist who has explored this fascinating topic is Dr. Steve Peters. He gained recognition through his work with British Cycling. His book, *The Chimp Paradox*[43], was published in 2012, shortly after the release of the previously cited work by bestselling author and Nobel Prize laureate Daniel Kahneman.

Peters further emphasises that the human brain comprises two fundamental modes of thinking that frequently come into conflict. Even when we understand what the most rational response would be, we often act contrary to reason.

The psychiatrist differentiates between the rational thinking part of the human brain, which is fact-based, and the 'inner chimp'. This chimp aspect does not make decisions rationally, but rather based on feelings and emotions. The limbic system, which is older than the rational part, operates more quickly and generates stronger impulses for action.

Peters' model allows the brain to be divided into a 'human side' and a 'chimp side'. The chimp functions as an emotional machine that can be both beneficial and destructive. Therefore, it is essential to learn how to manage it, in order to deliberately harness its power.

To achieve success, we must first understand ourselves and learn to regulate our emotions. In brief, our chimp acts emotionally, illogically and irrationally, thinking in a 'paranoid' and 'catastrophic' manner –

driven by fundamental instincts. In contrast, our human side values evidence, self-actualisation, success, happiness and the pursuit of meaningful contribution. This side respects honesty, compassion and conscience.

The chimp is an integral part of us, yet it does not always act in our best interests. When it takes control and causes problems, it can be destructive. The solution lies in accurately identifying and controlling the negative aspects of our chimp.

Certain thought patterns of the chimp are well recognised in the corporate context, as it tends to think in black-and-white terms – that is, right or wrong. To perceive shades of grey, we require the 'human aspect' of our brain.

Peters emphasises that initially, "all information is directed to the chimp". The limbic system operates more rapidly and sends stronger impulses to act. The principle that we are first emotional and only subsequently rational applies here. Emotional 'triggers' typically precede rational decisions. Frequently, we make decisions emotionally, and subsequently attempt to rationalise our choice. We have previously encountered this hindsight bias in other contexts. It appears prudent to manage our response to emotions in a manner that supports our success or, ideally, the team's success.

Managing the 'Chimp'

We cannot prevent emotions from arising before we have the opportunity to evaluate and consider them rationally. The question, therefore, is: How can we regulate our response to these emotions?

The simplest approach is to assist the 'chimp' in calming down, by allowing it an outlet to release energy. Peters insightfully observed that the chimp is content when it has an audience. Ideally, however, this should occur neither on the playing field, at the sidelines, nor in the meeting room. Seek a 'safe' space and a trusted listener who knows you well and refrains from judgement.

Dr. Tom Kossak, sports psychologist for the German national ice hockey team, humorously referred to his professional role as the "nation's trash can"[44] – a description he certainly did not intend to be disrespectful. Such a space can be highly beneficial for both players and coaches. Many leaders also value having a sparring partner who offers this kind of space. Emotions contain valuable information. Who supports your employees in harnessing them?

Labelling Emotions

There are ways to tame our inner chimp. However, this requires becoming aware of these emotions – a task that deserves more attention from many individuals.

This exercise is by no means trivial. In fact, more people than we might expect have never truly learned to perceive their emotions. All too often, these emotions have been suppressed to conform to an assumed ideal.

"These are feelings that are difficult to describe," remarked Jürgen Klinsmann following the home World Cup in Germany in 2006. These words capture what many individuals struggle with today, including head coaches and managers. In particular, those raised with traditional notions of masculinity often find it difficult to adequately articulate their emotions.

It is almost like learning a new language – a lost skill that transcends social stratification, genders and generations, often rooted in profound, individual reasons.

A technique known as 'labelling' exists in sports psychology. There is a scientific consensus that identifying negatively charged emotions such as anger, fear or shame, as well as positively charged emotions such as joy, interest or satisfaction, positively influences our health and well-being. David Rock, whom we have previously encountered in the section on motivation (SCARF model), observes that in high-pressure situations, stress levels can be reduced by up to 50% simply by articulating our feelings.

The method of 'labelling' is founded on the understanding that it is difficult to control and regulate something if it cannot be named. By distinguishing and describing our emotions more precisely, we find it easier to regulate them. As Dr. Dan Siegel states: "Name it to tame it" – assign a name to the experience, in order to manage it[45].

To name emotions effectively, we must engage System Two – the rational aspect of our brain. In essence, we step outside the emotion, creating a distance between the emotion and the resulting feeling. Does it sound simple? It is. Nonetheless, it takes practice to transform an impulsive actor on the field into a composed player who responds appropriately to the referee's whistle or to verbal attacks – or chooses not to respond at all.

Athletes who engage in mindfulness training develop the ability to become aware of their emotions and behavioural patterns that hinder them from fully realising their potential – a form of training that encourages greater use of System Two, as described by Kahneman.

Conversely, athletes who tend to overanalyse situations require support in trusting their own rapid, automatic decision-making processes governed by System One.

Coaches and athletes can be effectively supported in appropriately adapting their cognitive styles. This not only enhances control but can foster increased self-efficacy. Responding appropriately to emotions is not an innate skill but one that can assist us in achieving healthy and sustainable performance development – both in sport and business. Successful athletes and coaches have, over time, learned to perceive their emotions and thoughts with greater awareness. This process does not occur overnight, but is the result of consistent effort. While it certainly requires some repetition, it is by no means complicated. Various methods can assist athletes, such as the well-known and easy-to-implement 'STOPP' method.

The 'STOPP' Method

The 'STOPP' method[46], a technique commonly employed in cognitive behavioural therapy, has also proven highly effective in sport. Its benefits, however, only manifest once we learn to consciously recognise and acknowledge the emerging emotions. In this section, we explore the steps of the STOPP method – 'Stop', 'Take a breath', 'Observe', 'Pull back' and 'Proceed' – in more detail to foster a deeper understanding of its application.

Stop: Consciousness as the Key to Success

The first stage of the STOPP method, conscious pausing, represents the essential step towards emotion regulation. Without this mindfulness, it is impossible to consciously manage our behaviour. It involves becoming aware of ourselves and recognising our own emotions and thoughts.

Take a Breath: The Signal to the 'Chimp'

Taking a deep breath at this stage signals to our inner chimp that there is no immediate threat. This simple action has proven to be highly effective. We leverage evolution by signalling to ourselves that we no longer need to flee from wild animals. Through this conscious breathing, which many athletes successfully employ, we activate System Two and establish the foundation for emotional control.

Observe: Emotions as a Source of Information

Observing our emotions enables a deeper understanding of the information they convey. These feelings are primarily informative. It is essential to categorise both thoughts and emotions. For example, nervousness in sport can be interpreted by athletes as a sign of readiness, rather than being suppressed or resisted as a perceived weakness. The objective is to consider every emotional state as valuable information and to utilise it accordingly.

Pull Back: Gaining Distance and Reviewing Thoughts

The next stage involves creating distance from our thought patterns. This entails questioning thoughts and assessing their validity. Rather than convincing ourselves to struggle with nervousness, we should train our thoughts to perceive nervousness as a supportive element. The motto, 'Don't believe everything you think', serves as a guiding principle in sports psychology and coaching to foster a more realistic perception. It is essential not to compare our internal emotional state with the external behaviour of others – in most cases, this unequal comparison can cause problems.

Proceed: Get it Done

Only once thoughts are properly organised should we advance to the behavioural level. The quality of our thinking determines the quality of our behaviour. It is futile to resist emerging emotions. Instead, the focus should be on rituals that cultivate the desired mental state to win a game – confident and focused. Coaches and sports psychologists can assist in developing and reinforcing these practices. Managers, however, are often left to navigate these challenges on their own.

The STOPP method provides a structured approach to emotional self-regulation in sport by integrating awareness, breath control, self-monitoring, psychological distancing and purposeful action.

Sports psychology offers a comprehensive range of self-regulation techniques tailored to address the individual challenges faced by athletes. It is important to emphasise that categorising players simply as 'self-confident' or 'insecure' is insufficient. Frequently, when there is an abundant pool of talent, less focus is placed on the mental development of those perceived as less self-confident players – after all, the games are won regardless. In sport and clubs where talent is plentiful, the selection process tends to be quicker, and investment in the athletes' mental resilience is often neglected. This situation differs in disciplines that must compete for every talent.

In times of skilled labour shortages and increasing competition for talent, companies must carefully consider which area of sport can serve as an exemplary model.

Imagine if employees were empowered to consciously recognise emotions and respond to them effectively. This would not only reduce unhealthy, counterproductive friction within companies, but it would foster a more positive atmosphere in meetings and lead to more efficient decision-making.

To realise this vision, we must cease categorising employees as either strong or weak. Rather than making 'those who can' more self-assured and 'those who cannot' more humble, we should invest comprehensively in the mental development of our employees. Such an investment not only promotes healthy and sustainable performance improvement, but it significantly widens the pools of talent and high potential, without the need for elaborate employer branding or costly recruitment efforts.

In the context of resilience – and this may come as a surprise – those with high or excessive self-confidence particularly benefit from this mental work. Resilience fundamentally involves the ability to question our own emotions. It is not about experiencing fewer or no emotions, but rather about experiencing more of the 'right' emotions, better understanding them, and utilising them effectively.

Values

Currently, there is considerable discussion about values and value-based leadership. This does not refer to the corporate values displayed on glossy posters, which are often subject to individual interpretation, but rather to the conscious awareness of our own values.

These are often key to the regulation of emotions. Values are highly individual and significantly influence our actions and overall satisfaction. When the values we consider important are met, it feels positive – accompanied by positively perceived emotions. However, if these values are disregarded or violated, the consequences are severe. Emotions arise that signal to us: 'Something is wrong here.' Awareness of our values greatly facilitates self-regulation. Athletes and coaches frequently receive support to increase their awareness of their values. It is equally important for coaches to understand the values of players, as this can shed light on why certain behavioural patterns are more disturbing than others.

It is fascinating how a simple discussion about our values – whether in individual coaching, team coaching, sport or business – can lead to numerous lightbulb moments.

We have already explored several overarching models that assist us in understanding our inner drivers. When it comes to values, we take a further step. They have developed over time, remain constant companions, and influence our actions in a subtle yet pervasive manner.

As we look to align with our most important values, we often encounter obstacles. The environment in which we find ourselves, or social expectations, can hinder us from fully embodying our values. We attempt to coordinate with the value system of our environment, and experience discomfort, assign blame or suspect reasons within ourselves, without first of all considering if our values have been violated.

Let us be more specific. An athlete for whom 'fairness' is important will not understand why a teammate who has not trained all week is still in the starting lineup, simply because they are regarded as an important success factor. Similarly, these players often respond to referee decisions they perceive as unfair.

Another player, whose values are grounded in transparency and logic, expects an explanation when they are not selected to play. Empathy and honesty, however, are decisive for some players, who accept not being selected if the coach demonstrates compassion for their situation.

An employee who details health and sustainability as his core values in his application will soon be disappointed once he realises that the same mechanisms are at play as in his previous job. Here, short-term results are favoured over long-term, sustainable decisions. The focus is not only on healthy and sustainable performance but on working harder – preferably in a way that is noticed. Why did he change his job in the first place?

The most-costly employer branding is the one which fails to deliver on its promises. When what is advertised does not reflect reality, it is misleading and disappointing.

Our individual values provide important insight into why we experience certain emotions or do not. On the journey towards improved self-regulation, it is essential to confront our deeply ingrained values.

It is remarkable that many companies assume that simply displaying value posters will cause employees to embrace the same values. For instance, a managing director was initially surprised when we addressed the topic of values during a team workshop. He considered it a waste of time, believing the values were clearly accessible on the intranet. Only after I convinced him to reflect on his own values did he appreciate the potential embedded in such discussions. From that point forward, he encouraged his employees to engage with this topic, to foster improved self-regulation and a deeper understanding of conflicts within the team.

It is essential to recognise that values are not universal. Each person is uniquely shaped and has had diverse experiences, resulting in the development of distinct value systems. The focus is not on whether these values are good or bad, but on becoming aware of them to leverage team diversity and reduce unproductive friction.

Perhaps the reason handball players accept referee decisions differently is because they were raised with a different value system within the sporting context. In many of my workshops with handball teams, the word 'respect' secured a permanent place on the team poster, often without debate. While this is not representative, it illustrates how profoundly values can influence emotions and behaviour.

In the preceding sections, we have extensively discussed the process of becoming conscious. This involves becoming aware of our own values, emotions, thoughts and self-talk, and employing this consciousness for self-regulation. As a result, there are fewer unhealthy conflicts, more constructive discussions and, ultimately, better decisions. This involves engaging our analytical thinking (System Two) to effectively harness our human aspect.

Such consciousness constitutes a critical success factor for head coaches and leaders. It enables them to regulate themselves. It also helps them to coach their players and employees, recognising their unhelpful reactions and considering alternative responses to their emotions. Consciousness is a key factor for healthy and sustainable performance development.

Potential Tactical Errors

Tactical error 48: We confuse emotion with passion.

Tactical error 49: We are unaware of our emotional 'triggers'.

Tactical error 50: We underestimate the significance of individual values.

Tactical error 51: We attempt to suppress emotions instead of using them.

Tactical error 52: We inadequately utilise the space between emotion and behaviour.

Tactical error 53: We rationalise our emotional decisions.

Developing Performance

If there is a clear distinction between sport and business, it is that in sport, the majority of time is dedicated to training, whereas formal training in companies remains the exception. Nevertheless, performance should be continuously developed within companies. Continuous improvement is a core principle of many successful companies. We have learned to critically examine, optimise and digitalise processes. We have learned to enhance our system landscapes and, in some cases, develop structures that support rather than constrain us in our work. But what about the development of employees? The model of professional sport is based on improving individual players and leveraging their strengths for the collective. This is part of the success definition, and therefore it is unsurprising that we can learn from sport in this area. What, then, prevents us in business from focusing on the unlocking of individual potential and effective teamwork?

Shirkers and 'Know-It-Alls'

Anyone who has participated in a team sport will undoubtedly recall the various player types and be able to describe their characteristics. My former coach used to say: "Every team has its odd one out." He meant the player who frequently drew the displeasure of their teammates – not intentionally, but simply because of their personality. If you are unsure who this odd one out was in your team, it is likely that it was you.

If you were not this odd one out, you can certainly remember such a teammate, as well as the charismatic leader, the unwavering fighter, or the thoughtful strategist. And there was the one who regularly arrived late to games or training sessions, or who forgot something. Sometimes, it was just shower gel or a towel, but occasionally he forgot essential items such as football boots or shin guards. In the worst case, the entire set of jerseys was absent – taken home by mum or dad after the last game for washing.

For the sake of illustration, let us call this player Clemens, inspired by the former Austrian football player of Kaiserslautern, Clemens Walch.

He was prepared to be substituted on to help his teammates prevent the impending defeat against Werder Bremen. Unfortunately, this did not occur, as seconds before the substitution, he recalled that he had left his jersey in the dressing room. While the desperate Clemens searched for his jersey, his coach brought on another player. Clemens remained on the bench until the final whistle, helplessly watching as the Werder players scored in the 81st minute to mark the 2–0 final score. Two instances of misconduct within a minute: first unprepared, then too late. Unfortunate.

In team sports, Clemens understands by the second incident that such behaviour is unacceptable. He should refrain from offering excuses and take personal responsibility for his actions. In youth teams, well-intentioned educational measures are employed to address individuals like 'Clemens'. The older the players become, the more frequently fines are introduced to replenish the team's funds. Even misconduct assumes a character of solidarity. However, in the professional setting, such players are becoming increasingly rare, as those with insufficient learning curves are typically excluded.

Tardiness as a Self-promotion Strategy

In the corporate environment, behaviours that would result in a disciplinary in district league teams are increasingly tolerated or, more accurately, openly 'glorified'. Arriving late to meetings and inadequate preparation are no longer regarded as faux pas but rather as elements of a self-promotion strategy intended to highlight an individual's workload. The meeting begins, but we've just come from back-to-back meetings and need a comfort break, or we were just in a meeting with 'Ms. Important'. Ms. Important naturally occupies a higher position in the hierarchy than all other meeting participants. The creativity of excuses knows no limits.

If we are late, this opportunity is used to position ourselves, rather than appear as someone who does not manage their time effectively. Similarly, a lack of preparation is dismissed with comparable arguments. In some companies, there is a sense that those who are well prepared and have read the document distributed in advance are criticised: 'Do you have too much time?'

This trend then spirals. The more delays are tolerated, the more frequent and longer they become. The attitude, 'Why should I be punctual if Clemens is going to be late again?' becomes accepted practice. What results in fines even in amateur teams tends to provoke frustration inside organisations.

My Italian manager once remarked that Germans are punctual only because they have no other way to demonstrate respect. There may be some truth in that. Nonetheless, I prefer to align with the former German national basketball coach, Gordon Herbert, who is known for granting his players considerable freedom within certain boundaries, yet regards punctuality as one of the non-negotiable 'basics'. A lack of discipline in meetings indicates the absence of a performance culture. Numerous studies address this issue. Although the figures vary, the authors concur on one point: unproductive meetings constitute a significant cost factor for companies. According to some studies, up to 70% of participants consider meetings ineffective and inefficient. The opportunity costs associated with these meetings are substantial. More than half of the respondents report that meetings not only hinder them from engaging in actual work, but also impede 'deep thinking'. Equally concerning is that over 60% of respondents felt their meetings did not foster closer team cohesion[47].

Tardiness and lack of preparation, as exemplified by 'Clemens', represent only the tip of the iceberg. These behaviours not only incur financial costs for companies but have a lasting negative impact on performance. Even masters' teams of advanced age warm up together before a game, stretching their muscles and ligaments prior to competition. In business, however, it is generally accepted that colleagues attend meetings unprepared and effectively enter discussions, cold. In sport, such practices would not only increase the risk of injury, but prevent the team from unlocking its full potential. This phenomenon occurs within companies worldwide.

Behavioural patterns such as tardiness and lack of preparation are challenging to measure, as they predominantly take place beneath the surface. As a leader, it is your responsibility to find ways to ensure that employees arrive punctually and prepared for meetings. Perhaps you never conclude meetings exactly on the hour, but always ten minutes earlier, allowing managers time to pause and mentally prepare for the next session. Alternatively, you might follow the example of Jeff Bezos, who introduced the 'Meeting 6-Pager' at Amazon. The initial minutes of the meeting are dedicated to reading and understanding the document, establishing a shared foundation for discussion.

Observable behaviours such as tardiness and lack of preparation should be openly discussed and addressed. It is essential to examine the reasons and develop appropriate solutions. Even more importantly, this behaviour must no longer be glorified nor exploited for self-promotion at the expense of team performance.

Attitude Makes the Difference

Let us assume that, regarding preparation and punctuality, we have elevated ourselves to the standard of a disciplined veteran league team. We now move beyond the basics and focus on what generally distinguishes professional athletes from the players of a veteran league team. The distinction lies not only in the level of play, but more significantly in the attitude with which players approach training. NBA legend Kobe Bryant emphasised that success depends not on the number of hours you train, but on the extent to which your mind is fully engaged during training.

Ulrik Wilbek, one of the world's most successful handball coaches from Denmark, once stated that the difference between companies and sport lies in the fact that athletes spend 99% of their time training and only 1% competing. In companies, however, 99% of the time is devoted to the 'game' and only 1% to training. While this fundamental idea is valid, there are numerous opportunities within companies to 'train', without sending employees on costly training programmes. Meetings serve as spaces for reflection and provide an excellent opportunity to learn from one another, experiment and optimise decisions. Just as every training session contributes to team success, every meeting should contribute to the collective success of the company. However, without the appropriate attitude and a vigilant mind, this endeavour is bound to fail.

In recent years, I have engaged in conversations with numerous professional athletes to uncover the secrets of sustainable success. Most athletes shared one common trait: the training was driven by a clear purpose. The coaches of these athletes reported that the players approached each session with curiosity and a willingness to learn, aiming to improve incrementally or to be better prepared for the next game.

I contend that this same motivation drives most colleagues in meetings. They strive to contribute optimally for the benefit of both the team and the company. They value the opportunity to acquire new knowledge and feel satisfied when the meeting leads to greater clarity. They take pleasure in making sound decisions, demonstrate conflict and teamwork skills, and can effectively endure controversial discussions, provided these are conducted with mutual respect. I am convinced that the majority of meeting participants approach meetings with a positive mindset.

Naturally, I do not wish to be overly idealistic by attributing a certain 'fun factor' to every meeting. Work should occasionally feel like work. However, if we substitute 'fun' with 'satisfaction', that ought to be our standard – both for the work we perform and for the numerous meetings we attend. Meetings occupy a substantial portion of our working hours – depending on the industry and corporate culture, and according to various studies, up to 90%. This roughly corresponds to the amount of time professional athletes dedicate to training and to delivering their performance in competition, as Ulrik Wilbek observed.

At this point, I could fill pages with well-known meeting standards or agile working methods, all of which are justified. In sport, new training methods continually emerge, promising greater efficiency and effectiveness. However, one factor is always present: the attitude of the players when they step on to the training field.

The attitude determines the effectiveness of the training session. No coach in the world can sustainably improve a team if the players are frustrated during most training sessions, merely waiting for them to end, and regard the shower as the most desirable part of the session. Similarly, the attitude of meeting participants directly affects the quality of a meeting.

In a business context, we expect highly effective meetings with participants who are purposeful, focused, eager to learn and collaborative. Employees display the attitudes of a 'hard trainer', a 'procrastinator', a 'shirker', an 'animated straight-talker', a 'know-it-all', a 'show-off' or a 'first-to-do-everything' type. Although these employees are in the minority, they have a considerable impact on the quality of the meeting. The story of the bad apple is well known. But first, let us proceed step by step.

Five Steps Towards Healthy and Sustainable Performance

The 'Hard Trainer'

We have all had them in our teams: the so-called 'hard trainer'. They train tirelessly and are always present, come rain or shine. Nothing prevents them from signalling to the coach that they are ready: "I am here. You can count on me." Yet, why do they fail to improve and often fall behind the other players, despite training more frequently and consistently? This stagnation can stem from their attitude towards training. For them, the tick in the coach's book represents the goal, and once it is achieved, their motivation dissipates. This attitude, well known among sports psychologists and often unconscious, does not lead to outstanding performance. On the contrary, it diminishes the quality and intensity of training. Merely being marked present in the coach's book has never made anyone better. Of course, it has not harmed anyone, but only in combination with enjoying the process, willingness to learn and goal orientation – a clear understanding of the purpose behind it all – will it yield sustainable results.

Hand on heart, within companies, we recognise equivalents to the 'hard trainers'. Those who attend every meeting yet are not truly present. They are like a fly on the wall: they do not disturb, but they also contribute nothing. However, since they were invited, they attend to demonstrate appreciation to the person who invited them, or reliability to their manager. They are present, albeit with the unfortunate impression that the employee, the team nor the meeting gains any benefit. This is not only costly but frustrating for everyone involved.

The 'Procrastinator'

Procrastination is arguably one of the most widespread 'ailments' in company offices. Procrastinators are pleased to attend meetings, as this excuses them from being elsewhere and allows them to defer other burdensome tasks with justifiable reason and without guilt. Often, this results in them being notably good-humoured. Much like the 'hard trainers', they neither significantly disrupt the meeting nor, in most cases, contribute positively. For a sustainable performance culture, this implies that some employees do not focus on the issues that would have the greatest impact on collective success. Instead, when attending a physical meeting, they pour coffee into their personalised mugs, snack on delicious cookies or sweets and inconsiderately push the accumulating sweet wrappers to their neighbour.

The 'Shirker'

The situation is similar with 'shirkers'. Perhaps you recall from your active experience, players who skilfully operated under the coach's radar. They bear no responsibility off the field, nor do they contribute to setting up the goals on the field before training. They neither inflate balls nor collect them after training. Yet, somehow, they manage to avoid detection or simply appear too occupied – because they are still with the physiotherapist, engaging the assistant coach in conversation, tying their shoes, adjusting their shin guards, or taking a comfort break. These players have typically never organised a Christmas party, nor have they stood for election as treasurer. Positively stated, they are 'focused' on other matters; in other words, they are social freeloaders. However, they are often so talented and indispensable during the game that coaches and teammates have learned to tolerate this 'antisocial' behaviour.

Genius aside, and excluding those few experts with specialised knowledge, it is rare in companies for individual employees to overshadow others solely because of their talent. Nevertheless, we often encounter those meeting participants who consistently avoid taking on tasks when responsibilities are being assigned. Whether it is the tedious task of writing meeting minutes or other agreed-upon activities, the shirker's definition of success is: 'I attended the meeting without receiving any additional tasks.' This description aligns with what football coach Bernd Stange once remarked about Mario Basler, who was then playing for Bayern Munich: "He is like a parking meter; he just stands there, and Bayern throws money in." Occasionally, companies inadvertently foster such meeting participants by placing excessive demands on their employees, causing any additional task to be perceived as overload. Thus, the once social and responsible employee transforms into a 'shirker' – and the prevailing environment encourages this antisocial behaviour.

The 'Animated Straight-talker'

Since we are discussing Mario Basler, let us also mention another well-known figure from the successful Bayern Munich team at the turn of the millennium – Stefan Effenberg. While the nickname 'Tiger' was certainly more favoured during his time, some journalists and teammates labelled him 'the animated straight-talker'. I am far from diminishing the contributions of 'Effe' to German football. Nevertheless, this nickname often features in meetings. Bad-tempered, frequently due to preceding meetings, the 'animated straight-talker' enters the room. Their objective is not to enhance the quality of the discussion but rather to vent frustration and criticise others. Unlike the previously described attitudes, 'animated straight-talkers' can undermine both training sessions and meetings. Entering training with such an attitude is strictly prohibited in professional sport; it is toxic and dangerous. In some companies, it is tolerated and accepted, to the detriment of all involved.

The 'Know-it-all'

This type of meeting participant resembles self-proclaimed TV experts who, particularly during widely watched World Cups and European Championships, attempt to assert their bold opinions. I am not referring to the intelligent, objective comments of some of the professional and wise experts. Rather, I speak of those who, after a typically brief and unsuccessful career as head coach or assistant coach, have finally discovered their true vocation: explaining in hindsight how others could have done better. Their concern is not the matter itself, but primarily to display their alleged expertise – preferably at the expense of others. And, naturally, without having to assume any responsibility themselves.

While such unpleasant individuals are gradually becoming less common in sports TV, they are on the rise within companies. One possible explanation is the ubiquitous availability of standard leadership knowledge, always just a click or podcast away. Forming an opinion on what constitutes 'good' leadership behaviour is easy nowadays – quite unlike its practical implementation, which the self-proclaimed experts prefer to leave to others. Nevertheless, it is highly satisfying for them to demonstrate to their supposedly incompetent manager how things could be done better. Loyalty is entirely absent. Much like TV experts, they toss theoretical knowledge into the discussion and desperately strive to appear the smartest, without ever assuming responsibility. However, as in sport, theory and practice are often separated by a considerable gap in leadership. When some of these 'know-it-alls' assume leadership roles themselves, they frequently present a rather disappointing image.

The 'Show-off'

"Today, the national coach is sitting in the stand, so demonstrate what you are capable of" – a motivating piece of advice to many emerging talents who sense the opportunity to catapult themselves into the elite level of sport. The young player attempts to convince the critical observer of their abilities, shooting from all positions and performing every trick they know. Some talents overdo it, to the point of appearing rather ridiculous. It would be better to apply their abilities in a way that serves the team, but the desire to be 'seen' is stronger.

A similar situation occurs in meetings, with 'show-offs'. The primary objective of the meeting – to exchange ideas and reach decisions – fades into the background. Instead, 'show-offs' wait for the opportunity to showcase their insights or supposed heroic deeds. Those who miss the initial opportunity do not hesitate to take another turn in order to establish their position. Regrettably, this behaviour rarely enhances the quality of meetings; in most cases, it diminishes it. This leads to less focused and often prolonged discussions.

The 'First-to-do-everything' Type

The 'first to do everything' on the football field during my youth was the player permitted to take the first penalty kick, the first free kick and the first corner. Not necessarily because he appeared most suitable, but because he declared it. Confident and often physically dominant, he perceived himself as a leader – a role rarely questioned: "Ronald is the 'first to do everything'." Such personalities are also found in business. Quicker and louder than others, they impose their supposedly decisive mark on proceedings without thinking of the consequences, and disregarding the most constructive contributions. When other participants remain silent, it does not mean they have ceased thinking. The 'first-to-do-everything' type, however, pays little attention to this. Even after many months of video conferences, he has not learned to raise his virtual hand before sharing his insights – regardless of whether the group wishes to hear them at that moment.

Science offers an explanation for this behaviour: the so-called Dunning-Kruger effect[48]. This cognitive bias describes the tendency of certain individuals to significantly overestimate their own knowledge and skills – often precisely when they lack essential expertise in a given area. In other words, the less a person knows about a subject, the more likely they are to overestimate their own abilities, fail to acknowledge the competence of others, and remain unaware of their own ignorance. Consequently, these people often dominate meetings not out of malice, but due to a lack of knowledge. Their surprised or intimidated colleagues tend to pause respectfully, or prefer to reflect before contributing. If team leaders fail to coach the 'first-to-do-everything' types, the organisation risks losing valuable perspectives and misses the opportunity to make well-informed decisions.

I emphasise that I do not rely on stereotypes, as personality tests do. A 'shirker' in one meeting can become a 'first to do everything' in the next. While personality traits shape our behaviour, it is only the context that leads to the expression of preferred and cultivated behavioural patterns. The fact that organisations often regard a convincing appearance as competence makes it less appealing for 'first-to-do-everything' types to refine their competence as curious listeners.

It is essential to recognise that everyone can work on their attitude to influence their behaviour. Unfortunately, this is often overlooked, and employees are labelled as show-offs, animated straight-talkers or shirkers instead of being supported in developing their attitude and, thereby, continuously enhancing their value to the company.

Checking Attitude

Every behaviour serves a purpose. Therefore, it is not possible to categorically label a behaviour as good or bad. It depends on the intended outcome being pursued. In sports psychology, the distinction is not between good or bad, but between effective or non-effective, supportive and non-supportive. For the animated straight-talker, expressing their thoughts does support the intended outcome, as it provides relief and prevents persistent internal unrest. The shirker prefers not to take on additional tasks to avoid extending their to-do list. The 'know-it-all' derives energy from sharing their knowledge and seeks to avoid the discomfort of not being recognised as an expert. These behavioural patterns stem from fundamental human needs and should not be categorically condemned. However, they do not contribute to the collective success, assuming the intended outcome has been clearly defined for the meeting.

Let us assume that the meeting's goal is clearly articulated. Let us further assume that the success definition for the meeting is as follows: 'We have developed options for securing the million-pound deal with the client and have established activities with clearly assigned responsibilities.' Achieving this requires cross-functional collaboration among sales, marketing, development, quality, procurement and production – a challenge that many companies face in various forms. Without clear goal and team orientation, a meeting can turn into a scenario where everyone ends up as 'losers', particularly the client. The cause tends not to lie in meeting techniques, inappropriate selection of participants or insufficient time allocation. In most cases, there is a lack of shared understanding regarding the purpose of the meeting. More often than not, failure stems from the individual attitudes of participants.

Our focus must be on collective success. A shared understanding of what constitutes a successful meeting is indispensable. The ego stays outside, and the only appropriate attitude is: 'How can I contribute to our collective success?' Rather than asking how we can be the best in the team, we ask how we can be the best for the team and the meeting. It is as simple as that.

Raising Consciousness

Initially, it is about developing a shared understanding of the intended outcome of the meeting. This is generally not an insurmountable task, yet it is often overlooked. We must align our attitude with this 'purpose'.

Before and during the meeting, with some self-reflection and practice, I can assess whether my behaviour and contribution support the collective goal. In case of doubt, it is advisable to pause and adjust behaviour – just as players in successful teams do. Here, individual needs are less important than the team's success. This is a task that demands as much commitment as physical training or video analysis. It requires working on ourselves, understanding our drivers, motivations, deeply rooted needs and behavioural preferences.

In sport, this work is frequently undertaken by sports psychologists to assist individual players or coaches to fully realise their potential for the benefit of the team. This work always begins with an awareness of a person's attitude, which equally influences behaviour on the playing field, during training, and in the meeting room. The quality of training largely depends on the training objectives and practised content, but above all on the attitudes of the players.

In business, by contrast, we often move from one meeting to the next, unprepared and without a clear understanding of why we are present. We lack a sense of purpose and a shared understanding of how success is defined for these gatherings. The greatest challenge, however, relates to attitude in meetings. There is much we can learn from sport in this regard. If every meeting participant reflected on the attitude they brought to meetings, much would already be achieved. If we realise that people are attending a meeting merely to be seen, to avoid tasks, to vent frustration or to assert their expert status, it would be better not to attend. Such attitudes have no place in team sports. It is the responsibility of each person to critically examine their own stance.

Each participant brings a unique dynamic to the room. Rather than striving to be the 'smartest' person present, the 'know-it-all' should share their knowledge for the benefit of the team when it is needed. The 'first-to-do-everything' type should leverage their natural curiosity to understand others' perspectives before offering unsolicited solutions. The 'show-off' should approach every meeting, regardless of the attendees, with a consistent attitude focused on the team's success. The 'animated straight-talker' should find ways to redirect his energy constructively for the benefit of the team. The 'shirker' should reflect on what is preventing them from taking responsibility. The 'procrastinator' should carefully consider whether to accept the meeting invitation and whether they can genuinely contribute. The 'hard trainer' should critically examine their inner attitude. If the focus is on 'compliance' or ticking a box in the coach's record, it would be better to not participate.

Every behaviour in a meeting either contributes to the collective success or does not, just as the behaviour of players on the field determines victory or defeat. This awareness should be held by every meeting participant and serve as the benchmark for what is said or left unsaid during the meeting. As a brief checklist, it is recommended to answer the following questions before committing to a meeting:

- Do I understand the purpose of the meeting, and is the investment worthwhile for the company?
- Can I contribute to the meeting's success?
- Can I learn something that will benefit me in my current role?

- What added value does the team or company gain if I prioritise this meeting?
- With what attitude do I approach the meeting?

The meeting organiser should clearly articulate the purpose of the meeting to facilitate answering these questions. When selecting participants, he should also be guided by the same questions:

- Can the participant contribute to the success of the meeting?
- Can the participant learn something that will benefit them in their current role?

The leader is responsible for supporting team members to reflect on their behavioural patterns, review their attitudes and consistently align these with the company's interests. Thus, it begins once again 'at the top'. When the leader demonstrates one of the specified attitudes, other employees will align themselves accordingly.

There will continue to be undeserved victories, mudslinging and unfair contests. There will also be games without a clear winner, and tedious draws. There will be meetings in which no one progresses, despite everyone being present – meetings that resemble intellectual arm wrestling rather than open, constructive dialogue. However, with the methods mentioned above, we will significantly reduce the likelihood of such occurrences. We will cultivate an attitude that embraces the principle that there are no winners or losers in meetings. Each meeting should have only one winner – the company – whether through an informed, effective decision, or through employees who have mutually enriched one another. In this way, we lay the foundation for sustainable performance development.

Potential Tactical Errors

Tactical error 54: We lack established behavioural guidelines.

Tactical error 55: We interpret 'tardiness' as a sign of 'busyness'.

Tactical error 56: We tolerate colleagues entering the
  game unprepared.

Tactical error 57: We lack clarity on the meeting's purpose.

Tactical error 58: We fail to review our attitude prior to
  a meeting.

Tactical error 59: We fail to use meetings as
  learning opportunities.

Positivity Circles and Perfectionists

The winter break has firmly taken hold of the youth team of SC Weiche Flensburg 08. The football pitches of the northernmost (and my former) club in the German republic have been transformed into a waterlogged landscape due to persistent rain. Outdoor training sessions? Not feasible in the short term. Indoor training takes place in a sports hall that is far too small and must be shared with another team. A challenge that generates discontent among the young footballers, particularly when compared to the leading academies of Bundesliga football clubs. How are they expected to keep pace? The confidence of the young footballers is undermined by the unequal conditions.

Yet, amid such adversity, something remarkable occurs. After a few words from their coach, the players begin writing on small notes and affixing them to their teammates' jerseys. The notes bear encouraging messages such as 'You make the best passes', 'No forward can get past you' and 'It's a pleasure to play alongside you'.

Such an exercise is unquestionably more effective than any kind of incentive or motivational speech by a coach. Within just 20 minutes, it substantially enhances the self-awareness of the individuals and the entire group. Becoming aware of our abilities – a practice often carelessly overlooked in the hectic workday – is like discovering a magic potion. Such measures are, however, quickly dismissed as mere 'softening'. Though they prove effective even for seasoned NBA professionals. The former national basketball coach of Germany, Gordon Herbert, for instance, describes a positivity circle that he introduced for the national team. In this exercise, the players sit in a circle and each player names three things they appreciate about their neighbour[49].

What appears playful at first glance is an expression of a deeply rooted attitude. Rather than focusing on weaknesses, attention is consciously directed towards strengths, which are then emphasised. This does not imply that weaknesses are ignored. On the contrary: If they are limiting, they are acknowledged. However, the focus always remains on strengths. Thinking and acting are resource-oriented.

This resource-based approach has delivered impressive results in elite sport. Legendary basketball coach John Wooden, known as 'the Wizard', might not have started coaching had he allowed himself to be distracted by his team's apparent weaknesses. None of his players were taller than 1.80 metres – a seemingly insurmountable obstacle in a sport largely defined by height. Yet Wooden had a clear vision: He did not view his team through the lens of weaknesses but regarded them as a group of players striving to reach their maximum potential.

The outcome was an impressive season. On five occasions, his team scored more than 100 points. The opponent came within five points only four times. They remained undefeated and secured the first NCAA championship under Coach Wooden – marking the beginning of a legendary success story with a total of ten titles between 1964 and 1975. However, this first title was the most meaningful for Wooden, as it realised his team's potential through their own development[50].

This resource-oriented approach is also evident in structured development discussions within the professional academies of football clubs. Athleticism, technical skills, technique and tactics, as well as mental and social components, are thoroughly discussed. Time is taken to reflect on individual development, identify top competencies and plan measures that enable players to continue their development.

These measures are incorporated into an action plan at the beginning of the season, which is regularly and individually adjusted according to the season's progress. It is not solely about what the player can do to improve. It also involves examining what the coaching team can do to support the player's ongoing development. This is fundamental, as the path to achieving the goals is more important than the goals themselves. What is preventing me today or in the future from achieving this goal? Which teammates can assist me in reaching this goal? How can I recognise that I am on the right path? These discussions contribute

Five Steps Towards Healthy and Sustainable Performance

to the personal development of the participants. Every player should be better after the season than they were before it.

Success is Making Others Successful

These individual and structured development discussions are part of the ethos in performance-oriented sport. The intention and the quality demonstrated distinguish good from outstanding 'academies' and coaches.

In companies, such discussions are often only conducted in a structured way when it is almost too late – when an employee consistently falls short of the usually vaguely defined expectations. In organisations, these measures are referred to as 'PIP', which stands for 'Performance Improvement Plan'. It is ironic that many managers only begin to address an employee's performance when the situation seems hopeless. In many cases, however, the focus is no longer on their ability to perform but rather on the willingness to perform – a distinction that is not always fully understood.

Leaders also conduct development discussions with the motivated 'average' and 'high performers'. However, the quality of these discussions varies considerably. How frequent and for what purpose are these discussions conducted?

An examination of many companies reveals a leadership mindset predominantly shaped by short-term objectives and bonus calculations. A (naturally fictitious) example:

It is 9th December. Only two weeks remaining until Christmas. Time to unwind and recharge. Until then, I still need to accelerate. The budget has still not been approved, the year-end rally is entering its final phase, we need to reduce inventory levels, and there are still orders that must be finalised. Otherwise, I can forget about the bonus this year! Let's get started! But wait – first, I will take a look at the email from the HR department that I have been postponing for weeks. Argh! I am expected to schedule one hour for a one-on-one meeting with each employee! Who on earth invented these employee development discussions?! Apparently, the HR department assumes I have nothing better to do during this hectic period! Well, the email is from August, but it was no less busy then. Nevertheless, if I do not do this, I jeopardise my bonus and risk casting my leadership competence in a negative light. So, eyes closed and push through!

In sport, one-on-one conversations between coaches and players are regarded as essential investments in the future. They aim to optimise performance and support the personal growth of every individual. Before forming and developing a team, the individual is taken care of. For players, the motto is, 'Side over self', but for the coach, this order can be transposed. Ultimately, it is the individual players who achieve success together. Without a strong goalkeeper, the chances of victory are slim. If a player who delivers the perfect pass at the decisive moment or a forward with the right instinct is absent, the prospects for success decline rapidly. Therefore, the individual is initially at the centre of all efforts.

Football coaches who have achieved long-term success, such as José Mourinho, Jürgen Klopp, Arsène Wenger and Sir Alex Ferguson, are renowned not only for building teams but for enhancing the performance of each individual player. The best coaches derive their energy not only from the pursuit of victories and titles but, above all, from the commitment to unlocking the full potential of every player. It is reported that Pep Guardiola was indifferent to the previous successes and heroic deeds of his players when he assumed leadership of Barcelona. His sole objective was to advance the development of every individual. Also, the only German coaches to have won the treble – that is, the domestic league and cup, and the Champions League, Hansi Flick and Jupp Heynckes, unanimously affirm that success for them means enabling others to succeed.

Quarterly discussions are indispensable over a season of sport. Unfortunately, these valuable opportunities are often insufficiently recognised in many companies. These discussions are often perceived as a burdensome obligation, driven by entrenched limiting beliefs. The focus is often on 'compliance' rather than 'commitment'.

Focus on Self-efficacy

Communicating to employees how to intentionally leverage their strengths for collective success, while simultaneously identifying and addressing their areas for improvement, promotes self-efficacy. In sport, high self-efficacy entails confidence in our abilities and, above all, the awareness that our actions contribute meaningfully to team success. This principle is equally effective within the corporate context. Enhancing self-efficacy establishes the foundation for healthy and sustainable performance development. Motivation emerges from experienced self-efficacy[51].

Success coaches therefore begin with the player's strengths. They deliberate on how the player can further develop their existing skills and, subsequently, how to optimally deploy these talents for collective success. Weaknesses are acknowledged but only addressed when they become limiting factors. This attitude differs markedly from the typical approach in business, where there is often an inherent focus on weaknesses.

Those of you who are parents may recognise this. Your child proudly brings home their report card. Yet, instead of appreciating the many good grades, our attention is immediately drawn to the one outlier. "What do you plan to do to prevent this from happening again?" We are constantly seeking opportunities for optimisation. It is almost ingrained in us to first focus on the negative. Subsequently, strategies are devised to eliminate these weaknesses.

In the corporate context, weaknesses are frequently emphasised during employee appraisals. Driven by deeply rooted beliefs and the desire to continuously improve employees, leaders tend to focus on their employees' weaknesses. These, after all, can be thoroughly documented. Following a brief introduction, acknowledging the employee's considerable workload and achievements during the evaluation period, the manager quickly imposes their perspective on the 'process', despite an explicit request to prepare a self-assessment. Quite often, and without any bad intent, our own template is applied. Unsurprisingly, this template lacks a scale. The focus is frequently on extremes rather than considering nuances. This results in misunderstandings and a one-sided perspective, which we are already familiar with.

Thus, the employee who is committed to high quality and holds high standards is told to be a 'perfectionist' who must learn, regardless of context, to occasionally 'let things slide'.

The employee who, unlike her extroverted colleagues, reflects before speaking in lengthy meetings and only contributes when she truly has something meaningful to say, is labelled as 'introverted'. "Ms. Jones – you rarely participate in our discussion rounds. You need to learn to push back occasionally if you wish to progress here."

The employee with strategic foresight, who is able to connect various aspects and balance opportunities with risks, leaves the employee appraisal with the understanding that she should simply 'take action' – just like her manager. "You think too much, Ms. Petersen. The higher you advance, the faster you must make decisions. I simply do not see that quality in you. You need to move away from being perceived as a worrier."

Many managers proceed to share their own experiences, coupled with an uncontrollable tendency to offer unsolicited advice.

Unconsciously, the focus shifts away from the employee and the development of their potential. The original question of how the manager can better utilise and further develop the employee's existing skills is no longer addressed.

The art of self-reflection is lost. Rather, the proportion of speaking time clearly shifts in favour of the manager, although he had planned otherwise. The focus is now on what the manager would expect from their employee. Subtly, this indicates the leadership style being employed and how the employee can best adapt to it. It is not stated explicitly, but those who can read between the lines hold a distinct advantage.

At the end of the day, the manager leaves the employee appraisal satisfied, firmly convinced that they have done well. Through rigorous analysis and advice, the manager was able to demonstrate their added value and clarify why they are in charge – and why the other person is not (yet).

The anticipated 'win-win situation' often becomes a losing scenario, as both parties gain little insight into what would foster sustainable performance improvement. No genuine collaboration emerges. Unfortunately, the conversation often deteriorates into emphasising the manager's desires and their own leadership style, rather than fostering the actual development of the employee.

The so-called 'outliers' are thoroughly analysed, while positive outcomes are taken for granted. Focusing on optimisation potential results in the true strengths of an employee being overlooked.

Even worse, this leads to the self-confident becoming more self-confident, while the humble become even more humble. In sports psychology, there is an alternative approach that pursues precisely the opposite goal. It draws on a quote from the theologian, Dietrich Bonhoeffer: "Comfort the troubled and trouble the comfortable" is his guiding maxim.

In sport, support is provided to those at risk of becoming overconfident and underperforming on the field, helping them remain grounded and maintain their effort, while those whose confidence has diminished due to a lack of success are encouraged to believe in their strengths once again. It is recognised that a healthy trust in our abilities and self-efficacy constitutes the optimal foundation for continuous development.

Learning from Resource-oriented Coaches

Despite criticism that some academies develop players to become conformist robots lacking individuality, many coaches adopt a resource-oriented approach. Successful coaches interpret an apparent weakness as an exaggerated or contextually misplaced natural strength. This understanding allows for the preservation and deliberate development of existing strengths without restricting individual capabilities.

A dribbling specialist is not called 'greedy' but learns to apply their strengths more effectively for the benefit of the team. They work together to determine in which situations dribbling is ineffective or could even pose a risk to their own team.

The objective is not to transform an introverted midfield conductor into a vociferous leader. In this manner, Toni Kroos repaid the trust of his club, Real Madrid, with numerous titles. At Bayern Munich, the concept of a 'playmaker' was still heavily influenced by aggressive leaders such as Lothar Matthäus and Stefan Effenberg, which led to his departure – reportedly without significant efforts to secure this talent for Bayern Munich in the long term. At Real Madrid, Kroos' calmness and composure were clearly regarded as strengths.

Even in cases of perceived 'weakness', such as a goalkeeper's small stature, efforts are made to compensate through other strengths. A case in point is Yann Sommer – until summer 2023 the smallest goalkeeper in the Bundesliga and currently playing for Inter Milan. Through his remarkable leaping ability and well-developed anticipation skills, he effectively compensates for his physical disadvantages and raised his market value to 13 million euros at his peak[52].

How can this attitude be applied in the corporate context?

It means that we do not advise a perfectionist to 'let things slide' but rather discuss with them how their attention to detail can be leveraged more effectively, detailing the situations where they can be most effective, and committing to their development. A respectful and motivating employee appraisal should result in sustainable performance improvement.

Rather than advising an introverted employee to express dissent, an appreciative dialogue is conducted to explore options for how the team can integrate their perspective into decisions. All too often, managers consciously or unconsciously attempt to change an employee's personality. A better approach would be to establish the environment that enables the employee to fully realise their potential. Adjustments to the meeting structure, such as one-on-one conversations or 'brainstorming', could contribute to better integration of the quieter 'thinkers' or introverted colleagues.

An employee with strategic foresight should not be criticised for being overly hesitant. Instead, it would be worthwhile to discuss how their ability to perceive connections can protect the team from launching ill-considered projects.

Have you completed a personality test in recent years? Then consider the weaknesses identified therein and reflect on which exaggerated strengths might be concealed behind them. You will be surprised. Many successful athletes share a common trait: an awareness of their own strengths and the ability to deliberately develop these and apply them to achieve team success.

They often perceive their apparent weaknesses as exaggerated expressions of their strengths. Success coaches employ the '1% rule' in this context to help players avoid overextending their strengths or misapplying them in inappropriate contexts. This rule, which has led numerous sports teams to remarkable performance improvements, emphasises small, continuous changes that are consistently implemented. The British Cycling team, under the leadership of Performance Director Dave Brailsford, applied this method over several years, resulting in a revolution within the team. Following disappointing outcomes at the Olympic Games in the 1990s, an era of success ensued that made the British Cycling team virtually unbeatable. The eight gold medals won in 2008 and 2012 serve as tangible evidence of the continuous performance development of both individuals and the team as a collective.

In business, we are familiar with the '1% rule', primarily in the context of process optimisations aimed at enhancing productivity. However, what prevents us from applying this principle to employee development?

How is it in your organisation? Are you able to identify the hidden strength behind an employee's apparent weakness? Can you uncover the 1% potential within your employees? How can you support them in discovering this potential and consistently working to develop it? Are structured development discussions conducted only for those requiring rapid change, or do they embody an attitude that proactively fosters long-term development?

This is by no means about conducting 'softened' conversations or overlooking problematic behavioural patterns. Rather, it concerns changing the attitude – shifting away from 'judgement' towards 'development'. Employee appraisals grounded in this attitude not only foster the individual's performance development, but often also enhance their sense of self-efficacy. This is not only a success factor for sustainable and healthy performance, but a prerequisite for feedback to be effectively received. It is precisely here that we establish the connection to the next tactical error, which the following section addresses – the establishment of a feedback culture.

Potential Tactical Errors

Tactical error 60: We allow structured employee dialogues to become an annual obligation.

Tactical error 61: We focus on weaknesses.

Tactical error 62: We attempt to make employees fit, instead of leveraging their strengths.

Tactical error 63: We make the self-confident more self-confident, and the humble more humble.

The Breakfast of Champions and the Sandwich Technique

A youth handball match of SG Flensburg-Handewitt astonishes the spectators. The team dominates the game, and the coach enthusiastically encourages them: "Well done! You are performing excellently. Keep it up!" Suddenly, the father of one of the players approaches me, fully aware that I provided psychological support to the team during pre-season. "Markus, that is not how I was taught to give feedback in my company. The players find such general statements difficult to relate to. It is not specific enough. Shouldn't they learn this differently during coach training?"

His spontaneous criticism inevitably reminds me of my experiences with feedback training in companies. Many leaders leave such training sessions with the word 'specific' as a key takeaway – just like this father. Everything should be immediately actionable, forward-looking and clearly understandable. Armed with this knowledge, newly trained managers eagerly dive into practice, giving feedback relentlessly, whether it is requested or not. "Feedback is the breakfast of champions," as management guru Ken Blanchard once said.

However, this breakfast is not always as enjoyable as we might hope. Only a limited number of methods can be conveyed within one or two hours of feedback training. The focus is often on immediately applicable techniques to deliver quick results to clients. Short-term and measurable – a familiar pattern.

Consequently, the newly trained manager often perceives the youth coach's words as insufficient, or not as feedback at all. Yet, a "Well done, keep it up" constitutes valuable feedback. These words signal to the players that they are on the right track and that their efforts are bearing fruit.

'Feedback', in this context, is just praise. At many leadership levels, this simple yet powerful information is missing. Praise is a form of appreciation that openly acknowledges effort without demanding behavioural change.

Interestingly, high-performing teams tend to praise each other more frequently than lower-performing groups. Research shows that teams in which positive feedback significantly outweighs negative feedback achieve measurably better results. The so-called 'sweet spot' is approximately six times as much positive feedback as negative. This principle applies not only to successful teams but to stable partnerships and marriages. Consequently, a manager does not need to make substantial adjustments when commuting from home to the office, and back again in the evening.

A 2022 study by Gallup and Workhuman[53] compellingly demonstrates that a culture of recognition and appreciation is essential for employee engagement. Employees working in an appreciative environment are four times more engaged, four times more likely to recommend their employer, and five times more motivated to pursue a career within the company.

Moreover, empirical studies demonstrate that individuals with high self-worth and strong self-efficacy utilise feedback more effectively. They enhance their performance more significantly following both positive and negative feedback than individuals with low self-worth[54]. An environment of recognition provides the essential foundation for this development. Several approaches to fostering the self-efficacy of your employees were introduced in the previous section.

A thorough understanding of these dynamics is crucial for establishing a sustainable learning culture within an organisation. In the absence of self-worth and self-efficacy, newly trained leaders, despite their well-intentioned feedback techniques, may inadvertently diminish their teams' engagement and performance. The 6:1 rule – meaning six positive responses to one negative – should, as with successful sports coaches, be an integral part of every leader's repertoire. If the ratio falls below 2:1, the feedback culture enters a critical zone.

What is the ratio of positive to negative feedback in your company? How does it appear in your personal environment? When was the last time you received recognition from your supervisor or a colleague? How often have you personally praised your employees or colleagues? Ultimately, it is not only important that feedback is given, but how it is delivered.

Feedback Culture as a Means to an End

The term 'feedback culture' yields over one billion Google results. Most leaders have participated in at least one feedback training course during their careers and have experimented with various models. Yet, despite its frequency, the topic remains far from trivial.

The challenge in cultivating a good feedback culture lies in the fact that individuals are constantly torn between the desire to improve and the need to be accepted[55]. An analysis conducted by David Rock and his team demonstrates that none of the 35 feedback concepts studied resulted in sustainable behavioural change[56].

This failure often stems from organisations treating feedback as an end in itself, rather than as a tool to achieve wider objectives. A healthy feedback culture aims to foster a learning organisation. It focuses on enabling continuous improvement, mutual support and inspiration. In such an environment, employees are able to reflect and develop healthily – benefiting the entire organisation. This is precisely what young people now expect from their employers.

But why do so many well-intentioned transformations towards a genuine feedback culture fail? A key factor is that not all feedback is the same. It is important to examine more closely and differentiate between the various types of feedback to avoid one-size-fits-all solutions and errors.

Three Types of Feedback

Praise and Recognition
This form of feedback does not aim to change behaviour but serves to affirm. It strengthens employees' self-efficacy and forms the foundation for the other two types of feedback.

Evaluation
Evaluating means assessing performance. It provides insight into an individual's current standing. This type of feedback, often delivered through performance reviews, is deeply embedded in many companies.

Coaching
Coaching, by contrast, focuses on optimising behaviour and exploring new possibilities for action. Its objective is to elevate teams and individuals to a higher level of performance – to the top.

The Second Type of Feedback: Evaluation
We move beyond praise and recognition to focus on evaluation – the second form of feedback. Companies generally handle this with ease

and are well-practised in it. Evaluation is, so to speak, their 'daily bread'. Assessing performance is a fundamental aspect of everyday business. However, what is often measured is not the actual performance but goal attainment. Companies excel at evaluating raw KPIs (Key Performance Indicators). In traditional corporate cultures, evaluation is therefore the primary focus. Consequently, many companies have already established a feedback culture. However, this culture primarily concentrates on assessing results – which, at worst, can cause stress for employees.

We possess a wealth of data points, yet these are seldom utilised for the other two forms of feedback: praise and targeted coaching. These KPIs can serve as a valuable foundation for recognition and focused coaching – more on this later.

Instead, we focus on dashboards and allow ourselves to be guided by the red warning signals. We judge, condemn and deliberate on how to return the 'red lights' to the green zone. Often, these approaches remain superficial because we focus too much on the symptoms rather than asking the right questions to identify the causes, find answers, and work on them continuously.

In the weeks leading up to internal 'business reviews' or quarterly meetings, a great deal of energy is expended on creating precise and watertight PowerPoint presentations. Trial runs are conducted to ensure perfect preparation for the forthcoming 'negotiations'. For indicators that are difficult to measure, the traffic light is pre-emptively switched from red to amber to avoid uncomfortable questions. I have observed senior leaders who did not sleep a wink shortly before a business review, as if facing a decisive final exam. This excessive focus on such reviews consumes not only time but energy – resources that could be more effectively allocated to continuous performance development.

This behaviour reveals much about the leaders, as well as the true purpose of such business reviews. They resemble less a forward-looking reflection, as advocated by Kobe Bryant, and more an assessment in which one either wins or loses. Consequently, individuals tend to avoid uncomfortable feedback or prepare justifications in advance. Neither approach brings us closer to a genuine learning culture; on the contrary, it distances us further from it.

The Third Type of Feedback: Coaching

You may be familiar with scenes where Pep Guardiola interrupts training to passionately convey to his players that they are not performing in a way that will lead the team to success over the weekend. The intensity and clarity with which such coaches provide feedback to their team or individual players leaves no doubt about their motivation: they want their players to improve. This is precisely the purpose of this form of feedback. Without this intention, any attempt to establish a healthy feedback culture is bound to fail. Feedback should never be given for any other reason. If feedback is not aimed at improving the recipient, it is better not to express it at all.

A sustainable feedback culture is not an end in itself; it should always aim to create a learning environment where employees can grow and continuously improve. Only in this way does feedback truly become the 'breakfast of champions'.

Even in sport, we encounter coaches who – like the father at the beginning of this section – give little consideration to the true intention behind their feedback. The situation is similar in companies: feedback often becomes an end in itself, with the technique of delivering feedback sometimes receiving more attention than the underlying intention.

It is essential that the ego of the feedback provider remains excluded. Feedback should only be given when there is a clear intention to support the recipient. Even the slightest doubt about this motivation should be sufficient reason to reconsider the feedback and to instead withdraw. However, if the intention is sincere, employees and players can tolerate even harsh feedback – provided the feedback is honest and not contrived.

A concept that has gained increasing attention since 2017 is 'radical candour'[57]. The fundamental idea is straightforward and insightful: we do not have to choose between being a 'softie' or a 'tough manager'. When the intention is genuine, it is possible to be clear and compassionate at the same time. This is precisely what distinguishes successful coaches – or more accurately, success coaches.

I have observed teams that achieved significant improvements through deliberate reflection on their feedback behaviour. Nonetheless, this 'invitation' to provide feedback often results in unsolicited advice or casual remarks being shared. Frequently, this leads to the feedback giver's self-satisfaction: finally having the opportunity to tell a colleague how they could improve. Feedback providers are frequently motivated by the belief that it would be better for the recipient to handle matters exactly as they do.

Whether this assumption is always valid remains questionable, particularly when considering diverse personality structures. This phenomenon is often observed in head coaches who attempt to imitate their mentors. It is almost tragic when introverted tacticians suddenly transform in the dressing room into loud motivational speakers, causing embarrassment to their players. These cases reveal that we often overestimate the quality of our advice.

Research confirms that only a minority of employees receive genuinely helpful feedback. This issue has deeper underlying causes.

The Stress Experienced by the Feedback Provider

Not only is the feedback recipient under pressure; the situation can also be stressful for the feedback provider. Leaders often seek ways to alleviate the discomfort of the situation for themselves. A common approach is to 'soften' the feedback to make it seem less painful. The so-called 'sandwich technique', where criticism is between two positive comments, was popular for some time. Although this may ease the burden on the feedback provider, it seldom results in profound reflection by the recipient.

It is equally uncomfortable when leaders deliver critical feedback with a smile. Such a brittle smile gives the impression that the team has achieved significant success, while the underlying message is negative. This apparent, sometimes toxic, friendliness dilutes the core message and causes clear communication to be lost. Players often prefer to be addressed honestly, even if harshly.

The Season is Long

'The season is long' – this is a common statement, but it is not always sufficient to resolve uncertainties for players who are rarely fielded. In many discussions, they seek reasons for their limited playing time. The coach's response that he currently relies on his gut feeling to decide the starting lineup raises more questions than it answers. This is especially true when the coach emphasises that the player is performing excellently in training and expresses satisfaction in having them in the squad. His opportunity will come in due course.

Some conversations between players who seek me out as a mental coach and their coaches are based on this intuitive feeling. I frequently encounter the challenge of addressing the coaching team to clarify that this style of coaching does not assist players in enhancing their self-efficacy, or in receiving constructive feedback for their ongoing development. Players lack ideas how to move closer to the starting lineup.

This phenomenon is also evident within companies. Employees often wait in vain for promotions, receive vague assurances, are sent on training programmes, and ultimately become frustrated when external candidates are favoured. Incidentally, everyone except the employee was aware that he was not a candidate for the vacant position.

What makes it so challenging for coaches and supervisors to speak candidly? The answer to this question is relatively straightforward. Feedback conversations trigger a form of 'social threat response' in both parties – the giver and the recipient. In stressful situations, we often enter 'survival mode', which causes our heart rate to increase and manifests in stress symptoms such as sweaty palms or flushed skin.

For the feedback recipient, this means that if they 'withdraw', they rationalise why the other party is mistaken. They feign interest in the criticism. Whether the subsequent reflection (if it occurs at all) will lead to sustainable changes in behaviour is often highly questionable.

Let us examine the three most common 'triggers' that prevent us from using feedback as an opportunity to change our behaviour. I am confident you are familiar with these situations, perhaps in a different context.

The Truth Trigger

The truth trigger is one of the most frequent reasons why feedback is rejected.

Here is an example: At half-time, the score is 2–0, and the coach provides Kevin with feedback in the dressing room, following all best practices: "Our defensive behaviour begins at the front. I expect you to implement what we discussed in the second half – and to contribute more, defensively." The feedback is precise, timely and accompanied by a clear assignment. Kevin gives his coach the impression that he accepts the criticism. However, already on the way back to the field, his perspective shifts. "Did the coach really say that? Has he not noticed that I am sacrificing myself like never before? I like the coach, but today he is mistaken. Never have I worked harder defensively than in this damn game!"

We are all familiar with similar situations when we believe statements from colleagues or superiors to be incorrect and simply dismiss the conversation. This is referred to as the so-called 'truth trigger'[58]. It is as if the conversation never took place – only worse.

The Relationship Trigger

Ronald, who is usually sceptical of my 'superfluous' sports psychology expertise, unusually and desperately sought a conversation today. He feels constantly criticised by the coach and is even considering leaving the club. He was always the key player at his previous clubs. Interestingly, the coach recently informed me again that Ronald has not yet fully realised his potential.

The dilemma lies in the relationship between the two. It is difficult to accept advice when someone believes the advisor dislikes them. The good intentions of the feedback provider must not only be genuine but trusted by the recipient. Athletes often flourish under new coaches, demonstrating that the chemistry between coach and athlete plays a crucial role.

Frankly, who has never rejected valuable advice simply because they disliked the advisor? This dynamic does not foster peak performance but rather undermines the recipient's self-awareness. Well-intentioned feedback does not lead the athlete or employee to reflect and respond accordingly. If we are unwilling to invest the time and energy required to sustainably improve the relationship, it is preferable to end it. Anything else results in stagnation and a loss of energy.

The Identity Trigger

"Ralf, be more aggressive!" demands the coach. However, Ralf, through his emotional intelligence, is a pillar of the team and a hard-working, competent player who always puts the side first. He speaks only when addressed, yet significantly advances the internal team discussions. He requires no displays of power on the field, focusing instead on his capabilities. An outsider might perceive him as insufficiently aggressive, though his 'duel' statistics indicate otherwise.

Ralf perceives the feedback as an attack on his personality, as the human brain processes such an 'attack' on deeply held beliefs in the same way as a physical assault. When our identity feels threatened, the brain activates the same defence mechanisms it employs to protect the body[59]. This may also involve a temporary change in behaviour to avoid further disturbance after the game. However, the coach cannot expect lasting changes. Ralf remains the player he is.

We observe a similar phenomenon in employee appraisals, where attempts to address a person's identity often prove futile.

There are numerous reasons why feedback fails to be effective. It is seldom perceived as a gift – more like an unwelcome Christmas present. It must be accepted despite its limited value, and is quickly forgotten.

Consequently, in many cases, a lasting, performance-enhancing behavioural change does not materialise. It is essential to consider not only behaviour but personality and relational dynamics to successfully implement constructive feedback. Only then can it become a powerful tool for sustainable performance development.

It is unsurprising that well-intentioned efforts to cultivate a feedback culture fail in the vast majority of cases, if not universally. Any attempt to 'implement' such a culture without simultaneously addressing employees' attitudes, consciousness and self-efficacy is futile.

A Growth Mindset is Required

In her bestseller, *Mindset*, Dr. Carol Dweck presents the concept of the 'growth mindset'[60]. She differentiates between a static and a dynamic mindset. Individuals with a static mindset believe their abilities are fixed and unchangeable. They aim to continually demonstrate their talents. In contrast, individuals with a dynamic mindset view the journey as the goal – they are convinced they can improve continuously.

Athletes regarded as great talents for years often plateau in their development, whereas those who cultivate a dynamic mindset, flourish. These athletes are willing to work on themselves, identify weaknesses and explore new approaches. The foundation for this mindset was established at the end of the 19th century by the French psychologist Alfred Binet. He observed: "If someone is the smartest at the beginning, it does not necessarily mean they will remain so until the end."

Renowned sports psychologist Michael Gervais, who has supported numerous world record holders and Olympians, highlights the significant difference between the statements 'This is who I am' and 'This is who I am right now, and I am a work in progress'[61]. Those who adhere to the former justify their immutable status quo, whereas those who embrace the latter strive for continuous self-improvement. Such individuals are curious, receptive to criticism, and transform it into opportunities for growth. Their willingness to explore their potential nurtures their enthusiasm for learning.

Examples from elite sport include players classified in the third category by Thomas Tuchel, as well as the quote from Ayrton Senna, who felt dissatisfied whenever his learning curve plateaued. These exemplify the 'growth mindset' in its purest form – an attitude grounded in continuous development.

A dynamic mindset entails that players or employees actively solicit feedback to foster their ongoing development. They do not require persuasion; rather, they proactively seek feedback to learn from it and enhance their performance. Therefore, energy should be directed towards fostering curious and eager-to-learn employees. In this way, we could avoid costly feedback training and concentrate on the essential fundamentals.

A Beneficial Climate Change

For this approach to succeed, companies must cultivate an environment that promotes a 'growth mindset'. In sport, this is known as a task-oriented motivational climate. In such an environment, not only the final result, but progress and improvement, are acknowledged at least equally[62]. Results are – as you may already be familiar with – regarded as a consequence, rather than the ultimate goal. This mindset encourages athletes and employees to actively seek feedback to foster their development.

What is crucial is not that criticism is accepted too easily; rather, it is about identifying and leveraging 'game-changing' potential. Many successful athletes report that only a few 'lightbulb moments' set them on the path to success – often supported by a coach, mentor or teammate. The 'growth mindset' provides the foundation upon which these 1% improvements can yield results – as exemplified by the British Cycling team's successful practice. In such an environment, praise, recognition and coaching replace evaluations and judgements.

In many companies, however, a result-focused or egocentric motivational climate prevails[63], as it is described in sports psychology. In this paradoxical situation, the focus is primarily on results, comparison with others and winning. While this is not inherently wrong, it is unfair to expect employees to adopt an attitude that contradicts the prevailing culture. This initiative is not only unfair and unrealistic, but also destined to fail.

In such an environment, how feedback is delivered is of great importance. Feedback must be communicated in a way that ensures no one feels personally attacked. Given that there are always winners and losers, fostering an open feedback culture is challenging. These deeply entrenched structures cannot be transformed overnight by simply introducing new methods or terminology.

In a task-oriented environment that prioritises progress and development, the way feedback is given is of less significance. Feedback is actively sought, rather than being randomly distributed or offered as a 'gift'. This growth-oriented climate distinguishes good teams from exceptional ones, and establishes the foundation for sustainable success. It is these teams and companies that maintain long-term success, while others become one-hit wonders in both sport and business.

To foster genuine growth and continuous improvement, more than just feedback methods are necessary. An environment that encourages curious, eager-to-learn behaviour and prioritises personal development is essential. Only in this manner can a 'growth mindset' truly flourish and ensure long-term success for companies.

'Learn-It-All' versus 'Know-It-All'

A compelling example of how a 'growth mindset' can be embedded within a company is provided by the technology giant Microsoft. When CEO Satya Nadella assumed leadership in 2014, he decisively promoted a culture of learning over knowledge. His well-known phrase, "Don't be a 'know-it-all', be a 'learn-it-all'," epitomises this mindset. Rather than sending employees to seminars on feedback techniques, Nadella personally embodied the principle of continuous learning.

By exemplifying a 'learn-it-all' mindset through his own behaviour, he created authentic examples that influenced all levels of the organisation. Thus, the new mindset was established not only through words but through concrete actions. Although it took some time for this change to permeate the entire corporate culture, Nadella's perseverance proved successful. Leaders and teams began to adopt his approach until it became an integral part of the corporate culture.

A significant contribution also came from Kathleen Hogan, the former Chief People Officer and current Executive Vice-President, Office of Strategy and Transformation. Her achievement was ensuring that this transformation was not perceived as a 'one-man show', but as a comprehensive change that permeated all leadership levels. The success of this profound transformation demonstrates that consistency and perseverance are key factors in sustainably embedding a new culture within one of the world's largest companies.

And Now?

A motivating work environment that enhances employees' self-efficacy can foster a culture of learning and performance. Feedback training alone is often insufficient and can prove counterproductive. Leaders must instead assume responsibility and model the desired change.

You may recall that feedback training often results in colleagues offering unsolicited and random advice, which places the recipient in a passive role. To avoid this situation, you should take the initiative and actively pursue your own development – just as Satya Nadella has successfully demonstrated at Microsoft. Embrace the 'growth mindset':

1. Define the Desired Behaviour

The first step is to clearly define which behaviour should be optimised. A specific goal helps to focus feedback. The behaviour may relate to a technical skill, such as a shooting technique in football, or something less tangible, such as body language, clarity in team meetings, or self-control in stressful situations with your 'favourite colleagues'. Creativity is limitless. It is essential, however, that the behaviour is observable – rather than abstract qualities like 'greater self-awareness' or buzz words such as 'inclusive leadership'. Consider the situation in which you wish to exhibit the behaviour.

2. Establish a 'Circle of Trust'

Select individuals within your environment who you trust, and who you can observe in relevant situations. Share your goals with them and request that they provide you with regular feedback. Clearly specify those you do not wish to receive feedback from, to avoid distraction by irrelevant opinions. Athletes in the spotlight must learn to manage the influx of feedback on social media and filter out only what is essential[64].

3. Provide Yourself with Feedback

Alongside feedback from others, it is crucial to incorporate your own perception into the process. Ask yourself: How did I experience the situation? What went well, and what could be improved? What has prevented me from acting differently? This self-assessment is a crucial component of reflection, enabling you to better understand your behaviour and intentionally modify it.

4. Enjoy the Process

Do not expect immediate success; instead, remain consistently committed. The journey of change demands patience and perseverance. Even if the desired outcomes are not immediately apparent, this should not be discouraging. Progress will become evident over the long term if you persist.

If, as a leader, you have fostered a supportive environment for the growth mindset, your employees may invite you into their 'circle of trust'. This greatly enhances the quality of employee appraisals. If you are not invited, return to the start, review the established working environment, and adjust as needed.

Utilise employee appraisals to gain deeper insight into your employees' ambitions. Remain curious and be prepared to support them in achieving their goals. This approach ensures that potential is not left untapped but is deliberately cultivated. In this context, performance is not merely managed but steadily enhanced – step by step, 1% at a time.

An organisation or team that nurtures a culture of continuous learning will not only collaborate more effectively but achieve greater long-term success. The key is to create an environment that fosters a growth mindset and embraces the courage to experiment with new behavioural patterns. The reward lies in the sustainable development of performance – achieved through an approach that empowers every individual to perform at their best.

Potential Tactical Errors

Tactical error 64: We use data points for evaluation rather than for reflection and coaching.

Tactical error 65: We provide insufficient positive feedback (1:6 instead of 6:1).

Tactical error 66: We focus on feedback techniques rather than on cultivating a learning mindset.

Tactical error 67: We neglect the foundation of feedback – trust and self-efficacy.

Tactical error 68: We underestimate the triggers that cause feedback to be ineffective.

Tactical error 69: We fail to examine our intention before delivering feedback.

Overconfident Managers and Outdated Mentors

Globally, companies continue to invest approximately 14 trillion US dollars annually in the development of their leaders[65]. A significant portion of these investments still goes into traditional training formats, although studies indicate that conventional seminars have limited sustainable impact[66]. In many cases, this is less attributable to the content itself and more to the nature of the issue. Knowledge alone does not result in behavioural change, particularly when participants return to their usual environment after training and have minimal opportunities to apply the newly acquired skills.

One possible reason for this is that the demands of a hectic workday leave insufficient time to practise and experiment with the learned material. Also, people in the work environment may be sceptical rather than curious, or they may lack appreciation. This may also fail because the supervisor does not recognise the opportunity presented by 'coaching on the job' and considers the training process complete upon payment of the invoice.

Consequently, many well-intentioned training initiatives dissipate, and participants often choose not to apply their newly acquired knowledge in practice – at least not within the professional context.

Nonetheless, training programmes retain their legitimacy in many respects. They constitute an essential foundation for the development of an organisation. In numerous areas, knowledge must be imparted before it can be effectively translated into practice. Nevertheless, companies often struggle to appropriately prioritise this form of professional development, to strike the right balance, and to accommodate individual needs. Only in this way can they ensure that their investment in professional development genuinely leads to enhanced performance.

Let us identify where the obstacles lie.

First Work, Then Play

It is hardly surprising that our thinking patterns play a central role here. The motto, 'First work, then play', continues to significantly influence our daily work routines. Professional development is postponed until workloads decrease, which rarely occurs.

"If we achieve the goals, we can afford a team workshop, invest in training – and, above all, work undisturbed. So, let us deliver results." Raised expectations mean results that were previously sufficient are no longer accepted. We therefore need to achieve better results with the same employees under the same conditions. Welcome to the hamster wheel.

The mindset that training and coaching should be postponed until they can be afforded resembles the absurd notion that a top club in crisis would suspend training until results improve.

The limiting beliefs are clear: short-term, measurable results are prioritised over the continuous discovery and development of potential. We think day to day, have no time for training, and yet congratulate ourselves for delivering exceptional performance – treating training as a kind of reward.

It is therefore unsurprising that employee development is recorded as a cost rather than viewed as an investment promising sustainable revenue and profit. Have we, then, fundamentally misunderstood something in the business world? Have we reversed the proper sequence? Or could it be that athletes are approaching it incorrectly?

Modern Training Methods

Perhaps we should embrace modern training methods, such as the diverse offerings of digital learning platforms. These are individual, easily accessible and cost-effective, adapting to the contemporary learning behaviours of younger generations. However, there are challenges. These offerings, which typically do not extend beyond knowledge transfer, often only reach employees who are already motivated and eager to learn, while others tend to disregard them.

Digital learning snippets may be efficient, but they cannot replace comprehensive training. These digital offerings focus on the 10% component of the 70:20:10 rule, which is based on a study conducted in 1996. This rule states that employees learn 70% through challenging tasks and 20% through appreciative and trust-based relationships at work. Only 10% of learning results from traditional training. In other words, 70% of learning occurs through practical challenges, 20% through interaction with others, and 10% within a formal framework.

Learning is an individual process; therefore, this 10% serves only as a rough guide. Nonetheless, this rule is often used to justify a reduction in the formal training budget, particularly when the desired outcomes are not achieved. A peculiar logic prevails: the game was lost, so training will be reduced, initially. However, genuine learning occurs in the workplace, informally and 'on the job' – and this is not necessarily incorrect. Regrettably, many leaders are uncertain about how 'coaching on the job' should be conducted, as it has never been explained or taught to them.

Overconfident Managers

Partly responsible is the fact that many leaders overrate their own coaching capabilities. The reality is that, rather than coaching, most managers tend to offer advice, driven by their knowledge and experience. Ultimately, these qualities are what have shaped them into who they are. However, this is more a case of micromanaging, albeit presented in a more motivating manner[67]. We have already encountered this phenomenon in the previous section. This does not facilitate effective learning. Managers focused on rapid results and activity have little time or space for genuine coaching, as it would distract them from delivering short-term, measurable outcomes. Effective for our careers, but neither sustainable nor forward-looking.

Typically, conscious development does not occur during everyday work. This is primarily cited by younger employees as a decisive factor when selecting an employer. The 10% allocated to formal training is either ineffective or reduced. The remaining 90% is neglected because the hamster wheel moves too quickly, or managers lack an understanding of how 'coaching on the job' could be implemented.

Individuality Instead of a One-size-fits-all Approach

Here is a perspective from sport. A sports psychologist shared that he sometimes sends his players – all professionals in the English Premier League – home, despite their urgent requests to work with him on their 'mental strength'. He does so when the players cannot convincingly assure him that they obtain at least 7.5 hours of healthy sleep – both during the training week and on the night before the match.

Mental improvement potentials in sport always compete with athleticism, technical skills, technique and tactics. Each year, new specialised positions such as set-piece coaches, neuroathletics experts and sleep coaches are introduced. The day of professional athletes is already fully scheduled, and with tightly packed game plans and new competitions driven by commercial interests, there is little room for 'new approaches'. Therefore, it is not only important but appropriate to consider individually which measures or interventions are most effective for each player. Which measures would enable him to better realise his performance potential in a healthy and sustainable way?

The detrimental impact of insufficient or poor-quality sleep on performance is significant, and this is well recognised among sports psychologists. Why should a sports psychologist begin mental training with a player to 'extract' the last percentage of his potential when improving sleep hygiene offers a far greater benefit for the athlete? Whenever there are doubts regarding the appropriate quantity and/or quality of sleep, a sleep coach would first seek to unlock this potential.

The focus is on setting individual priorities in the pursuit of continuous performance development. The one-size-fits-all approach may seem pragmatic and efficient, however, it is not only costly but ineffective. In elite sport, no player experiencing mental strain is assigned a strength and conditioning coach just because the coach is available. Instead, the player is offered the opportunity to work with a sports psychologist. In this context, the words of the former Argentine national coach Alejandro Sabella during the 2014 World Cup remain relevant: "One gram of neurons weighs more than a kilo of muscles."[68]

Unhealthy Trend-hopping

What we occasionally observe in companies is quite the opposite. There is an offer that is simply pushed on to individuals. There is a competent communication coach available, so, often, a lack of communication skills is identified as the root cause. A coaching programme is launched and urgently requires leaders to participate. Consequently, coaching is applied extensively, regardless of whether it is appropriate.

The same applies to company-wide initiatives: one year, they must be 'lean'; the next year, they must be 'agile'. Within a year, 'purpose' must be at the forefront[69]. In the 365 days that follow, leaders are expected to demonstrate vulnerability[70], while the year after, focus on dealing with ambiguity and developing resilience. This is accompanied by various change management concepts until we understand that change cannot truly be managed. A year later, empathy emerges for leaders, but only after the enthusiasm for emotional intelligence has waned. Equally important is the establishment of a feedback culture, followed by the acclaimed 'fuck up nights', where leaders are encouraged to openly share and celebrate their defeats and mistakes to foster a learning culture. Consequently, all leaders are required to develop their growth mindset[71]. All of this only occurs after the company-wide adjustment of the OKRs (Objectives and Key Results) the previous year. The 'open office' culture, introduced and heavily promoted several years ago, has been phased out in recent years, as it failed to meet expectations. Instead, there are table tennis tables and hammocks, similar to those at Google.

If you think these statements are exaggerated, rest assured that, particularly in the corporate context, this is more of an understatement. Each year, a new initiative is pushed through, and frustration arises when long-serving employees do not respond with enthusiastic applause. It may not be the age of these colleagues, but rather their experience that they are once again expending energy on something that does not sustainably contribute to the company's success. Experience can, in a negative sense, prevent us from experimenting with new approaches. However, it can also serve to protect us from 'wasting' our energy.

All the ideas and methods presented have their validity and can indeed produce significant impact, as I have experienced. Sustainable performance development requires, in addition to sound diagnostics, considerable dedication, perseverance and persistence. These well-intentioned initiatives will, however, result in few or no sustainable developments if the patient is given the same treatment regardless of the diagnosis. Even less can be expected when these initiatives aim for sustainable behavioural change but are replaced by a new initiative in less than 12 months. Activity in its purest form. The lasting impact on corporate culture will be negligible. Confusion among employees, and especially among leaders, has never been greater than it is today.

This is hardly surprising, as these initiatives are seldom launched by corporate leadership and even less frequently by the grassroots, but are often driven by the HR department or, as it is now called, the 'People & Culture' team. In their own pursuit of meaningfulness and self-efficacy, they attempt to imprint their mark on this peculiar process.

Entire movements emerge from a good book or an inspiring TED Talk, filled with self-fulfilling prophecies and numerous aspiring consultants and coaches, all eager to claim a share of the pie. We gladly incorporate these into our portfolio of well-intentioned performance enhancers. After all, more is better. Sensationalism instead of sustainability. Unfortunately, the true success factors – focus and consistency – are repeatedly neglected.

Mentoring as a Cost-effective Alternative

Additionally, there are mentoring programmes. While considered cost-effective, they often demand more resources than anticipated. Many of these programmes function as formalities, without delivering clear benefits. They connect individuals across hierarchy levels and demonstrate commitment to talent, yet they tend to be costly and inflexible. The value of these programmes is frequently undermined by mentors who embody outdated leadership qualities. Since Marshall Goldsmith's eponymous bestseller, we understand that "What got you here won't get you there", meaning that what has brought you to this point will not necessarily serve you in the future.

An effective alternative to mentoring programmes is to foster a culture in which young or inexperienced employees proactively seek advice from experienced colleagues. This significantly enhances career development, job satisfaction and self-confidence.

The tactical error lies in the established priorities: training is viewed as a reward rather than as an investment. In business, training is not only conducted at the wrong time – specifically after the work has been completed – but also far too infrequently. The reasons for this are varied. Some leaders are unaware of their role, others feel incapable or lack the imagination to envision what 'coaching on the job' could look like. There is a shortage of time and financial resources to give formal or informal training the significance it deserves.

Rather than questioning whether we can afford to invest in a learning organisation, we should consider whether we can afford not to. Can we afford to only engage in official matches without taking time to reflect, experiment or train in between? This brings us to the next section, which will focus precisely on this topic.

Potential Tactical Errors

Tactical error 70: We rigidly separate work and learning under the principle of 'either/or'.

Tactical error 71: We do not take time to train, as every day is a match day.

Tactical error 72: We restrict targeted education to a minority.

Tactical error 73: We regard training as a reward rather than as an investment.

Tactical error 74: We mistake 'coaching on the job' for giving advice.

Tactical error 75: We initiate 'one-size-fits-all' training initiatives without diagnostics.

Tactical error 76: We rely on digital self-help and traditional mentoring programmes.

Learning Zones and Moments of Silence

"The reason many people have good ideas in the shower is that it is often the only time of day when they are away from screens long enough to think clearly. The lesson, however, should not be to shower more often, but to deliberately set aside time for reflection"[72].

In other contexts, we have already examined the consequences of constantly fixating on the scoreboard and frantically attempting to outpace the opponent. The prevalent practice of managing results rather than fostering sustainable performance creates numerous obstacles and shortcomings that impede healthy development. One of the most significant shortcomings is the lack of reflection. Our preoccupation with results prevents us from entering the so-called learning zone.

To be candid: How much time do you genuinely have for thinking, learning, reflecting and experimenting?

As we understand, learning does not occur through experience alone, but through conscious reflection upon experience. Why do we learn more from defeats or mistakes than from success? It is not the mistake itself that makes the difference, but rather the fact that we engage in deeper reflection after defeats than after successes. This extended dwelling in the learning zone is crucial. The focus is on reflecting on the 'how' – our behaviour – rather than acknowledging that we, for example, conceded too many goals.

The unilateral focus on result-oriented objectives within companies hinders this appropriate reflection aimed at enhancing performance. In short, companies concentrate too much on the 'what' and neglect the 'how'.

The focus on result-seeking deprives us of the opportunity to reflect on behavioural patterns that may lead to either positive or negative outcomes. This tendency is further reinforced by the cognitive bias known in psychology as 'hindsight bias'. Humans possess the ability to understand an event only after it has happened. Consequently, assumptions made prior to the event are often distorted in memory to align more closely with the actual outcomes. This phenomenon can be clearly observed in social settings around the world. At the conclusion of a game or championship, it is common for experts to assert that they had foreseen the outcome all along. Though their predictions beforehand do not align with this assertion.

This hindsight bias means individuals, after an event, are unable to evaluate the circumstances and reasons that led to the outcome. The tendency to view everything positively when the outcome is known leads to a superficial assessment. This effect has already hindered many managers and coaches from advancing their development. Many leaders are trained to manage results rather than to cultivate sustainable performance. However, accurate reflection is essential for sustainable performance development, regardless of victory or defeat.

This awareness of our cognitive biases enables us to understand that both victory and defeat offer valuable insights – albeit sometimes with different implications. The learning experiences can be equally significant, regardless of the outcome. To avoid this error, successful coaches learn early on, not to trust the result.

Coach or Trainer?

In sport, reflection describes the athlete's process of being in the learning zone and acquiring new insights. Coaching is the discipline that guides the athlete into precisely this state. The significance of reflection as an integral component of performance development must not be underestimated. While repeated training undoubtedly yields positive effects, targeted reflection enables players to achieve significant performance breakthroughs.

This insight is not new; nevertheless, both head coaches and managers struggle equally with its implementation. Many head coaches inherently maintain a rather outdated perception of their profession – and this is not limited to older people. In many instances, they perceive themselves, much like some leaders, as conveyors of knowledge. This perception echoes the traditional teacher-student relationship. A teacher imparts knowledge to their students, just as a head coach imparts skills to their players, or at least ensures that training and practice occur. The concept: Teachers and coaches always possess greater knowledge and skills than their students or players, and they impart knowledge by demonstrating 'how it is done'. They know things better and are, so to speak, 'know-it-alls' – without this necessarily carrying a negative connotation.

However, this often results in a misunderstanding. In business, this perception is frequently reflected in the role of leaders. The manager is presumed to know everything, issue instructions and, at a minimum, ensure that employees arrive at work punctually. This mentality results in the continued emergence of player-coaches in business, with the best engineers and salespeople being promoted to department heads.

But why are head coaches called coaches and not trainers (like in Germany) or teachers?

This linguistic nuance provides an important insight. Coaching is not just about imparting knowledge or organising training, but primarily about unlocking potential and bringing out the best in the team. Even in today's world of work, there is a growing demand for 'learn-it-alls' rather than 'know-it-alls'. This demand has long-been established. Numerous studies confirm that employees prefer leaders who respect them, and from whom they can learn. Google's 'Project Oxygen' identified the key characteristics that define an effective leader. At the top of the list: 'Be a good coach'[73]. This aligns with the 70:20:10 rule of employee development, which states that 70% of learning success is achieved through 'coaching on the job'.

What Does 'Coaching on the Job' Mean?

Do you recall the previously cited Bonhoeffer quote: "Comfort the troubled and trouble the comfortable"? Effective coaching should be the art of encouraging those who have settled into their comfort zones to step out, while instilling self-awareness in those who doubt themselves. What, then, is the goal of coaching? The Greek philosopher Socrates once stated: "I cannot teach anybody anything; I can only make them think." This encapsulates a fundamental principle of coaching: encouraging individuals to reflect, facilitating new insights, and subsequently motivating them to take action. The objective is to assist the individual – whether manager, player or coach – in becoming the person they aspire to be. This requires a clear and precise vision of the desired state, while the current state must be honestly and transparently disclosed at the outset.

It is not my intention to transform every leader into a certified coach. Nonetheless, I firmly believe that contemporary leaders should develop essential coaching skills to effectively support the sustainable performance development of their teams. These skills stand in contrast to the qualities often valued in today's executive levels, and involve listening, asking questions, enduring silence and refraining from giving advice – simple, yet not easy. Therefore, let us proceed step by step.

The Art of Listening

As a coach, I am convinced about the power of listening – which, incidentally, was one of the primary motivations for my career choice. Coaching creates a space for unconditional listening; a practice frequently overlooked in the hectic pace of daily life. Anyone who has had the privilege of a conversational partner – whether in a professional, family or friend context – understands how beneficial it is to be heard unconditionally. The true art, as bestselling author Simon Sinek states, lies in giving the other person the feeling of being understood[74]. The emphasis is less on the word 'understood' and more on the word 'feeling'.

Listening is arguably one of the most demanding skills for a modern leader. As part of a development programme for globally operating sales teams, I have facilitated numerous workshops for emerging and experienced sales managers. Regrettably, many sales employees struggle with listening, despite clear evidence from studies that this skill is essential for sales success.

Our challenge was to impart fundamental coaching principles to successful sales managers. This programme spanned more than five years. A key phrase that stayed with most participants was: 'There is a reason you have two ears but only one mouth.' To illustrate this, we presented participants with the 'coach potato', featuring oversized ears and a relatively small mouth, prompting reflection on the role and importance of listening. This somewhat unconventional, yet expressive and highly effective 'coach potato' can still be found today, many years later, on office desks.

It is no coincidence that companies are increasingly initiating programmes focused on the theme of 'listening'. An example of this is the German automotive supplier Webasto. Then Chief Financial Officer (CFO), Dr. Philipp Schramm, initiated, as part of a cultural transformation, a training programme entitled 'Listen Like a Leader'. Within the first 16 months, more than 500 employees participated, many describing the programme as 'life-changing'. This proved to be a crucial element in the successful turnaround of the Webasto Group, which, among other objectives, sought to enhance employees' capacity for reflection[75].

It is also no coincidence that numerous successful sports coaches are recognised as exceptional listeners. Nancy Kline's assertion that the quality of attention we offer to another determines the quality of thinking[76] is accurate. Listening constitutes an integral component of what we understand as communication. Therefore, it is surprising that many leadership training programmes allocate considerable attention to communication, yet often neglect the importance of listening. The assumption that this skill is inherently present is misleading.

Numerous concepts exist regarding the art of listening, many of which attempt to surpass each other in complexity. Let us remain pragmatic and confine ourselves to a simplified twofold classification. The first form of listening, erroneously labelled as such, is referred to as 'selective hearing'. In this mode, we only hear what confirms our own biases, or focus on statements that do not diverge from our conventional beliefs. This type of listening is often driven by self-interest, and as a result, these discussions frequently conclude with one party winning and the other losing. The so-called listener remains in a kind of holding pattern, waiting for the right (or wrong) moment to present their arguments and insights.

The second form of listening, however, suspends our ego. We initially set aside self-interest and place ourselves in service of the other person. We begin to see and feel the world through their eyes. I refer to this as 'listen to understand'.

The first form of listening is likely familiar to you from most meetings. Meetings are often used to clarify or shift power dynamics rather than to harness collective wisdom and collaboratively make the best decisions. The ego often unconsciously takes its place at the meeting table, even though it was not invited. The same applies, incidentally, to talk shows around the world.

But what about the second form of listening? When was the last time you truly felt you were being listened to? A conversation in which the other person's ego had disappeared, and you were the sole focus. In their autobiographies, athletes occasionally recall such moments with coaches, companions or sports psychologists, and regard them as transformative. If you were fortunate enough to experience this, how did it feel? What results or insights did it yield?

At the risk of being unpopular with other coaches, I suggest that better training in the simple technique of listening could lead to a significant redistribution of resources. However, leaders must dedicate necessary time to this. Once they have discovered the power of listening, and experience what happens during phases of unconditional listening, they will not want to forgo it again. Those who embrace this discipline become witnesses to individual and sustainable potential development. This is, after all, one of the reasons why these individuals chose a leadership role, is it not?

Our Curiosity

Human beings are curious by nature. During our childhood, we feed our curiosity by asking questions. We constantly try to learn and explore. Over the years, however, many of us have 'unlearned' to actively ask questions and harness our natural curiosity to comprehend the world.

In business, we tend to conceal our perceived incompetence, driven by deeply ingrained thinking patterns and the image of a 'know-it-all' manager. According to bestsellers, after 100 days in an office, asking questions becomes rare. At that point, it is expected to have developed a comprehensive understanding of the situation and to have addressed pressing questions. Now it is time to pull up our sleeves and take action – preferably on all fronts.

More effort yields greater results, as we have learned. In companies, asking questions or challenging assumptions are often deliberately avoided. Questions are seen as a waste of time, and a questioning manager might appear insecure or incompetent. The urgently needed reflection is replaced by rapid decision-making and execution.

Nevertheless, there are moments when even experienced managers rediscover their curiosity – following failed projects, disappointing product launches or employee appraisals with so-called low performers. Suddenly, they exhibit a marked eagerness to learn and embark on an investigative search, much like sports reporters who pose uncomfortable questions after a lost game.

The Manager as an Investigative Reporter

"Why did you lose the game?" This question from sports journalists often triggers the brain's justification mode. The interviewee instinctively searches for reasons usually beyond their control: the referee's decisions, misfortune, or the injury list. Ultimately, it boils down to: "If you have bad luck, you have bad luck."

Reporters favour questions that place their subjects into an emotional justification mode. A notable example – at least for German football fans – is the legendary interview conducted by Waldemar Hartmann with then national head coach Rudi Völler following a disappointing international against Iceland in September 2003. Völler accused Hartmann of excessive wheat beer consumption and allowed his emotions to run free. The audience continues to enjoy and stream this to this day, and Hartmann is rumoured to have secured a long-term advertising contract with a brewery. It is said that every year on 6th September – the day of the aforementioned interview – he sends Rudi Völler a text message thanking him for his 'volcanic eruption' in Iceland.

It is not the reporter's role to extract a fact-based, forward-looking, solution-oriented match analysis from the coach immediately after the final whistle. And who among the viewers watching at home would genuinely be interested? Ultimately, it should be noted that in such situations, the person questioned is often deemed the 'loser' rather than being supported in the search for a solution.

In sport, emotions often take precedence over facts. This explains why many interviews begin with the pivotal question, "Why?" The question of why the match plan was not apparent compared to previous games immediately places the respondent in justification mode. However, what if the question was skilfully reframed? For instance: "What factors contributed to the match plan being less clear today than usual?" or even: "What prevented you from executing your match plan?" This approach circumvents justification mode and facilitates a solution-oriented diagnosis. The task now is to identify a better, effective and supportive approach to increase the likelihood of success at the next attempt. This subtlety in how the question is asked may go unnoticed by neutrals, but it can make a significant difference.

Success coaches master the art of continuously enhancing their players' performance. Criticism is intended to guide players towards reflection and thereby into the so-called learning zone. These coaches often ask themselves "Why?", but they frame their questions in a way that encourages players to think carefully.

Consequently, they never ask their players why they failed in a game. It is likely that players will offer explanations that serve as self-justification in such moments. The space for excuses is limitless – whether it be the field, their boots, the tactics, the referee, or the opponent. In this cycle of blame, the team misses the opportunity to learn from defeats and to better prepare for similar situations in the future. This is a missed opportunity to develop potential – and to do so in a sustainable way.

Let us imagine a success coach who instead addresses the team with the question: "What caused you not to perform at your usual level yesterday?" Suddenly, there is silence in the dressing room, as if the players are holding their breath. Thoughts begin to form, and the players start to reflect. What truly held us back? Was it the referee or our reaction to his decisions?

Perhaps an introverted player speaks up – let us call him Ralf, inspired by the 'football professor', Ralf Rangnick. Ralf does not say much, but what he says is sound and well-founded. He breaks the silence and states: "We have lost our focus on what truly matters and what we can influence."

At this point, the success coach intervenes: "So, team, what could we do going forward to maintain our focus until the end of the game?" The question is subtly different, yet it means everything. The coach avoids the question of why, as his goal is to look ahead and support the team in identifying options to improve next time.

Perhaps another player dares to speak up: "The tactical instructions at half-time were effective, coach. When we lost focus midway through the second half, a few words would have helped us to regain focus on what matters most." Fact-based, forward-looking and focused on growth – this is the path to success.

Naturally, the above example is simplified, but it illustrates the critical difference that a single word can make. A new quality of reflection emerges, characterised by solution- and future-oriented insights, without minimising or dismissing past mistakes. 'What instead of Why' is a simple principle that can foster sustainable performance improvement, rather than sowing frustration or encouraging excuses.

What can tomorrow's leaders learn from this? The choice of question influences not only the answers but the mindset. If you seek excuses and explanations for failure, you will continue to ask "Why?". However, if you aim to uncover the true causes and explore future-oriented, solution-focused options – which I naturally assume – then from today onward, abandon 'Why' questions and instead pose questions beginning with 'What'. The question should align with the respondent's interest, not that of the questioner – as was the case in Iceland with Waldemar Hartmann.

Therefore, next time, do not ask your employee: "Why didn't you speak during the meeting?" Rather, ask: "What prevented you from speaking in yesterday's meeting?" You will be surprised by how much more productive the response will be. This form of questioning encourages thinking in terms of possibilities rather than limitations and obstacles. The justification mode is circumvented, allowing us to begin thinking in options and solutions.

The Manager as an Expert

Our tendency to offer advice causes greater harm than using 'why' questions. When leaders are asked whether they are effective coaches, one often observes an almost embarrassing degree of overconfidence. Many believe that their success as managers automatically implies that they are also excellent coaches. Coaching is frequently misunderstood as merely 'dispensing good advice'. Interestingly, the issue does not stem from ill intentions on the part of leaders, but is deeply ingrained in human nature. We enjoy helping others and believe that advice is the most effective form of support.

Yet, all too often, we listen only until we believe we have a solution for the person in front of us. We frequently attempt to act as 'mind readers', endeavouring to decipher the most complex and dynamic system of our time: the brain. It contains approximately 86 billion neurons, each connected by synapses to an average of 1,000 to 10,000 other neurons[77]. Such an endeavour appears nearly impossible.

Well-intentioned advice often hinders the other person from thinking independently and developing their own solutions. Unconsciously, we impose our own solutions on others – naturally with the best intentions. However, we overlook that every individual is unique, as is the problem itself and the context in which both exist.

The bestselling author Michael Bungay Stanier describes this almost compulsive tendency to offer unsolicited solutions to others as 'the advice monster'[78].

A study from 1984[79] shows that doctors listen to their patients for an average of only 18 seconds before offering advice. This appears representative of many leaders today.

Success coaches have adopted the principle of questioning their athletes at least twice as often to stimulate their thinking, rather than immediately providing advice. Asking questions is more effective than mind reading.

The Learning Zone

Good advice has its place in certain situations. However, in the majority of cases, it does not lead to a significant increase in performance, nor does it encourage the other person to engage in reflective thinking. As explained earlier, the likelihood that advice is received, processed and implemented is generally minimal and contingent upon numerous conditions.

Nevertheless, it remains part of the coach's role to provide answers. Success coaches, however, typically manage to withhold these answers and well-intentioned advice for a longer period. Within this brief yet critically important timeframe, authentic thinking and learning can occur. Welcome to the widely referenced 'learning zone'.

Successful coaches are not just 'coaches', but they have adopted a real coaching mindset. They have internalised the necessary attitude and do not revert to habitual patterns under stress. These coaches have mastered the skill of guiding their players into the essential learning zone, regardless of the time available. They are aware that this process yields the best results over the long term. 'Quick fixes' are considered options only when the fast pace of the game necessitates immediate behavioural adjustment; they are not part of a success coach's standard toolbox. This is because such 'quick fixes' may produce temporary effects, but will almost certainly not be recalled as viable options during subsequent competitions or high-pressure situations.

As I have previously emphasised, well-intentioned advice often amounts to a gentler form of micromanagement and 'quick fixes' that fail to support sustainable performance development. Therefore, it is advisable to withhold them for a longer period, allowing players and employees the opportunity to advance within the learning zone.

A Moment of Silence

"I love the sound when no one says anything." Do you consider yourself among those who embrace this saying, or do you find silence rather uncomfortable? At times, moments of silence are observed at sporting events to commemorate incidents or athletes. Yet, during this minute, it is rarely truly quiet in the stadium. The ambient noise may be subdued but is present, and it typically increases before the minute concludes. For many, silence is challenging; stillness is often perceived as uncomfortable.

If you identify with this group, you are in good company. In an increasingly hectic and noisy world, many people find it progressively difficult to achieve tranquillity. Silence becomes a perceived state of deprivation that must be endured. Even when we long for silence, restlessness often arises once it appears – except perhaps in certain meditation practices. The writer Paul Keller once observed: "The path to all greatness passes through silence." This insight remains relevant today, as the art of questioning also involves the ability to endure silence.

Enduring silence is a skill that many coaches and leaders find challenging. The avoidance of uncomfortable silence becomes a driving force that causes advice to be offered prematurely. A sense of guilt and responsibility compels them to break the silence as swiftly as possible.

In my role as performance coach, I collaborate with coaches to cultivate the ability to endure silence. Many coaches perceive silence as a sign of helplessness. However, what if players arrive at different conclusions than the coach? When a coach avoids silence, they deprive players of the opportunity to genuinely think, reflect and develop their own solutions.

Enduring this oppressive silence requires courage, particularly when it arises unexpectedly. Pressure generates oppression, and under pressure, we often revert to old, habitual patterns of behaviour. This is how we break through the threatening silence, offering prompts and guidance. At that moment, the focus shifts away from the team and returns to the coach.

The opportunity for young athletes to engage and develop within the learning zone is currently being lost. Therefore, it is crucial that coaches and leaders cultivate the ability not only to endure spontaneous moments of silence, but to intentionally create and appreciate them. Such moments serve as sources of new ideas and indicate that the individual has just entered the learning zone.

Silence should not be perceived as a sign of helplessness, nor as an opportunity to indulge in 'helper syndrome'. Instead, it signifies that something important is occurring at this moment, and that new options and solutions may be emerging. Allow it. These moments of silence are what a coach strives for – times when the individual thinks deeply and occasionally experiences a 'lightbulb moment'. These are moments in which sustainable performance is cultivated.

'Retrospectives' in Sport and Business

Lightbulb moments play a crucial role in the enthusiasm around so-called agile working methods, which have revitalised the practice of simple reflection. It is a shame that we had to wait until the emergence of 'new work' initiatives to bring reflection back into focus. Nonetheless, this trend presents an excellent opportunity for sustainable performance development. The so-called 'retrospectives' have enjoyed considerable popularity for some time.

In these 'retros', project members reflect – either after the completion of a project or on a regular basis – on what went well and what could be improved. They identify best practices to be maintained in the next project and consider possible adjustments. What essentially constitutes common sense had been lost to many companies over the years and now must be painstakingly rediscovered and developed.

Note: 'New work' summarises the many tools and attempts around modern work and leadership that have become popular over the last ten years. The method to reflect is called 'retrospectives', 'retros' or 'retro meeting'. This is common language in business.

In sport, reflection occurs after every match day or occasionally following training sessions. Success coaches dedicate time to meticulous reflection following victories and defeats. Even more importantly, the retrospective focuses on the elements identified as success factors. Observable behavioural patterns emphasised within the predetermined match plan are carefully reflected upon.

Was mutual support provided? Was sufficient effort made to execute tactical instructions under pressure? Was there adequate preparation of the opponent? Was the opponent impressed by our positive body language? Was focus maintained despite adverse field conditions and seemingly unfair referee decisions? Did the players on the bench do everything possible to support their teammates?

These questions prompt reflection on the success factors – which are then refined, enhanced or even replaced. Because the approach is performance-driven rather than result-driven, the focus shifts to the factors beneath the iceberg, rather than searching for external reasons above the iceberg for why the goal was not achieved. This represents 'coaching on the job' in its purest form.

Within the corporate setting, this means not complaining about delayed projects or seeking justification, and instead engaging in self-reflection. What prevented the team from saying 'No'? What made us initiate projects without adequate resources? This is, of course, only relevant if a realistic assessment of resources prior to project initiation was regarded as a success factor.

Rather than expressing frustration within the sales team over the revenue decline in the fourth quarter and attributing it to market unpredictability, a discussion could be held regarding a defined success factor. For example, the close cross-functional collaboration in large projects, which was not executed as planned, resulting in lost contracts.

The fundamental difference lies in reflecting in a solution-oriented and forward-looking manner, rather than seeking explanations in the past, which often serve as justifications.

Routines

This brings us back to the coaches frequently referenced in this book, who do not measure success solely by goals or league standings. They understand that results are often difficult to explain and that there is a sequence of causes. Hence, they do not trust the result. They focus on factors within their influence and analyse how to increase the likelihood of success. There is no black-and-white portrayal, no panic mode, no emphasis on going the extra mile, nor a reliance on the principle of hope. Instead, they carefully differentiate between the achieved, measurable results and the so-called success factors – that is, the behavioural patterns and principles of action to which the entire team has committed.

Success coaches typically follow a structured routine when reflecting on the previous game:

- What had we planned? (Definition of success)
- What did we achieve?
- Which of our identified success factors were we able to implement?
- What supported us in this process?
- Are there success indicators that confirm these outcomes?
- Which success factors did we find challenging to pursue?
- What prevented us from successfully implementing them?
- Are there success indicators that confirm these outcomes?
- Have we gained any new insights?

- How do we intend to apply these insights?
- Which behaviours would we like to improve?
- How will we implement these improvements?
- Which behaviours do we want to maintain in the next game?
- What actions will we take to ensure this?

Focusing on the success factors allows players and teams the additional benefit of being able to continuously self-assess. Rather than panicking in mid-season or reviewing performance only at the end of the season, feedback becomes a daily tool. Colleagues, employees and leaders can regularly exchange feedback without waiting for the annual employee appraisal. Reflection becomes a constant companion – an attitude that no longer needs to be scheduled but, like other routines, becomes part of everyday life. In this way, reflection becomes firmly embedded in the corporate culture.

This approach ensures that these coaches do not become unsettled by data. Instead, they consider their success indicators and analyse: Do the measured indicators align with our observations? Is the trend accurate, and how can we influence it in a sustainable way? These discussions take place within teams, where results are regarded as the consequence of a healthy and sustainable performance culture. Within these teams, indicators remain what they are: indicators. They serve to verify and enable teams to ask the right questions, rather than being treated as the definitive answer to success or failure. You are not 'reduced' to goals. Instead, the trends of these indicators are observed, analysed, discussed and then acted upon with due calm.

It should be emphasised that these reflections should not come solely from the coach. On the contrary, much of the reflective work should take place within the players' minds. Therefore, questions are asked, attentive listening occurs and, sometimes, silence in the dressing room is patiently endured. Advice and corrective measures from the coach remain valuable; however, for success coaches, they no longer initiate the team meeting.

Naturally, a match review cannot be directly compared to a project or quarterly review. Nonetheless, you may find some valuable suggestions on how to structure such meetings more as forward-looking learning sessions, rather than reducing them to 'examinations' focused primarily on justifications. Instead of desperately asking for the 'extra mile' or doubting the team's willingness to perform, you could identify other causes and tools that your team can willingly and responsibly apply.

This reflection routine is also ideal for your employee appraisals.

Potential Tactical Errors

Tactical error 77: We do not know how to reflect.

Tactical error 78: We reflect on results rather than on the behaviour responsible for the results.

Tactical error 79: We allocate too little time to reflection.

Tactical error 80: We only engage in reflection following defeats.

Tactical error 81: We ask 'Why?' questions instead of 'What?' questions.

Tactical error 82: We confuse 'coaching' with 'giving advice'.

Tactical error 83: We fail in listening to understand.

Tactical error 84: We talk too much and ask too little.

Tactical error 85: We fear silence.

Tactical error 86: We overestimate the quality of our advice.

Tactical error 87: We give advice too quickly and too frequently.

Sustaining Performance

When we speak of healthy and sustainable performance development, we do not mean clubs or athletes who rise meteorically, only to vanish just as quickly. The examples presented in this book demonstrate sustainable success. It is not enough to deliver extraordinary performance over a short period; rather, performance must be maintained at a high level over many years. This requires maintaining health and managing stress effectively. Sports clubs and businesses are increasingly criticised due to the growing demands placed on their employees. Can we learn something from sport here? How do professionals manage to remain ready to perform when it counts, while regenerating and managing their energy? And which of these insights can be applied within business?

Energy Drainers and Duracell Bunnies

When my phone's battery drops into the red zone, I become concerned – depending on the situation – and quickly look to charge it. Do you experience this? Anyone raising teenagers understands the significance of an empty battery: panic attacks, blame and even existential fears are not uncommon.

Even when driving, it is natural to stop at a petrol or charging station when the fuel or battery indicator signals the need. We wouldn't embark on a journey with an almost empty tank, or make an important phone call with a nearly depleted battery. The fear of running out of energy is too great. We have learned to recharge our cars and mobile phones when their energy is depleted. We often do this before it is necessary, thanks to the fuel and battery indicators.

However, when it comes to our energy, it becomes increasingly difficult to take notice of our internal fuel gauge. We either fail to recognise when we are operating at a low battery level or refuse to acknowledge it. Perhaps we do not want to admit to ourselves – or to others – that we are exhausted.

Prominent Examples in Sport

In sport, as in many companies, there are numerous examples of individuals who continue despite a depleted battery, or only speak openly about their mental health challenges after their careers. According to a study, one in ten competitive athletes suffer from burnout symptoms[80].

The former German ski jumper and current TV expert at ARD, Sven Hannawald, announced in April 2004, at nearly 30 years of age and in the midst of his career, that after winning countless titles on ski jumps worldwide, he was suffering from burnout syndrome.

During Hannawald's era, Sebastian Deisler was regarded as one of Germany's greatest football talents. Deisler missed several months of the 2003/04 season due to depression. His career ended in January 2007. He visited Bayern Munich's then-manager Uli Hoeness several times in his suite during a training camp in Dubai, repeatedly expressing that he could no longer continue and that he had nothing else to give[81]. Upon his return to Germany, he announced the end of his career.

Swimming legend Michael Phelps spoke openly at an early stage about his depression and suicidal thoughts following the 2012 Olympic Games.

Tennis star Naomi Osaka from Japan and professional cyclist Marcel Kittel are prominent recent examples – both have publicly disclosed their mental health struggles.

A Growing Awareness

However, there is hope. Beyond coaches and athletes who compete despite exhaustion and often only discuss it after their careers, an increasing number of individuals are responding promptly to their bodies' signals – frequently with the support of sports psychologists or psychotherapists. Such cases sometimes provoke surprise or indignation among fans.

Adam Peaty, the two-time Olympic champion in the 100m breaststroke, withdrew from the British Swimming Championships and subsequently did not appear at the 2023 World Aquatics Championships due to struggles with his mental health. He felt fatigued and recognised that he was not himself. He no longer derived the same enjoyment from the sport and took a break from competitive swimming. He now understands how to address this imbalance in his life and delivered peak performance once again at the 2024 Olympic Games[82]. He returned and missed his third Olympic gold by only 0.02 seconds in a heart-stopping finale.

Another notable example is Simone Biles, who withdrew from several events during the Olympic Games despite strong prospects of winning. She experienced 'twisties' – a spatial disorientation during complex aerial twists. This condition can impair movement control and increase the risk of injury. Stress, fatigue and performance pressure are common causes of this phenomenon. During a press conference, Biles stated: "We are always told that we somehow have to push through. At the end of the day, we are not here merely to entertain; we are, above all, human beings." This impactful statement sparked a discussion about the sports industry, which depends on people, yet often treats them as commodities.

The cases that have come to light in sport are likely only the tip of the iceberg. Meanwhile, public perception is beginning to shift. Jürgen Klopp's voluntary departure from Liverpool at the end of the 2023/24 season was met with widespread recognition and respect. Klopp explained his decision by stating that he owed it to the players and the club to always give 100%, which he could no longer guarantee for the forthcoming season. He said: "I cannot do it on three wheels[83]."

Energy is a Zero-sum Game

Not only coaches and elite athletes must know when to recharge their energy; managers and employees at all levels are equally responsible for monitoring their energy reserves. Energy is like time: a zero-sum game, meaning it is limited. If I expend energy on one activity, I cannot use the same energy for another. While managing time is a widespread misconception, it is possible to manage our personal energy levels. The fundamental prerequisite for this is the ability to accurately assess our current energy state. How does it feel to be bursting with energy – that is, at 100%? And how does it feel when running whilst not at your best?

In some clubs, this assessment is not left to chance. In the dressing room of successful German handball club SG Flensburg-Handewitt, players press a 'buzzer' before each training session to rate their energy level on a scale from 1 to 10. Many other professional teams across various sports employ similar tools to enhance players' awareness of their energy and performance levels in an engaging manner. These tools not only provide data points to assess whether the workload and stress levels are healthy and sustainable, or require adjustment, but they also serve as early warning signals for players against overload of any kind. The workload may stem not only from training but from diverse sources such as family issues or poor sleep quality. The causes are as varied and individual as the players themselves.

Athletic coaches, performance coaches and sports psychologists closely monitor these metrics and provide support when trends indicate a prolonged decline. They investigate the underlying causes to restore the player's energy to the necessary level for achieving outstanding performance. However, there is an unpleasant aspect to this method. The risk that players pretend to be 'in good shape' to signal to the coach that they are ready for the next game is significant. In sports where livelihoods depend on securing a position in the starting lineup, this should come as no surprise.

The Duracell Bunnies

In environments where strength, misunderstood self-confidence and 'busyness' are regarded as indicators of high performance and commitment, it becomes increasingly difficult to show vulnerability and admit when we are not performing at our best – as Jürgen Klopp anticipated for the 2024/2025 season. Too often, such honesty and the courage to say "no" are perceived as weaknesses, which can abruptly end a career. This person's resilience is questioned.

Those of my generation may recall the Duracell Bunnies from advertisements, whose batteries seemed inexhaustible, allowing the bunnies to keep 'digging' even when most of their peers had long since given up. Many of the so-called 'high performers' in companies increasingly resemble these Duracell Bunnies – they simply work longer and harder.

At first glance, this may not seem to be a problem, as some of them derive considerable energy from their work, feel effective, apply their strengths, enjoy their tasks, and value the social environment. I am far from intending to criticise or admonish these colleagues, as for some, their work represents fulfilment and a source of energy. I, myself, was such a manager for many years and have worked under such managers. I have enjoyed it in many respects. In other cases, however, this form of energy management can have far-reaching consequences and may ultimately lead to burnout. The boundary is often difficult to discern and therefore challenging to define.

Do Not Believe Everything You See

Some of these Duracell Bunnies confide to another person that they have no energy left for other areas of life. More often than not, it is social expectations that motivate them. It is considered desirable to juggle many tasks at the same time, to always remain busy, and above all, to be busier than others. This resilience and level of activity are often regarded in many executive teams as indicators of quality, whereas focus and composure tend to be less valued. Due to our thinking patterns, the inability to rest is often mistaken for a high energy level. This can be very misleading.

Just as you should not believe everything you think, you should not believe everything you see. In sport, athletes are advised: 'Do not compare your inner state with the outward appearance of your opponent.' A respected opponent may be extremely nervous, even if they appear confident on the outside. Just as your counterpart has learned to conceal their nervousness, you can learn not to be influenced by outward appearances and displays of power.

Many employees perceive the outward appearance and activity level of leaders as indicators of strength and resilience. These attributes are highly valued in business life, although they are often considerably overrated. We seldom consider that this activity may be accompanied by internal conflict. It strikes us as peculiar that even 'alpha individuals' might be motivated by the desire to be accepted and liked, to join the distinguished circle of high performers, or to secure their position within this elite group.

We hesitate to interpret the apparent ability to multitask (which we have already debunked as a myth) and relentless activity as manifestations of powerlessness and helplessness. Instead, we interpret these behavioural patterns as signs of strength and energy. Consequently, when one of our colleagues falls ill, everyone is surprised to discover that behind the hardened manager lies a human being.

Our Default Setting Prevents Us from Making an Accurate Diagnosis

Our limited perspective prevents us from considering that the employee's issue might be something other than a motivation problem or lack of willpower. We believe what we observe – that the colleague is not turning the hamster wheel as quickly as the rest of the team. Our default setting prompts us to act immediately without investigating the underlying causes. In many cases, 'the carrot and stick' method is the tool of choice.

We seldom consider that an employee's energy is insufficient to fully realise their potential. Nor do we often acknowledge that the environment can drain employees of their energy. How can we recognise when our employees are operating at minimal capacity? Unlike a car, it cannot be heard; unlike a mobile phone, it cannot be seen; and unlike the professionals at SG Flensburg-Handewitt, we lack an early warning system. Why is that?

Willpower Demands Energy

Asking the employee to exert more effort may be effective in the short term. However, willpower differs fundamentally from the intrinsic motivation to make a meaningful contribution to the team. While willpower is necessary in many respects, it requires significantly more energy than our intrinsic drive.

In this manner, we cultivate highly committed employees who give their utmost throughout the week, only to collapse exhausted on the sofa on a Friday evening. They hope that their family has not planned too many activities over the weekend, allowing them to recover from the demands of the workweek. On Monday, a new week filled with tasks and challenges begins. These employees perform to be liked, accepted and respected, thereby avoiding vulnerability. This is enough for survival, but it falls far short of healthy and sustainable performance development.

Well-being and Resilience Programmes

The increasing rates of illness and the rise in the number of burnout cases have not gone unnoticed. The number of unreported cases is undoubtedly higher, and it can be assumed that an increasing number of people come to work with depleted batteries. However, we are neither

Duracell Bunnies nor computers designed to operate at high speed with multiple programmes running simultaneously over extended periods.

The response of companies to rising sickness rates and absenteeism is the implementation of well-being initiatives supported by carefully planned internal communication. For some, applying sticking plasters and administering a broad-spectrum antibiotic may be effective, but often this remains a short-term solution that addresses only the symptoms rather than the underlying causes – in particular, when these measures are offered as a one-size-fits-all solution.

One cause is almost unanimously acknowledged: employees appear unable to cope with the changes in today's world. Partial responsibility is accepted by the responsible, and it is decided to do more for employees to better equip them for the daily challenges. Stress management seminars are offered, and hotlines to mental health first-aiders are established. The company's key performers are expected to become 'resilient', a term from physics, describing how objects return to their original state after an event, similar to a sponge. In other words, the status quo is restored once the crisis has passed. Is this really what we want to accomplish?

These events are allowed to occur, but they only affect us temporarily, as we have learned to respond in ways that prevent lasting harm. I contend that this approach carries the risk of the organisation failing to develop in a healthy and sustainable way. Accepting the conditions and adapting like a sponge may aid survival, but it neither awakens latent potential nor fosters innovation, nor does it establish a solid foundation for the future or advance the organisation's development.

Amidst all this adaptation, we often neglect to pose the fundamental questions. Why is it necessary for our employees to develop resilience in the first place? The organisation assumes a kind of victim role; however, the question remains: victim of whom? Victims of the ever-accelerating world, the so-called VUCA world. VUCA stands for Volatility, Uncertainty, Complexity and Ambiguity. We become victims of the rapidly accepted 'new normal' and the self-imposed conditions that accompany it.

Don't get me wrong, it is essential to prepare employees and teams for stressful situations and equip them with options to manage these challenges effectively. The objective is to empower them to realistically evaluate opportunities and risks, and to channel their emotional energy purposefully and efficiently – much like sports psychologists do with their athletes. Nonetheless, this does not exempt us from self-reflection and from establishing an environment that focuses not on mere survival, but on the healthy and sustainable development of performance. We should help our people to thrive, rather than just survive.

Without appropriate conditions, both parties knowingly or unknowingly accept 40, 50 or 60% performance because the energy required for optimal performance is lacking. One hundred percent energy? Many employees only reach this level after a three-week summer holiday, returning to work tanned and full of good intentions. Often, the weekends are only sufficient to recover from the deep red zone. Achieving 100% battery performance remains an illusion for many.

When asked about their personal energy level, the majority of participants in my team workshops indicate that their battery level is approximately 40–60%. When I highlight that this is unsatisfactory, most respond that energy levels are better on Mondays than at the end of the week. I am also advised to be grateful that I'm conducting the workshop in February rather than December, as many employees then operate in the red zone and yearn for the Christmas break.

Employees are not required to perform flips and twists like Simone Biles, and often they neither have the time nor the inclination for such aerial feats. Nevertheless, they can accomplish their tasks with a battery that is not fully charged. While this does not entail the same risk of injury as with Biles, it results in performance decline, errors and poor decisions – often a gradual process that can prove costly for companies. The resulting sick leave and burnout cases are relatively straightforward to identify. However, measuring the gradual decline in performance due to low energy levels among employees, teams or organisations is more challenging.

Energy Drain
In today's fast-paced and chaotic world, company owners and executive teams are often inclined to attribute energy losses to external circumstances. However, a considerable portion of our energy balance is influenced by the company's culture, which significantly shapes the overall energy level of the workforce.

During physical work, we expend energy. In mental work, our body requires substantial energy, particularly the brain. Although it constitutes only about 2% of our body weight, the brain consumes approximately 20% of our total energy.

The central thesis of this book is that, alongside necessary energy, we expend a great deal of unnecessary energy to achieve results. In the search for 'energy drains', we encounter familiar factors: the limiting beliefs and tactical errors outlined in this book. These not only diminish efficiency and effectiveness but deplete a significant amount of our energy. Many of these elements directly or indirectly impact our performance and have a lasting effect on our energy balance in both positive and negative ways. Let's proceed step by step.

Energy Drainer Number One: Our Result-driven Mindset

Anyone who has ever been involved in a relegation battle and absolutely had to win the next game knows what it feels like to have their back against the wall. In the short term, this can mobilise energy; however, in the long term, it impedes players and leaders alike, and strains nerves. Most are relieved when the ordeal finally ends. It scarcely matters whether the 'survival struggle' resulted in avoiding relegation or demotion to a lower division. Once the sword of Damocles that constantly reminds the team of inadequate performance is removed, they can take a deep breath and press the reset button. Finally, efforts can focus on developing a future-oriented vision, rather than clinging to outdated, fragile lifelines. A fresh start can evoke positive emotions, even if it might initially feel strange.

In business, it often does not take an existential threat or crisis to trigger the previously mentioned 'fight or flight' mode. Yet, despite sound financial health, many companies default to this 'survival mode'. Unmet goals or the fear of failure provoke peculiar reactions. Organisations, teams and employees operate continuously in 'survival mode', often without being aware. They have not learned to recognise their emotions or to manage them effectively. Instead, they suppress their feelings or attempt to resist them. Their dysfunctional and often unconscious self-talk, along with limiting beliefs, exacerbate this. Not only do decision-making and creativity suffer, but the constant 'fight or flight' also depletes the energy reserves of all those involved.

Do you reflect on your own mode from time to time? If you predominantly feel 'driven', metaphorically operating in 'survival mode', there is a risk that your energy reserves and those of your employees will be depleted more rapidly than usual.

It is time to become aware of the situation and take appropriate action. In most cases, this does not mean resigning impulsively, but rather thoroughly examining what causes this feeling of being 'driven'. An open conversation with the manager or the team, in which you share your feelings and observations, can make a significant difference. It provides clarity and creates space for change. A 'business as usual' approach must not be an option.

The same applies to teams and clubs that year after year attempt to avoid relegation, only to eventually be relegated. Running more than the opponent, hastily dismissing coaches, or abruptly changing the entire system, rarely result in healthy and sustainable improvements, just like relying on the principle of hope. This has not changed, despite the world seemingly becoming less predictable and spinning faster.

Energy Drainer Number Two: Our Focus on Weakness

A result-driven mindset often leads to recognition being granted only when outcomes are measurable. Monthly evaluations indicate whether efforts have been successful. So long as the dashboard does not consistently display green, our focus remains on the amber or red indicators that require attention.

In this process, we frequently overlook the small steps towards the overarching goal, as well as the subtle progress and behavioural changes occurring beneath the surface. Much like a runner who, fixated on results, fails to notice the beauty of nature or their elevated pulse, we lose the capacity to appreciate small details and derive energy from them, instead taking them for granted. Ironically, it is often these small actions that collectively produce the results.

Constantly focusing on even minor weaknesses consumes valuable energy. It requires more energy and willpower to address weaknesses than to leverage and enhance strengths. Repeatedly explaining our weaknesses is more draining than the positive feeling of being effective.

An often-overlooked benefit of focusing on strengths is the energy that praise generates for both the giver and the recipient. Observations should not be reserved for monthly or annual meetings. Small gestures and words of appreciation serve as genuine energy boosters for both parties.

This is by no means about adopting a 'soft approach' or offering praise merely for the sake of it. The culture of continuous improvement, in which I was raised, is valuable and brings satisfaction. However, these improvements should not come at the expense of recognising and appreciating small successes. These successes occur more frequently at the process and behavioural levels, and cannot always be substantiated by concrete evidence and measures.

A lack of success leads to the depletion of energy reserves. More concerning is the disregard for small successes, which prevent us from acknowledging and celebrating them. This is a natural consequence of our result-focused, or rather, result-driven, approach, which, as you may already suspect, leads to energetic exhaustion.

Energy Drainer Number Three: Our Insecurity

Psychological safety is a critical and non-negotiable asset that is widely discussed today, particularly following Google's 'Project Aristotle' study on high-performing teams. Psychological safety in the workplace, alongside a healthy learning culture, is not only a valuable economic factor because it fosters innovation and better decision-making, but because it prevents employees from expending unnecessary energy.

It consumes immense energy when we suspect a sniper behind every wall and must constantly remain vigilant for threats. Energy management is a zero-sum game: the more energy we invest in defending our value, the faster we become exhausted, leaving less energy available to develop ourselves and to create value within the company.

Individuals who expend their energy playing a role, fearing mistakes or saying the wrong thing will lose more energy throughout the workday than those who can authentically apply their skills without fear of errors or reprisal. Such individuals act with the hope and conviction that they are making a meaningful contribution to the whole.

The same principle applies here. Having to constantly justify ourselves consumes more energy than feeling effective. Accordingly, we have identified three primary energy drains rooted in organisational culture or leadership philosophy.

- Result-focused goal setting: The pressure to continuously deliver specific outcomes can be overwhelming and can deplete energy.

- Focus on weaknesses: Rather than fostering strengths, we often disproportionately concentrate on weaknesses. This also depletes valuable energy.
- Lack of psychological safety: An absence of a sense of security can make the work environment stressful and drain our energy reserves.

These energy drainers are deeply embedded in the corporate culture and result from our established limiting beliefs – both of which do not change overnight. The list is not exhaustive but highlights factors that are less individual and more universally applicable.

They cause us to drag ourselves exhausted into the weekend on Friday, instead of entering our free time feeling energised. The television evening, often described as cozy but abruptly ending in sleep on the beloved sofa, is preferred over visits from friends. Not only does our back suffer, but also the quality of our sleep. However, in 'survival mode', we tend to disregard this.

The good news is that you do not need to wait for large-scale well-being programmes or stress management seminars. Instead, focus on addressing the matters within your sphere of influence. In the following sections, I will provide you with reflective prompts and strategies to help identify and counteract your personal energy drains. Furthermore, you will learn to recognise warning signs and establish effective routines to maintain your energy balance. This way, you avoid the risk of entering the red zone.

Our Values

When was the last time you reflected on your personal values – that is, the principles that are most important to you in your actions and aspirations? If it has been a while or never, you are in good company.

Many individuals neglect reflecting on their values in everyday work life. Frequently, they begin to tolerate violations of their values and gradually distance themselves from them. We accept or engage in actions that normally contradict our inner compass. Even worse, we refrain from taking action.

The realities of everyday business often place us under pressure while simultaneously demanding flexibility. These constraints can challenge our willpower, as we seldom act from intrinsic motivation in such situations – often at the expense of our own authenticity and energy.

In this book, we have emphasised the importance of engaging with our own value system to achieve effective self-regulation. Nevertheless, we must not underestimate the significant energy loss that occurs when we consciously or unconsciously act against our values or are compelled to do so. Such conflict places a considerable burden on us and can severely deplete our energy reserves. This process often occurs gradually, and is only recognised and addressed at a late stage.

It is therefore unsurprising that defining team values and adhering to corresponding behavioural patterns is standard practice in preparing performance teams. These values serve as a guiding framework for every individual's behaviour. However, for those who comply because they have to – and without genuine commitment – the season can prove challenging. This is especially true when the coaching team actively embodies and reflects the values, rather than just displaying them as a faded poster on the wall of the clubhouse.

I am not referring to the official corporate values, which are proudly presented on the business' website, but to the values that are practised daily within teams or between departments and colleagues. If you feel compelled to mask your true self on a daily basis to fit into the system, you have already identified a significant energy drain. It may be time to reassess and reorder your priorities.

Our Purpose

The next potential energy drainer, which is not entirely beyond our influence, is our 'purpose'. In the opening sections, we stressed the importance of starting with the purpose to enable deliberate and targeted action. A clear purpose fosters motivation and ideally places us in a state of 'flow'. The work flows almost effortlessly and hardly feels like work. It requires little discipline and willpower to stay engaged. The joy of hard work arises because it advances our greater purpose.

It is unrealistic for a company to just employ intrinsically highly motivated employees with a clear purpose. Therefore, it is not inappropriate to deliberately adjust with extrinsic incentives, provided we remain mindful of the associated side effects, which we have already discussed in this book. However, we should also consider that this has an additional effect: tasks performed more from extrinsic than intrinsic motivation, demand more energy and willpower. This is not inherently negative but should be considered to avoid overtaxing the battery – and ultimately depleting it.

As previously explained, the purpose represents one of our intrinsic motivators. When we understand the purpose behind our actions and feel effective in making a valuable contribution, we typically do not require external incentives to maintain high performance.

A player whose goal is to become a professional and who is making consistent progress will not require additional motivation or energy boosts. Conversely, a player who has been on the bench for several matches and questions the purpose of continuing to play, requires considerable willpower and discipline to persevere. He does not feel effective, as he is unable to make a visible contribution either to the team or to his own sense of purpose. This situation is also evident among our employees, even though companies do not have a direct substitutes' bench. Nevertheless, there are ways to provide them with a similar sense of support.

It is beneficial to reflect on our purpose. Without a clear answer, the work to be performed will demand considerable willpower and energy. The same applies to our personal contributions to the overall objective. Without clarity, a lack of self-efficacy causes our energy reserves to diminish more rapidly than necessary.

Being aware of our purpose and core values enables us to identify factors that either drain or replenish our energy. This awareness is essential for effective energy management. Additionally, there are pragmatic and practical guidelines that help prevent burnout and maintain our energy at a healthy equilibrium. For this, we once again draw upon insights from sports science.

The Two Energy Zones

In sport, we refer to two zones: the 'performance zone', where physical or mental performance is delivered, and the 'recovery zone', where energy reserves – whether physical or mental – are replenished. Coaches ensure balanced load management. Players who exert themselves for 90 minutes on the field on Sunday subsequently train in a manner that prepares them mentally and physically for the next game. A performance phase is followed by a recovery phase to allow energy reserves to be fully recharged.

While this concept is easily understood in sport, it is often interpreted differently in everyday business life. Our Duracell Bunnies, to whom we dedicated the beginning of this section, are no exception. Once back in the manager's chair, most interpret the concept in a rather idiosyncratic way. The cycles in which these two phases alternate are often too long and become unbalanced.

In executive teams, the situation often appears as follows: from Monday to Friday, many work within the performance zone. On Friday evening, they switch to the recovery zone, gradually returning to performance mode by checking emails on Sunday evening. Even on weekdays, we leave the performance zone only briefly when fatigue overcomes us and we fall asleep, with thoughts of the next stressful day ahead. After typically only five to six hours of rather restless sleep, we are abruptly awakened by our mobile phones, often accompanied by the unpleasant default ringtone, as we have not taken the time to select a more soothing melody to gently rouse us from our (night)mares.

Alternating Between Energy Zones

Individuals perform most effectively when they rhythmically alternate between these two zones. This is in contrast to the practices of many executive teams, which often demand prolonged periods of intense performance until a well-deserved holiday, or a 70-hour workweek until the weekend off. Instead, it is advisable to balance our energy throughout the day and week by consciously alternating between exertion and recovery.

As with athletes, this approach to load management enables healthy, sustainable performance that can be accessed when it truly matters. It is essential to reconsider the definition of 'high performance' within the context of this book: here, it signifies delivering and cultivating performance in a healthy and sustainable way. A high performer is not someone who works until burnout and can only recover through an extended holiday. They are not the person who answers emails late into the night because they were unable to do so during the day due to an exhausting series of meetings. A high performer is also not someone who boasts in the morning about having slept only four hours because they have been agonising over a critical project since three o'clock in the morning.

A high performer is, rather, someone who successfully maintains a high energy level throughout the day to work productively. Such a person balances energy-intensive activities with restorative tasks. They recognise when their energy is depleting and take appropriate action to recover. When energy falls to a critical level, the risk of poor decision-making increases, and the 'monkey brain' takes control in stressful situations – a scenario high performers prevent by timely and corrective interventions.

'Self-care' as a Leadership Responsibility

Avoiding the tactical errors outlined in this book will support you and your employees to arrive at work full of energy. Often, companies' self-imposed conditions serve as energy drains. These include an excessive focus on results, concentrating on weaknesses, a lack of psychological safety, or losing sight of the 'purpose' due to excessive activity.

As a leader, it is your responsibility to positively influence the environment to ensure that your team's energy balance is not adversely affected. Lead and support, in terms of content and process, without becoming trapped by your goals or operating in 'survival mode' – or, even worse, reacting. Adopt a strength-based leadership approach that fosters confidence and trust while allowing space for mistakes and diverse perspectives. Ensure that your team members remain authentic. Maintain focus on the 'big picture' and thereby support the team and individuals, defining their purpose and contribution.

As a leader, demonstrate genuine confidence – not the version defined by organisational standards. Recognise your own strengths, values and goals. Only by truly knowing yourself can you effectively support your employees in identifying their values, strengths and contributions, and recognise potential energy drains.

Being self-aware also means taking care of yourself by monitoring your energy balance and knowing when it is time to take a break. Excel not through constant availability, but by managing your energy reserves skilfully – like elite athletes – and maintaining a healthy balance between exertion and recovery. This is how you set an example for your employees, who will ideally follow your lead, respond with a strong willingness to perform, and be satisfied.

In competitive sport, professional coaches, physiotherapists and sports psychologists work together to protect athletes from overload. It is understood that an empty energy reserve will sooner or later lead to underperformance or even injury, potentially ending a career. But how can we effectively manage our energy balance without such a team of experts? In the next section, we will explore how to spend less time in 'survival mode', and how to leverage the two energy zones to enhance our performance in a healthy and sustainable way.

Potential Tactical Errors

Tactical error 88: We spend too much time in 'survival mode'.

Tactical error 89: We manage our time rather than our energy.

Tactical error 90: We are unaware of our true energy drains.

Pit Stops and Power Naps

The famous phrase, "The game lasts 90 minutes", originates from Sepp Herberger, the legendary coach of the West German national football team in 1954. However, today we understand that this mantra does not always hold true. The referenced 1999 Champions League final, in which Manchester United defeated Bayern Munich during time added on, along with the extended times observed since the 2022 football World Cup in Qatar, demonstrate that the game often extends well beyond regular time.

Incidentally, a football match used to continue until a certain number of goals were scored, often resulting in prolonged 'battles'. This parallels our daily work routine, where we frequently continue working until tasks are completed, the manager leaves the office, or we must acknowledge that we have reached our limit.

While Herberger's assertion regarding the length of the game is outdated, scientists concur on the duration of the so-called 'ultradian rhythms'. These cycles last between 90 and 120 minutes, and describe the transition of our body from a state of high energy to a physiological low. At the end of each cycle, the body craves a recovery phase. Indicators include physical restlessness, yawning, hunger, daydreaming, emotional instability and diminished concentration.

Pause to Perform

In Formula 1, the 'recovery phases' serve to refuel the cars. A strategically timed pit stop can be the difference between victory and defeat. Athletes also need to replenish their energy reserves. In training theory, this is known as the 'rewarding pause' principle. Our body can regenerate within a short period from both physical and mental exertion. It is essentially refuelling – like the racing car in the pit lane.

During this time, the brain regenerates, similar to a muscle after exertion. Waste products and residues from previous energy production, as well as depleted enzymes and hormones, are expelled from the cell. The cell is maintained and reactivated, enabling it to be ready for the next phase of exertion after a short interval[84].

If a break is denied, the body can temporarily compensate through stress hormones; however, this effect is limited in duration. The consequence is a marked decrease in performance and concentration.

This occurs when we ignore the signals of ultradian rhythms and attempt to counteract declining concentration and increasing fatigue over extended periods with caffeine, sweets, nicotine or other 'substances'. This is accompanied by side effects such as irritability, nervousness and exhaustion.

Human performance is not linear but follows rhythmic cycles of 90 to 120 minutes. Recognising these rhythms is essential for healthy and sustainable results. Concentration and mental performance demand high energy expenditure. During a 90- to 120-minute high-performance phase, breathing, blood pressure and heart rate synchronise in a specific rhythm. After this phase, a recovery break is essential[85].

Regrettably, these biological fundamentals are frequently neglected in today's world of work. Many individuals have learned to ignore these signals and simply continue working. Leaders' schedules are often so packed that there is not even time for comfort breaks between meetings.

We constantly fall into the trap of believing that skipping breaks and restorative periods ultimately increases productivity. In reality, though, it has a lasting negative impact on both performance and health. Work becomes tiring and error-prone, making it difficult to maintain optimal performance.

Occasional 'pit stops' for refuelling are as essential for healthy and sustainable performance as they are in Formula 1. While a pit stop in Formula 1 lasts only a few seconds, we should allow our bodies 15 to 20 minutes to initiate and complete the regeneration process. A brief walk to the coffee machine is often insufficient, particularly as the distances to the coffee machine are now short, designed to avoid keeping employees away from work for too long or to accommodate their increased expectations. The principle of recovery dictates that the part of the body subjected to strain regenerates during the recovery phase, and that it does not bear further load at this time. While playing video games can be relaxing for an athlete after an intense strength training session, it is advisable to take a walk following a demanding mental effort.

The predominantly externally controlled workday does not always permit us to take such breaks. If 15 to 20 minutes is not feasible, we should still endeavour to incorporate brief recovery breaks. Establish a routine that suits you. Once you experience the positive effects of these breaks, you will take the next step towards greater self-determination, performance and well-being.

Sometimes, shortening meetings slightly or avoiding starting exactly on the hour is enough to break the vicious circle of meeting marathons.

Breathe to Perform

Given that relaxation is the goal, it is unsurprising that breathing techniques are key to success. Just as breathing exercises help an athlete to escape the 'fight or flight' mode, they can reduce stress and activate recovery mode in everyday work situations.

Breathing is a fundamental element in transitioning from stress mode to recovery mode: "Under acute stress, the respiratory rate increases to 20 to 30 breaths per minute, whereas in a relaxed state it ranges from six to ten breaths per minute. This clearly illustrates why breathing is the universal key to relaxation. All stress responses are regulated by the autonomic nervous system. Because it operates autonomously, we cannot consciously control our heartbeat, blood pressure or muscle tension. The only system over which we can consciously exert influence is our breathing[86]."

By breathing slowly and deeply, we deliberately influence the mechanism of the autonomic nervous system, whenever we choose. When we slow the rhythm of our breathing, our heart rate, blood pressure and muscle tension decrease automatically. This activates the parasympathetic nervous system, which functions as the brake pedal of the autonomic nervous system, while reducing the activity of the sympathetic nervous system (the accelerator pedal). This mechanism underpins all breathing techniques that have been employed for millennia across nearly all cultures for both relaxation and enhanced focus. Many elite athletes utilise this mechanism before and during competitions. Social media frequently depicts these athletes entering an almost meditative state during breaks in play. You benefit from the principle of 'reciprocal inhibition', which asserts that one cannot be anxious and relaxed at the same time. The undesired emotional state is effectively 'overwritten' by the intended state of relaxation.

Just a few minutes of conscious breathing through the diaphragm or abdominal region are sufficient to induce a state of relaxation in body and mind. Crucial is not only the reduction of the respiratory rate but the prolongation of the exhalation. A common guideline suggests that exhalation should last approximately twice as long as the natural inhalation reflex.

A detailed explanation of various breathing techniques would exceed the scope of this book. In recent years, the market for apps designed to help you breathe correctly and apply breathing techniques for relaxation has expanded rapidly. Even better, of course, is to consult experts who can assist you with your individual challenges through proper breathing.

Sleep to Perform

Another effective method to restore concentration and performance is the use of so-called power naps – short naps that enable complete relaxation and help recharge your energy reserves. These brief sleep phases not only positively influence your sense of well-being but have a proven stimulating effect on your productivity[87]. Consequently, the term 'nappiness' has gained attention over the years.

This book focuses on sustainable and healthy performance development. Nonetheless, power naps also produce remarkable effects in this context. Scientific research states that brief periods of sleep can significantly enhance concentration, creativity and productivity. A NASA study demonstrated that power naps can increase attention by a remarkable 54%[88].

As the understanding that recovery phases improve employee performance gains traction, companies such as Google, Microsoft and Salesforce have established dedicated 'nap spaces' where employees can replenish their energy reserves. The reality in traditional office environments, however, differs. In your office, you might be able to use a yoga mat, while working from home may be a more viable option to experiment with this sleep routine – and to adopt it, if it proves beneficial.

The effectiveness of power naps varies from person to person. The optimal duration and timing depend on individual needs. As a general guideline, power naps should not exceed 25 minutes to prevent disrupting the body's deep-sleep phase. Timing is just as important as duration. Individuals who follow a typical daily routine and wake up between 6am and 8am, should plan their nap for early afternoon. Sleeping too late risks artificially diminishing their natural need for sleep. As a result, they do not feel tired in the evening.

Experiment with what is practical and beneficial for you.

Good Sleep is an Integral Part of the 'Job'

For an increasing number of CEOs, the era of experimentation has come to an end. They now prioritise good sleep – not only because it promotes well-being, but because numerous studies demonstrate that sleep deprivation impairs the quality of our decisions.

Nevertheless, a significant number of leaders still adhere to the motto: 'I can sleep when I'm dead.' This casually expressed phrase often symbolises resilience and boundless energy. In reality, chronic sleep deprivation increases the risk of cardiovascular disease and, consequently, the likelihood of premature death.

Sleep is a fundamental human need and essential for high performance as well as overall health. Nevertheless, this aspect is sometimes neglected or underestimated, even in competitive sport.

The English football club Brentford recognised early on the importance of sleep and was among the first clubs to engage the expertise of a sleep specialist. Anna West, a renowned expert in sleep and regeneration, has been supporting the club's football players for more than eight years. From the outset of the collaboration, it was clear to her that both staff and players needed to learn how essential sleep is for their performance, and how it can be deliberately integrated into optimisation strategies. The focus was not only on understanding the theory of sleep, but on practically applying this knowledge to achieve tangible results. Brentford's leadership was quickly convinced – the facts spoke for themselves.

Today, many other professional teams follow this example and collaborate with sleep researchers to optimise their athletes' ability to perform and regenerate. For athletes in elite sport, healthy sleep has become indispensable and is now an integral part of their daily professional routine. With the increasing commercialisation of various sports and the rising number of competitions, the demands on players continue to grow. Anna West forecasts that an athlete's sleep and recovery capacity will become a key criterion in the football scouting process in the future[89].

Even beyond the realm of sport, such as within executive teams, physical and mental demands have been steadily increasing for years, as numerous studies have shown. Nonetheless, a different principle often prevails in this context: limited sleep is perceived as a sign of resilience and strength – like a badge of honour. However, this mindset impedes sustainable and healthy performance development. To understand why, it is important to examine what occurs during sleep.

Sleep Is More Than Rest

What mechanisms enable us to regenerate during sleep and begin the new day fully capable of performing? The pineal gland secretes the hormone melatonin, which signals to the body in darkness that it is time to rest and reduce energy expenditure. The brain sends signals to the muscles to facilitate relaxation, while the body reduces heart rate and blood pressure.

Contrary to popular belief, sleep is not an energy-saving mechanism of the body. During sleep, the basal metabolic rate remains nearly as high as when you are awake. Moreover, sleep is not a period of rest for the mind; the brain is, in fact, partially more active than during the day.

Simultaneously, metabolic processes are activated, cells perform repair functions, and waste products are broken down and eliminated. The immune system is strengthened, and the body secretes substantial amounts of growth hormones that promote the regeneration of bones, muscles and organs.

The brain utilises sleep to consolidate, regenerate and reorganise itself. Memories are strengthened, while irrelevant information is filtered out. The impressions, information and images gathered during the day are processed by the brain at night. New memories are formed during healthy sleep, and existing ones are reinforced.

Research indicates that dreams assist the brain in processing emotions, particularly those linked to emotional events from the previous day.

Sleep thus serves not only to provide the body with rest but to enable it to perform functions that would otherwise be neglected amid the demands of daily life. These performance-enhancing processes cannot be completed during short breaks or power naps within working hours. Moreover, the body cannot achieve this while lounging on the sofa at home, watching television, streaming content on Netflix, or passively consuming questionable videos on social media platforms. Healthy sleep provides the foundation for feeling physically, mentally and emotionally fit throughout the day.

As with many aspects of life, the significance of healthy and sufficient sleep is often only appreciated when it is absent. Many individuals who have endured sleepless nights or, like me, frequently travel across multiple time zones can attest to this: the following day is seldom productive. It is often accompanied by reduced concentration, limited patience, diminished empathy and increased irritability. Overall attention declines, as does the ability to respond effectively, make rational decisions and solve problems. You will undoubtedly agree that all of this is rather detrimental in the professional work environment.

Sleepless nights significantly impair concentration and cognitive performance. The quality of our sleep directly affects the brain's capacity to perform[90].

Unusual Sleep Habits

Let us return to the sports psychologist who does not support athletes until they can 'demonstrate' that they are sleeping sufficiently and healthily. What must an athlete demonstrate? Five, seven or nine hours of sleep?

The right amount of sleep for one person may not be the right amount of sleep for another. However, research largely agrees that adults generally require approximately seven to nine hours of sleep to develop their full performance potential in a healthy and sustainable way.

Exceptions, as always, prove the rule, although these are even more remarkable in the animal kingdom: flamingos sleep standing on one leg, sperm whales while 'standing', and cats for up to 18 hours. Elephants, by contrast, manage with only two hours of sleep. Therefore, sleep requirements do not appear to correlate with the size of the animal.

The most remarkable human exception is the five-time World Footballer of the Year Cristiano Ronaldo, whose extravagant sleep habits were widely reported by the media for several years and are now questioned by experts. Despite all extravagance, it is important to note that even Ronaldo's sleep routines appear to follow the 90-minute cycles we introduced at the beginning of the section as 'ultradian rhythms'.

Research concurs that humans adhere to these 'ultradian rhythms' during sleep. This is hardly surprising. In the early 1950s, researchers Eugene Aserinsky and Nathaniel Kleitman discovered that night sleep occurs in cycles averaging 90 minutes. Throughout the night, lighter sleep phases, characterised by intense brain activity, alternate with deeper phases, during which brain activity diminishes and the most profound recovery occurs.

The commonly cited 90-minute cycle is a statistical average. In reality, sleep cycles vary between 70 and 110 minutes for approximately two-thirds of individuals.

The duration of an individual's sleep cycle can be accurately determined in a sleep laboratory. Alternatively, you may choose to wake up naturally without an alarm clock for several days during a holiday. You will observe a pattern that reflects your unique sleep cycles. If you are among the 'average sleepers', you will notice that the highest likelihood of waking occurs after six, seven-and-a-half or nine hours of sleep. It is therefore advisable to set the alarm clock so that you are not awakened during a deep-sleep phase. For instance, if you fall asleep at 11pm, you should set the alarm for 5am, 6.30am or 8am. Try it and you will notice the difference, although the 5am option falls below the generally recommended sleep duration of seven to nine hours.

Identify your healthy rhythm that enables you to maximise your performance, both healthily and sustainably. It is essential to establish the necessary conditions to support this. There are few reasons – and certainly no valid ones – for employees to have to conform to the manager's internal clock. The cost is borne not only by the employees but by the company in the form of reduced performance.

Rituals in Sport

For competitive athletes and employees, getting sufficient sleep on a daily basis can be challenging. Late games, long working sessions, uncomfortable hotel beds, jet lag from crossing time zones, or children who are unable or unwilling to fall asleep, are just some of the factors that complicate this. Although our need for sleep has remained constant over the centuries, living conditions have changed considerably. Modern demands often conflict with natural needs and are less compatible than in the past. So, what can be done to address this?

Sleep expert Anna West, who has been working with the German Football Association since 2021, is well acquainted with the challenges faced by athletes through her work with professional clubs. After an exciting evening match under floodlights, many players often only find rest at the hotel in the early morning hours, making it nearly impossible to obtain sufficient restorative sleep.

West recommends focusing not only on the duration of sleep but, above all, on the quality of the restorative hours. An overly rigid focus on the quantity of sleep can induce additional stress and, in the worst case, cause panic – particularly if the sleep schedule cannot be maintained before important competitions. Instead, the objective should be to achieve adequate sleep on as many days as possible, allowing the body to better compensate for any deficits. Moreover, West advises employing positive activation strategies in the morning upon waking. A walk in daylight and adequate hydration are simple yet effective methods to support the body after a restless night.

While lost sleep cannot be fully recovered, the body can be prepared for the forthcoming night. As in many other areas of sport, routines and rituals play a crucial role in sleep. They provide stability in a fast-paced and often unpredictable world. West highlights the importance of translating scientifically grounded insights into practical applications to enhance sleep quality. A clear example illustrates the significance of establishing a structure through recurring habits that support long-term sleep improvement.

Teams often form a circle after a match, regardless of the outcome. This circle helps coaches and players to close off the match without analysing it in detail. This enables players to end the day with a positive mindset and to prepare for the next game with an optimistic attitude. It is a routine that has proven to be effective.

Just as players risk taking their problems home after a defeat, employees face the risk of taking their professional or personal concerns to bed. Individual rituals can help release distressing thoughts before sleep and clear the mind, before those thoughts take control.

We have already encountered this scenario when addressing self-regulation. Writing down thoughts or practising a breathing technique can help in processing worries. Your creativity and willingness to experiment know no bounds. Moreover, there are numerous sleep apps offering a variety of methods. If all else fails, qualified sleep experts are available to assist you in developing effective routines for sufficient, healthy sleep.

Establishing Conditions for Good Sleep

Even when there is insufficient time for adequate sleep, we can at least ensure that the available time for healthy sleep is fully optimised. Here, as well, healthy sleep results from our actions and the conditions we establish. The classic recommendations for healthy sleep are as follows:

- A darkened, quiet room
- A cool bedroom (between 16 and 20° Celsius)
- No heavy meals approximately three hours before going to bed
- No alcohol or nicotine
- No caffeine in the late afternoon or evening
- No use of mobile phones or tablets for approximately 60 to 90 minutes before going to bed.

In line with the principles of this book, focus on what you can influence and accept what you cannot. You may already be familiar with the advice from the sleep expert. As previously discussed, it is essential to establish the appropriate conditions, apply scientific insights and cultivate behavioural patterns that support the goal of healthy sleep.

So, what hinders us?

You can probably guess.

Our thinking patterns cause us to view sleep as a necessary evil or an unwelcome interruption – a pause that prevents us from being productive. In fact, the opposite is true – the faster we turn the wheel, the more the ability to regenerate becomes a key competence, as exemplified by the football players mentioned earlier.

Neglecting regeneration prevents us from realising our full potential. It results in poorer decision-making, reduced empathy, diminished creativity and a quicker depletion of willpower. The more employees push themselves to their limits, the longer and more intensive the recovery phases must be. However, this boundary is often difficult to delineate, as it is fluid. Sports psychologist Sebastian Altfeld vividly illustrates this state[91] by comparing it to a sunburn. By the time we realise we have overexerted ourselves, the damage has already been done.

Just as elite athletes benefit from proactive management of the balance between stress and recovery, companies also gain from such an approach. Only through this can long-term success be ensured in a healthy and sustainable way.

Naturally, companies cannot and should not intrude into employees' privacy to the same extent as is common with highly paid athletes. However, what prevents us from enhancing awareness, challenging our limiting beliefs and establishing an environment that facilitates effective regeneration?

Become the CoE for your team – the 'Chief of Energy' – and support your employees in managing their energy levels. This responsibility is ethically and economically significant. In doing so, you will gain valuable insights into how to optimise your employees' energy levels to foster healthy and sustainable performance.

The encouraging news is that an increasing number of companies are recognising their responsibilities and the benefits responsible conduct brings. As a result, a variety of apps and survey tools – from simple to more advanced solutions – are gaining traction, marking a positive trend.

It doesn't have to be complex. At times, a simple enquiry as to somebody's well-being – extending beyond the typical greeting of "How are you?" – is enough. A genuine interest in employees can work wonders. It demonstrates appreciation and helps identify and, where necessary, eliminate or reduce energy drains, fostering healthy and sustainable performance development.

Potential Tactical Errors

Tactical error 91: We overestimate the length of our performance cycles.

Tactical error 92: We neglect recovery phases.

Tactical error 93: We consider breaks as preventing us from performing.

Tactical error 94: We glorify the 'tireless'.

A New Mindset

What Makes a Great Coach?

"A good head coach can improve a team by 10%, while a bad one can make it 50% worse." This is how football coaching legend Giovanni Trapattoni emphasised the significance of the coach – both positively and negatively.

In elite sport, the selection of the coach is of paramount importance. This decision is analogous to appointing individuals to critical leadership positions in business. It is often said in sport that the 'chemistry must be right'. There are often intense debates about whether a down-to-earth coach truly suits a prominent club. Patience with a coach is limited; sometimes they are only given one season. Would a 'great' coach have been a better appointment than the current assistant coach, or would a charismatic coach who promotes attractive football have been preferable? Opinions on appropriate coach selection are as varied as those regarding the performance of the national football team, goal-line technology or a referee's decisions.

If we consider that these endless discussions fail to do justice to the responsible role of a coach, we should take a moment to reflect. The selection of leaders within companies is often even more simplistic.

What is the opposite of black? Is it white? No, it should correctly be stated as: everything except white. Thus, it could be blue, green, yellow or pink. We tend to think digitally, rather than in scales – except, of course, during our annual performance evaluations.

Regarding leadership, our evaluation scale often consists of only two poles: either 'this person can lead' or they cannot. Sometimes, though, we are more nuanced. We might say: "He is too lenient," or "She has a reputation for being tough." Occasionally, we refer to age, asserting that someone is either too young or old for a leadership position. At times, we rely on our familiar thinking patterns: "The young guy is excellent; he's a diligent, hard worker who is willing to go the extra mile." In sport, we would say 'he puts himself where it hurts'. This makes me think of the legendary 2014 football World Cup final between Germany and Argentina, in which the German leader Bastian Schweinsteiger gave his all despite a head injury, until Mario Götze scored the winning goal. At this time, Schweinsteiger was the ultimate example of an 'aggressive leader' on the pitch. In business, we do not use the term 'aggressive leadership'; we call it 'executive presence'.

We often use this term without fully understanding its meaning. We seem convinced that people either possess 'executive presence' or they don't. Many leaders believe it cannot be taught or developed. They simplify their world, which had become too complex, anyway. For leadership, we can get away without any nuances – the common belief is that a person can either lead, or they cannot.

It is remarkable that in business we seldom reflect on the compatibility between a leader and their team. We have just as many leadership archetypes as there are coaching profiles in sport. Perhaps some of these are familiar to you?

The Player-coach

Some of today's leaders may recall the rare player-coaches who brought themselves on for the final ten minutes when the team was losing. A species long extinct in professional sport, for good reason, yet increasingly popular in business. Rather than focusing on, and taking pleasure in, developing the skills of employees – which are neglected – emphasis is placed on the leader as they become the hero.

In companies, player-coaches remain popular among leaders. They typically do not request new 'players', as they secretly await moments when they can take the spotlight. This renders them somewhat indispensable and provides them with the reassuring feeling of still being needed, much like the player-coaches of former times. Occasionally, these leaders are advised to delegate more effectively, yet they are not genuinely supported to do so. If the work is completed and targets are met, that is all that seemingly matters, so long as they do not experience burnout. This type of leader aligns well with our common thinking pattern: they consistently deliver, work diligently and get things done.

The Legendary Player

How many national players do you know who have been genuinely successful as coaches following their professional careers? And how many names come to mind of those who have failed spectacularly? The most renowned example from Germany, Lothar Matthäus, is in distinguished company – spanning across various sports and continents.

In 1969, a book was published that became a global bestseller: *The Peter Principle*[92]. In this book, the authors explore the hypothesis that within every company hierarchy, employees are promoted until they reach positions for which they are incompetent. This phenomenon, observable in nearly every company, is termed the 'incompetence principle' or, as the book title states, the 'Peter Principle'. It posits that, in companies, every position is eventually filled by an employee who is entirely overwhelmed by their responsibilities. Although originally intended as satire, it often contains a significant element of truth. A clear example in sport is the fallacy that an exceptional football player must inevitably be a good coach. Equally mistaken is the assumption within companies that the most successful salesperson inherently possesses the best qualifications for team leadership. It is also misleading to assume that the highest degree in engineering automatically qualifies someone to lead the research and development team. While expertise and experience are valuable, leading a team demands entirely different skills than those that made an individual the star performer. In such a scenario, everyone loses. The company loses its best salesperson and its best worker, and may gain 'leaders' who do not feel equipped for the role.

What, then, motivates a successful salesperson or star worker to apply for a leadership position? Ideally, they possess the motivation to lead and develop the team further, aiming for greater collective success. If this is the case, the future appears very promising.

Motivation, however, often consists of obtaining a better company car, a higher salary or a lucrative bonus scheme. It is no surprise that many individuals strive to advance, regardless of whether they genuinely desire leadership. They simply accept assuming leadership responsibilities. Consequently, it is not always those leaders with the appropriate motivation who advance, but often those whose primary motivation is self-reward.

There is another reason why star workers aspire to reach the executive level, and it again relates to our thinking patterns. These star workers feel compelled to protect their careers, just as the legendary player looks to do when they can no longer keep up, physically. Those who do not prepare in a timely manner for life beyond their professional career will become 'experts' or coaches. The career of a successful salesperson or star worker may end sooner than anticipated. It is therefore important to consider what occurs when they neither apply for an open position nor accept the manager's offer to advance into a leadership role. "Does he really not want to pursue a career?" or "He lacks sufficient ambition" are among the more benign remarks. The star worker shifts from being regarded as 'the best choice' to someone who doesn't warrant further investment. Many of these employees attempt to rise to leadership positions without genuinely feeling the passion for it. According to our rooted beliefs, it appears almost inevitable to conform to expectations and follow the career ladder.

Thus, the 'formerly successful' individuals populate the executive levels, exhibiting little interest in fully developing the potential of their employees. Typically, employees suffer under the leadership of a leader who assumes these responsibilities for reasons other than a genuine commitment to employee and team development. This vicious circle frequently results in unmet expectations and untapped potential.

The Firefighter

The firefighters among coaches and leaders are called upon when urgent issues arise, as the term implies. They are generally coaches who temporarily instil new energy or necessary self-confidence into the team. In every league and in every sport, there are head coaches who have built their reputation as firefighters. They are frequently hired mid-season or later, to save clubs from relegation. These managers are typically experienced, pragmatic and good at quickly organising struggling squads, motivating players, and grinding out results. These managers are typically hired not for long-term projects, but to survive the immediate crisis.

In the corporate environment, such profiles would typically be referred to as 'turnaround' managers. They do not come to stay, but to avert the worst. At best, they navigate the ship back into calmer waters before it becomes too monotonous for them. They are not expected to develop their employees. This concerns bare results – survival itself. Accordingly, firefighters align well with how we like to think about leadership. They deliver short-term, measurable results and perform remarkable feats through their skill in motivation. True heroes, indeed.

The Coaching Leader

The joy of leadership stems from witnessing people achieve more than they ever thought possible. This concept, articulated by leadership expert Simon Sinek, echoes what is frequently expressed by successful coaches at world-class level across various sports. These are not merely empty buzzwords, but a deeply ingrained philosophy that sets exceptional coaches apart from the wider field. It might be assumed that at this level, players have reached their peak and that the focus is on maintaining the stars' morale and refining tactical subtleties. However, this is a misconception, as demonstrated by the significant increase in these teams' market values over the years – even without expensive transfers. Under the guidance of these coaches, not only does the team develop as a whole, but each player progresses within months and enhances their value – regardless of their role.

These coaches pursue two primary objectives: collective success and the joy derived from unlocking their players' potential. They embody the ideas of Sinek, whose assertion underlines the desire to establish an environment that advances the entire team, rather than just serve the individual's advancement as a head coach. Such coaches do not just regard players as athletes but show genuine interest in the person. Players under these coaches consistently report feeling valued, which enables them to accept even difficult decisions[93]. They adhere to the principle that has elevated Belgian football in recent years: "First the person, then the player, then the team"[94]. These coaches succeed in making their players feel unique and empowered, fostering belief in their strengths and the ability to access them even under pressure. They treat their players as if they truly make a difference – and are seldom disappointed. Moreover, they create an environment in which players feel comfortable, develop and deliver peak performance when it matters most.

These coaches are distinguished not only by the typical competencies of top managers, but by qualities more commonly associated with HR experts, as found in many large companies. Naturally, they master their sport and can manage pressure and media attention. What unites them is their passion for the continuous development of their players. They stand on two solid pillars: delivering performance and unlocking potential, ideally in that order. They take pleasure in winning, while simultaneously nurturing their players and teams.

Some began their careers as youth coaches, while others accumulated extensive experience as assistant coaches. There are notable examples in my home country of Germany. World Cup-winning coach Joachim Löw served as assistant coach at Stuttgart and supported Jürgen Klinsmann during his tenure as national coach at the 2006 World Cup. Prior to his breakthrough as head coach at Bayern Munich, Hansi Flick spent 13 years as assistant coach at Red Bull Salzburg, with the German national team, and at Bayern Munich. Similarly, Julian Nagelsmann worked for many years as a youth and assistant coach before taking charge of his first professional team, Hoffenheim. The list of successful head coaches who have honed their craft in these roles is extensive. These experiences have undoubtedly enabled them to evolve into head coaches who understand the needs and motivations of their players, successfully integrating them into the team, without the individuals feeling overlooked. They perceive the pulse of their team, listen attentively, ask insightful questions, foster their players' reflection, and remain consistently curious. Naturally, there are exceptions – Jürgen Klopp, for instance, experienced a more rapid ascent. His passion for identifying and nurturing potential likely stems from his playing career, in which, with all due respect, there was little more to be achieved. Integrating this type of 'coaching leader' into your team requires courage and, above all, patience. This investment typically yields long-term benefits – the success will be enduring.

Naturally, such leaders also exist within companies; we simply need to look more closely. Employee and team development are usually included in the job descriptions of contemporary leaders; however, reality often takes over. As German football legend Alfred 'Adi' Preissler might have said: "All theory is grey – what matters is on the pitch." When pressure mounts or results fail to appear, development plans are abandoned as swiftly as New Year's resolutions.

The manager who can use both feet is a rarity. You have likely already worked out why. Unfortunately, our deeply ingrained beliefs call for a different type of leader. We seek swift results and someone who takes decisive action, motivates the team and is not a 'soft' empathiser. Even more crucial is the ability to market themselves as a winner, which does not necessarily align with the nature of this coach type. They are the unsung heroes of these clubs, often unrecognised for their contributions. Their energy is dedicated to daily training and the commitment to improve every individual and the team as a whole. For these coaches, the result is a natural consequence of their daily work.

Many managers find it more effective to lead in a way that aligns with expectations of the executive level: that is, being result-focused (in reality, rather result-driven), hardworking and pushing employees to deliver. Accordingly, player-coaches, legendary players and firefighters are commonly found at the executive levels. Coaching leaders rarely make their way there – a regrettable circumstance.

So far, we have observed that leadership qualities are often regarded very rigidly, and that the compatibility of the leader and the team plays a subordinate role in the selection process within companies. The appointment of a new team leader often occurs like this: the manager explains their leadership style to employees during the first week, and what does not fit is made to fit. This somewhat recalls José Mourinho's attempt with Zlatan Ibrahimović before he decided to move on. However, not every employee is as highly sought-after as Ibrahimović. Typically, employees adapt in one way or another, make the best of the situation, and await the arrival of the next leader, as this will not be long in coming.

Whether this next leader will be more of a legendary player, player-coach, firefighter or a coaching leader cannot, of course, be predicted. This said, the candidates on the coaching carousel are known. While in sport, coaches who assume their roles due to a lack of alternatives or because of their achievements as players are replaced relatively quickly and often fade into the lower leagues after two or three failures, the situation in business is often different: once a leader, always a leader.

The prevailing conditions in many companies result in leaders being selected not for their motivation and passion, but based on traditional attitudes they perpetuate. For this reason, we should not categorically condemn today's player-coaches, legendary players and firefighters among leaders, particularly as they do fulfil their roles in certain situations. Rather, we should support those who seek to rediscover the joy of potential development, whose fundamental human desire to help others has simply been suppressed. This approach serves the interests of all parties involved and, above all, benefits companies aiming to achieve healthy and sustainable performance improvement within a transforming work environment.

Frequently, today's leaders are constrained by the conditions and beliefs of society. This is precisely why I do not condemn managers who are used to the more traditional way of leading their people. It is our responsibility to positively shape the world of work, to make 'coaching leadership' possible and more likely, today and in the future. Let us chart a course for all stakeholders, rather than perpetuating the same black-and-white thinking as our predecessors.

Potential Tactical Errors

Tactical error 95: We promote employees to leadership positions without examining their motivation.

Tactical error 96: We promote individuals based on past heroic achievements and solid self-promotion.

Tactical error 97: We recognise only one direction of promotion (once a manager, always a manager).

Tactical error 98: We pay insufficient attention to the compatibility between the manager and team.

Tactical error 99: We expect employees to conform to the leadership style of the manager.

Tactical error 100: We promote and demand 'result managers' rather than success coaches.

HR – From Personnel Manager to Performance Coach

Why have most Human Resources (HR) departments so far failed to cultivate these success coaches, to effect lasting changes in mindset at the executive levels, to assist decision-makers in avoiding tactical errors, and to establish a corporate culture that adequately addresses the challenges of our time? In many companies, the three-pillar HR model has been established, separating operational, transactional tasks from the strategic responsibilities of the HR department. However, this model is increasingly viewed as unsuccessful, and new concepts are being discussed to empower the HR function with the necessary effectiveness. It is noteworthy that HR departments have been exchanging ideas for years regarding their organisational structure.

In this section, my focus is not on the operational duties of HR professionals but on strategic HR management; the significance of which, according to numerous studies, is expected to continue growing[95]. I will refer to individuals working in this field as 'HR professionals' or 'HR specialists' – because this is the affectionate terminology used in the majority of organisations.

Originally, this section was intended to be brief, but it evolved into a passionate appeal to the HR community, of which I have been a member. As I articulated my thoughts, it became increasingly clear to me the opportunity HR departments have to sustainably shape tomorrow's world of work. The journey towards healthier and more sustainable performance development will be challenging to realise without the support of HR professionals. The limiting beliefs of today are deeply entrenched, trapping many of us in a hamster wheel. When we speak of attitude and behaviour, we are also addressing culture – a topic that is on the agenda for most HR professionals.

HR in Transition: From 'Human Resources' to 'People & Culture'
Although HR departments have not yet fully determined how they wish to organise themselves internally, many have at least undertaken efforts to drive transformation. Office doors no longer bear the labels

'Personnel Department' or 'Human Resources', but instead terms such as 'People & Culture'. While 'People' is self-explanatory, it has been less evident until now that the development of corporate culture also falls within the remit of HR departments, which certainly makes sense.

Who else should ensure that the 'right' individuals are supported and promoted? Who else should prevent the hiring or dismissal of the 'wrong' employees? Who else should enhance the effectiveness and efficiency of internal collaboration? Who else should ensure that corporate values do not remain lip service, ultimately fostering only cynicism within the workforce? Who else should guarantee that at least once a year, conversations take place between managers and employees that focus not only on project milestones and financial metrics, but on the individual, their goals, motivations and development opportunities? Who else should ensure that all of this is meticulously documented, only to be ultimately disregarded? Who else should ensure that salaries are aligned with performance and do not escalate, unchecked? And who else should ensure that every manager can, at the push of a button, identify their potential successor – at least in theory?

These tasks should ideally be managed by the leaders themselves, provided they operate in a supportive environment. However, as we know, this is unfortunately not always the case in organisations. Often, the 'wrong' individuals are promoted, and these leaders encounter conditions that scarcely allow them to operate effectively on both fronts – namely, delivering results while simultaneously fostering the healthy and sustainable development of their employees' and teams' performance.

HR as a Guardian of the Status Quo
Rather than establishing these conditions and working to improve the 'system', HR specialists frequently operate within the existing system. They compensate for what leaders are unable to accomplish due to their profiles, lack of experience, unwillingness or an unfavourable environment. In doing so, they do the organisation a disservice. It is as sad as it is true – they contribute more than almost anyone else to ensuring that nothing changes, that the status quo is preserved, and that the existing culture is solidified.

In this, they are in good company, as the executive level is often unwilling to examine the corporate culture and infuse it with new life, whether partially or radically.

In most companies, the term 'culture' has become a buzzword – something elusive, expected to develop organically, and occasionally taking on a life of its own in one direction or another. Culture cannot be managed, to the displeasure of result managers. Therefore, it is easier to look away or accept things as they are. If someone does not agree with this way of working, they are free to leave, and their position will be filled by another person.

The problem is that this 'someone else' may have different expectations, perhaps demand a higher salary and prefer to work only four days a week, two of them remotely. Alternatively, this 'someone else' may not exist at all – at least not here, where our office is located. Alternatively, we rely on the principle of hope, believing it will somehow work out. HR will handle it.

This is precisely the misconception. If any function in today's companies is neither empowered nor capable of initiating cultural change, it is the HR department – and I say this with the utmost respect for all HR specialists worldwide who dedicate themselves daily to positively shaping corporate culture, as I have done over many years.

Some protagonists are unable, while others are unwilling. We have discussed at length in this book why some of them are unwilling. Their mindsets hinder them, and the consequential tactical errors entrench habits that are far removed from a healthy and sustainable performance culture.

What, then, prevents many HR departments from effecting change? It may sound ironic, but it is our passion that blinds us. This is the 'reward' for our hard work, our adherence to the system, and our service-oriented mindset. But let us proceed step by step.

HR as a Kitman

In the context of diversity and inclusion, HR specialists often employ striking phrases such as: 'It does not help to be invited to a party if you are not allowed to dance.' Yet, we frequently forget that we are the ones to whom this fate applies. Not because we are black or white, young or old, male or female, but because we have placed ourselves in a position where we are tolerated but not always respected.

The situation appears even more disheartening: occasionally, we are invited to dance – to music we did not choose and often do not enjoy. Rather than having the courage to decline the dance or propose different music, we resign ourselves to our fate and dance until our partner leads us back to our seat. From here, we can observe proceedings from the outside. And when someone passes by with a half-empty beer glass, admitting they do not like the music either, we at least no longer feel alone. The celebration does not improve because of this, but it becomes more bearable.

Many HR specialists become either accomplices or complainers. Neither role is fulfilling, nor is it a worthwhile investment for the company. 'People & Culture'? Perhaps a little 'people', but hardly any 'culture'.

To console ourselves, some of us believe that we would only be missed if we were no longer present. I have heard this many times since choosing to support companies from a HR perspective. Its meaning has never been completely clear to me. Instead, this thought troubles me, as it always sounds somewhat defensive, helpless and frustrating. It appears that many HR specialists are not sure about the contribution they make. The notion that 'others would surely notice if we were no longer here' may offer short-term comfort, but it does not improve the situation in any way.

The Comparison: Kitman or Assistant Coach?
Which do you believe would affect a team the most? The absence of the kitman, who prepares the drinks, washes the jerseys and listens to personal concerns and problems, or the absence of the assistant coach, who occasionally challenges the players, encourages them not to remain in their comfort zone, and consistently emphasises the importance of the right attitude and mindset? Whom would they miss more? The answer is clear – it is the kitman.

When you suddenly have to mix your own drinks, wash the dirty mouthguards yourself, and carry your kitbag on to the team bus because the dressing room key is missing and the showers remain cold, the absence of the kitman becomes significantly more noticeable than that of the assistant coach, whose admonishing words you could go without for a few more days.

Many HR specialists function more as kitmen than as assistant coaches. While this may seem client-centred, it is no coincidence – most leaders prefer a kitman to an assistant coach. The problem, however, is that this mindset keeps the company exactly where it is.

In most cases, HR professionals are only as effective as the leaders they support. Why is this? The influence of most HR specialists on their managers is minimal. They tend to act – or rather react – as accomplices. This is precisely why they would be missed if they were no longer present – just as players would miss their kitman.

In many ways, HR professionals often resemble a kitman. They ensure that the leader shines and, quite literally, looks their best. They deliver documents to the leader and ensure that everything is ready for when the 'game' begins. And when it concludes, they help the leader return to a state of happiness and strength. In the worst case, they clean up the equipment scattered across the office following an emotional outburst.

HR as a 'Cone-setter'

Once or twice a year, HR professionals may assume the role of an assistant coach – though not as a modern assistant coach operating on equal terms with the head coach, rather as an old-school assistant coach who sets up cones and distributes bibs.

This opportunity typically arises for HR professionals when a team meeting is scheduled. Usually, this occurs in the first quarter, when no one anticipates that the 'stretched targets' will once again be missed. Then, it confidently resounds from the manager's office: "Ms. Thompson, we will dedicate the first two days of the meeting to business matters. You are welcome to listen if you wish. On the final day, we have a few hours without a set agenda. Please take responsibility for the 'people aspect'. I am sure you will come up with something. In my previous company, we often engaged in enjoyable activities, perhaps something designed to build trust."

The manager's request often resembles a Kinder Surprise – a combination of excitement, play and chocolate. And who could deny a manager with such sparkling, childlike eyes, this wish? Thus, the team meeting is arranged. Colleagues are allowed to do some climbing or rowing, and if the budget allows, conclude the evening by the campfire or at the hotel bar. This pleases many participants – at least for a day. Naturally, we do not refer to it as a team party but rather as team building, which sounds more professional. Although such events often fail to have a sustainable impact, the HR department has nonetheless delivered. When things go well, colleagues recall Ms. Thompson's dedication at the Christmas party and express their gratitude for her efforts. Speaking of the Christmas party, it has to be held virtually due to unfavourable market conditions. This event is also organised by Ms. Thompson.

Ms. Thompson does not consider this to be problematic. She takes pleasure in supporting the executive level to the best of her ability. She is not alone in having this attitude. Fundamentally, there is nothing wrong with this. So long as the manager fosters the culture he demands, Ms. Thompson can contribute to developing this in a sustainable way. But what if the manager is an unpleasant person? In this case, 'tidying up afterwards' tends to count for nothing.

When I decided to pause my corporate career and step into the world of HR, I contacted a friend who held a similar position in an international company. Since my previous career path did not align with the typical profile of a HR partner, I asked her which job would be ideal for this role. Her answer was prompt: "A nursery school teacher."

I suspected what she meant but did not press further. Instead, I smiled awkwardly.

HR as a Treasurer

The HR department can adopt different roles than we might be accustomed to. It is almost a dilemma: the more the workforce has demanded appreciation and development opportunities over the years, the faster the hamster wheel has turned within companies. The ever-increasing focus on results has led to the introduction and management of more performance-enhancing 'measures' in the form of bonus systems and goal agreements. However, the more energy devoted to increasing employees' willingness to perform, the less time there is to genuinely focus on the development of their potential, let alone to develop and unlock it progressively and sustainably. Leaders, and consequently the HR department, have become victims of their self-imposed conditions.

In order to address the reluctance of result managers to engage in the development of their employees, strict regulations were introduced. Initially, the frequency of employee appraisals was established. Because many managers struggled to fill these conversations with meaningful content and questions, conversation templates and checklists were developed. These measures do not necessarily enhance the quantity or quality of the conversations, but they assist some leaders in overcoming their perceived helplessness. This approach was effective until the advancement of digitalisation (through personnel management systems) enabled the tracking of whether these conversations took place. Beyond planning the 'people components' in team meetings, HR professionals were now able to address critical issues directly. In many instances, however, they acted not as assistant coaches but as admonishing treasurers – some because they were unable to do otherwise; others because they were not permitted.

What remained were processes that continued to grow increasingly complex. Conversation guides that became lengthy and complicated, alongside a multitude of frustrated leaders. On one hand, there were those who would have conducted such conversations regardless, or did so far more regularly than the HR process required. On the other hand, there were those who did not understand the purpose of these measures and, moreover, had a manager who felt the same way.

I do not wish to be overly critical of HR specialists, as it is true that many of today's managers fail to fulfil their role as 'developers' and have not fully embraced this responsibility. The issue is that the efforts of many HR specialists do not foster increased self-responsibility among leaders. On the contrary, team leaders are almost conditioned to wait with their conversations until the representative from the HR department initiates them. Questions beyond the standard protocol? They are frequently absent. It resembles completing a digital registration form. The primary concern is that all fields are completed and pass the plausibility check. The objective is to press the 'submit' button without any red fields appearing. The only thing missing are the images to prove you are not a robot. As you might expect, this fosters compliance rather than commitment. The contribution to sustainable performance development is virtually nil.

We in HR adhere to traditional processes that no longer serve us but instead constrain us like a corset. Strict rules and processes are designed for those who require them, and such individuals seem to multiply within companies almost magically. Conversely, these rules often frustrate and alienate those who would perform their roles effectively without rigid guidelines. HR departments today navigate a narrow, perilous path.

However, as a by-product of this 'monitoring function', HR specialists have ironically acquired an engaging responsibility – they are now the experts in managing these HR systems. They understand which buttons to push and when. Regarding designated low performers, they know precisely where to locate the so-called 'Performance Improvement Plan' on the intranet. Some have even succeeded in translating HR corporate jargon into language that every manager at every leadership level can understand.

And when appreciation fails to materialise despite all expectations, at least one thing is certain: "They would surely notice if we were no longer here." In this way, HR specialists are superior to the modest kitman and treasurer.

This is how we cultivate helpless leaders who are accustomed to being reminded of their responsibilities by their HR specialists, just as they are reminded at home by their spouse to take out the rubbish. Nowadays, most HR departments are reduced to service organisations, preoccupied with justifying their added value. Incidentally, neither the kitman, nor the treasurer, experience this sense of urgency.

HR as a Tactical Coach

Year after year, HR specialists are presented with fresh ideas. Yet, as in other fields, the purported holy grail often proves to be old wine in new bottles. Upon closer examination, many ideas over the last few years are more accurately described as a 'new word' than genuine 'new work'.

On the one hand, we strive to justify our existence; on the other, we experience the euphoria of what seems to be the last straw offered by numerous thought leaders in the form of a new bestseller, an easily digestible TED Talk, or a podcast.

With regularity, such HR topics reach the executive levels. This cycle roughly aligns with the book industry marketing a new 'HR hype', and the speed at which the community of leadership coaches can transform the original book concept into actionable and scalable frameworks to the point of it becoming unrecognisable.

HR professionals then assume the role of tactical coaches, presenting the 'head coaches' with the latest concepts and standards. The longer it has been since the company visibly invested in people development, the more likely the executive level is to heed the advice of the self-appointed standards coach and approve the project. However, having signed up for the project, the 'head coaches' and executive team rarely oversee it, and it can become resigned to the past, much like that new-year gym membership. If the organisation does not evolve, motivation can soon decline, and we can lose sight of the big picture and purpose of our efforts.

Open offices, agile working, feedback culture, psychological safety, OKRs (Objectives and Key Results) – these topics will remain prevalent for some time. However, we should not expect a lasting impact. This is not only because these topics are treated as projects, and the initial enthusiasm quickly diminishes, but because project leaders tend to lose sight of the context between milestones and dashboards, or have never fully understood it.

We avoid the one-size-fits-all approach by distributing the new 'medicine' only to those who need it, without a thought for the executive level. They tend to be too busy and/or believe their learning process is already complete. The fact remains: as long as our limiting beliefs remain unchallenged, sustainable performance development will continue to be a challenge.

Consequently, it rarely takes long before we revert to 'business as usual'. In such cases, the sustainable contribution of these well-intentioned initiatives to performance development is not only negligible but often detrimental. Resources are consumed, hopes are raised, insecurities grown and expectations not met – all of which hinder healthy and sustainable performance development.

In hindsight, everyone knew that such an approach would not succeed within their organisation. What was once the advertising department is now 'People & Culture'. Everyone has a voice and an opinion. All these failed 'projects' serve to fuel the 'know-it-alls'. Consequently, the HR department ends up achieving the opposite of its intended goal. Rather than challenging outdated limiting beliefs, we inadvertently reinforce them.

HR as a Physiotherapist
"The poorer the leadership within business, the more active the HR partners become." This remark from one of my clients caused me to pause and reflect. I had observed similar dynamics. When HR partners

become particularly busy, it is not necessarily a positive sign. It may instead suggest that HR remains the sole entity upholding humanity. "If we do not stand up for our values, who will?" HR often compensates for leaders who do not act in a balanced manner but primarily focus on results. The more overtime is demanded from above, the more HR strives to counter this and support leaders in maintaining their work-life balance. The less appreciation middle-management receives, the more opportunities HR provides to vent frustrations, address complaints and seek emotional relief.

It almost appears as if HR partners deliberately adopt a counter-position. 'Yin and Yang'; 'good cop, bad cop' – call it what you will. Their role resembles that of a physiotherapist in sport, albeit without the massage table. The primary responsibility of a physiotherapist is to restore athletes to full fitness. However, in practice, they do far more. Particularly in environments lacking sports psychologists, the 'physios', as they are affectionately known, undertake much more than merely massaging tight calves. Whether they wish to or not, they listen to the concerns of injured, overtrained or frustrated players. Often, the act of attentive listening by physiotherapists produces remarkable results. Some even assert that it is more effective than the massages or exercises themselves. Others report that players visit physiotherapists primarily because there is finally someone who listens to them and understands them.

It feels good to get everything off their chest – at least in the short term. It provides relief and can lead to greater clarity. It is essential that players and employees have a safe space where they can speak openly; a space in which they feel understood. However, this is precisely the point: they are understood, but very rarely coached. It more closely resembles what a physiotherapist offers.

Naturally, such conversations are confidential. The HR partner oscillates between sympathy for the exhausted managers and employees, and loyalty to their own manager. Although this manager may occasionally disregard certain values, they themselves are under immense pressure. Consequently, everyone feels understood by the HR partner. However, the effect on sustainable performance development is negligible.

What Ensures the Sustainable Success of Transformation?

Following my rather sobering and admittedly one-sided analysis of today's HR departments, let us now examine successful cultural developments. In the next step, we aim to determine the role that the HR department can – and should – assume to pave the way for a healthy and sustainable performance culture. In doing so, we avoid common tactical errors and build upon the insights from the preceding sections. If you work in HR, I encourage you to begin implementation immediately. If you do not hold HR responsibilities, I hope you will forward this section to your HR department, provided you identify with the evolving role of your 'People & Culture' division.

The successful cultural transformations referenced in this book reveal remarkable parallels. One example is German football club SC Freiburg; a club that, despite limited resources, has consistently secured a single-digit position in the Bundesliga standings for years. Athletic Bilbao is a club that fosters unparalleled identification through its unique youth development philosophy and, despite – or precisely because of – its limited talent pool, has been among the most successful clubs in Spain for decades. Belgian footballers have advanced to the top position in the FIFA World Ranking through a so-called 'coaching switch' – a transformation in the attitude of coaches across all age groups. FC Midtjylland and Brentford also merit mention in this book, as both clubs have successfully challenged long-standing myths and limiting beliefs. They not only gather data and scientific insights but apply them strategically to achieve success.

Similar examples have been observed in business. In this book, we have presented two exemplars of other successful transformations. Firstly, there is Netflix with its 'Culture Deck', which did not remain confined to the HR department as its principles were cultivated across all levels of the company. Equally noteworthy is the example of Microsoft and its CEO Satya Nadella, who transformed the company from a 'know-it-all' mentality to a dynamic 'learn-it-all' culture.

The successful initiatives I have had the opportunity to support also reveal four fundamental parallels:

1. A clear definition of success: It was precisely established who one aspires to be and what is worth dedicating effort to.

2. Translation into concrete principles of action: The success factors were transformed into clear, action-guiding principles and behavioural patterns.
3. Leading by example: The corporate culture was not imposed from above but was exemplified by the leadership team.
4. Long-term perseverance: Those responsible demonstrated stamina and consistently remained engaged.

Often, these transformations were preceded by a change in the company's top management. However, there are numerous examples where such a change did not result in a cultural transformation. What accounts for the difference? Among many other conditions, the difference lies in the fact that the 'new' leadership recognised the need for action concerning attitude and behaviour. They did not merely set ambitious growth targets to define the new direction. Instead, they asked themselves: 'Who do we want to be?' They recognised a gap between their envisioned future and current reality, which they began to close gradually and with perseverance.

This gap served as a crucial impetus. They understood that the existing culture, employee attitudes and behavioural patterns would not deliver the success they sought in the long term. For decades, leaders have employed so-called 'burning platforms' to drive change and rouse their organisations from inertia. However, although fear is a powerful motivator, its impact diminishes over time. This often results in a stop-and-go dynamic.

From Ambition to Aspiration: The Crucial Difference

The protagonists of successful cases generally did not require a 'burning platform'. According to Agnes Callard's philosophy, they possessed not only ambition but aspiration. While ambition denotes a desired outcome, aspiration defines who we hope to become. The 'who' represents a powerful motive worthy of being pursued with focus, discipline and perseverance.

Many CEOs possess both ambition and aspiration – much like the numerous athletes we never see at world championships or the Olympic Games. They simply overlook points 2 through 4. Some fail to identify the success factors and translate them into concrete principles of action and observable behavioural patterns. Others are unable to embody the new principles of action they expect from others. Finally, some lose patience prematurely. They stop practising the desired behaviour before it becomes ingrained in the subconscious. In stressful situations, they revert to old habits, causing their good intentions to be short-lived and preventing sustainable development. Athletic coaches often adhere to the slogan: 'Use it or lose it'. With new habits, it is like muscles: they must be used regularly, or they will be lost.

People & Culture: A New Mandate Requires New Content

If HR specialists wish to rightfully carry the label 'People & Culture' in the future (and they should certainly aspire to do so), it is insufficient to serve as a 'kitman' supplying the leaders with their jerseys, as an inexperienced 'treasurer' establishing rules for the workforce, as a 'physiotherapist' helping to heal, or as a 'tactics coach' offering half-formed advice. This is by no means intended to diminish the importance of these vital roles within clubs. However, the kitman's door sign does not read 'Equipment & Culture'. Similarly, the treasurer does not hold the title 'Finance & Culture', the physiotherapist 'Health & Culture', nor the tactics coach 'Tactics & Culture'. While all these roles significantly influence a club's culture, this influence alone does not justify a new, wider professional designation.

Once again: The new designation 'People & Culture' is indeed meaningful. However, for this to be justified, the content defining this role must evolve. Otherwise, unrealistic expectations are raised, inevitably leading to disappointment. Let us therefore review the four steps of successful culture development and consider the role of HR in this process.

The Definition of Success: New Questions for New Answers

The transformation of the German national football team shortly before the 2024 home European Championship demonstrates the critical nature of new questions and a new way of thinking. Within a few weeks, the new national coach, Julian Nagelsmann, succeeded in instilling a renewed sense of identity in both the team and the nation. This was not primarily the result of tactical ingenuity or solely the return of Toni Kroos, who had retired after the 2021 European Championship. Rather, Nagelsmann challenged himself and his environment with new questions and fostered fresh, optimistic thinking – an influence that proved contagious for the team and football throughout Germany.

Naturally, you could wait for a new CEO to take up office and, like Nagelsmann, challenge the mindset of the entire workforce. That would be a straightforward solution, but one beyond your sphere of influence – and therefore inconsistent with the philosophy of this book.

What happens when a new CEO joins a company? Is it their charisma, or their ability to inspire employees to give a little more, to rapidly steer the company in a new direction? Or is it that the new CEO – much like Nagelsmann – poses different questions and introduces new beliefs?

Those of you who have changed companies or departments may recall how, as the 'new kid on the block', you asked questions that surprised seasoned employees. Perhaps you held back out of fear of appearing ignorant. If that was the case, you missed a significant opportunity. It is precisely these seemingly 'stupid' questions that long-term employees often no longer ask themselves. Their behaviour operates on autopilot; their thinking has become rigid. The 'work' that new colleagues undertake during their first weeks is a valuable opportunity for every department to reflect and continuously improve. Therefore, fresh perspectives in manageable doses benefit every company, especially when these new colleagues bring cognitive diversity, meaning different beliefs and perspectives – and are genuinely heard.

The Time is Now

According to a study conducted by the executive search firm Egon Zehnder, nearly 80% of CEOs acknowledge the necessity of self-questioning, reflecting on their blind spots, and pursuing deeper personal development[96]. Only in this manner, according to the CEOs' assessment, can they successfully lead their companies into the future. Executive coaches and sports psychologists apply precisely this approach in their daily work. They assist their clients in challenging entrenched limiting beliefs and encourage them to regard this critical examination of deeply rooted beliefs not as a threat, but as an opportunity – an opportunity to unlock new spaces for thinking and acting.

It remains to be seen how committed leadership is to actively fostering this reflection and questioning outdated mindsets, or whether the observation of Harvard psychology professor Daniel Gilbert will once again prove accurate: "Human beings are works in progress that mistakenly think they're finished"[97].

However, one thing is certain: the opportunity to experiment with new approaches is now – the windows are as wide open as they once were for the pioneers of football when they developed 'counter-pressing'. Coaches challenged the old notion that players must immediately retreat to defend their own goal after losing possession. Instead, the new principle was immediate attack – lasting approximately four seconds after losing possession. Traditional beliefs were challenged to foster innovative strategies.

To enter and effectively utilise new spaces for thinking and action, it is essential to ask the right questions. Those who consistently ask the same questions often receive the same answers. In the pursuit of new answers, we should occasionally shift perspective and pose different questions – just as executive coaches and sports psychologists do. Pose the questions you would expect from the future CEO. Ask questions that encourage reflection and stimulate discussion. Raise the questions you might overhear in the corridors when leadership is absent. Be the coach who introduces new enquiries and thereby initiates developmental processes.

Even if you have been trained for years to be seen as a problem solver, avoid relying on tactical solutions or attempting to impress with expertise or partial knowledge, or philosophising about the latest management practices. Instead, ask the essential questions: Who do we want to be? Or alternatively: Who must we become? Who must we become to remain competitive in the market, retain our best employees, attract new specialists and young talent, enhance workforce engagement, and reduce absenteeism?

Ensure that these questions are addressed and that you are present at the table when they are discussed. Make certain that you are not only invited but actively engaged in the process. You want to participate fully. Assume responsibility for the music, the rhythm and the direction of the discussion. I have observed many management teams surprised by how narrowly they defined success. The definition of success changed significantly when a new perspective was embraced and the collective wisdom in the room was harnessed. In today's world, it is essential to promote diversity and inclusion to make better decisions. The time has come to experiment and apply these insights in practice.

What might be preventing you from doing so? You can probably guess – your outdated understanding of roles. Liberate yourself from your previous role as kitman, treasurer or physiotherapist. If necessary, assume the role of groundsman – you decide on which field the team is allowed to play. Do not be the traditional assistant coach who merely sets up cones, but rather the assistant coach who operates on an equal footing and notices what the head coach does not. Be the assistant coach who gathers information others miss, and possesses knowledge that others lack. Be the assistant coach who supports the manager in making even better decisions.

Would German football have experienced the 'summer fairy tale' in 2006 if Jürgen Klinsmann had been acting alone? Assistant coach Jogi Löw was an essential part of Klinsmann's coaching staff at the time. And there are many other good examples of coaching teams around the world. In many cases, the head coach and assistant coach complement each other so well. Dual leadership or job sharing is increasingly common in business and politics. Given the heightened demands on leaders, this approach is sensible. If you aim to sustainably influence corporate culture, rather than rely on your title, then assume the assistant coach's role is as an equal partner. If you are unwilling to do so, at least reconsider your title.

Do you require a compelling reason for such a conversation? Perhaps you believe that a crisis or a 'burning platform' is necessary. However, this crisis differs from the typical crises of recent years. It is not yet a 'burning platform', but rather a smouldering fire, the danger of which is often only recognised when it is too late. This 'burning platform' presents itself in a different form. It is like a Trojan horse that only becomes apparent when other companies advance, while you remain stagnant. When you lose your most loyal employees to the competition and rely solely on glossy brochures to mislead emerging talent with the allure of past glories. When employee turnover in your company reaches record levels and you are compelled to implement unpopular measures, such as in football, switching from a back four to man-marking with a sweeper. These things cannot be seen in the weekly financial metrics.

The encouraging news is that executive boards have recognised that this is not just a HR issue, but a significant risk to the entire business. This awareness is increasing, although it has yet to be fully embraced across all executive levels. It is time for HR departments to take a proactive stance, rather than waiting for directives to be assigned.

The best time to initiate this dialogue with your executive team was several years ago. The second-best time is now – much like planting an apple tree.

Find the Gap

It is essential to identify which levers need adjustment, or which major challenges must be addressed. How far are you from a 'good' state? Do not simply bring a sheet of A4 to the meeting – the list of deficiencies is often much longer nowadays and warrants more paper.

If your response is, "There is potential for improvement, and we will manage that", and you agree with the outcome of the discussion, then I congratulate you.

However, if you cannot agree with the outcome of the discussion, you have at least fulfilled your duty and should begin searching for a new position as soon as possible. Otherwise, you risk becoming an accomplice to something in which you do not believe. You set up markers and rules instead of making a meaningful contribution to the sustainable performance development of your company. Do not waste your time.

If your executive level recognises that the new definition of success is appealing and intends to pursue this path with the support of HR, then do not plan much else for the coming years. This journey will demand considerable energy. By avoiding the tactical errors outlined in this book, the coming years will yield significant positive energy for you, your executive level and, most importantly, all employees of your company. There will no longer be questions as to why your door sign reads 'People & Culture'.

Identifying Success Factors

The second step involves identifying the success factors that will bring you closer to your definition of success and bridge the gap between aspiration and reality. To achieve this, you must persuasively demonstrate that it is the mindset and actions of the individuals involved that render your organisation effective and efficient. Sustainable transformation revolves around attitude and behaviour. Such changes require time, but prove to be more enduring and impactful than any restructuring or 'burning platform'. Insist on the necessary time, fully aware that successful transformations have typically been initiated by CEOs with planning horizons beyond two or three years. Many of these remarkable leaders remain in their roles for ten years or more – a duration in which attitudes and behavioural patterns can evolve and become so deeply embedded that they become second nature, or, as sports psychologists describe, run on autopilot. This consistency may seem somewhat unusual, yet it is admired in successful clubs, whether it be the long-standing, stable leadership of the club or the continuity on the coaching bench. In many cases, this continuity has been a guarantee of long-term success and sustainable performance development.

Decode and Promote the New Culture

As explained earlier in this book, you do not necessarily obtain what you measure. Rather, you receive what you focus on, what you value and what you tolerate. As Aristotle wisely stated: "We are what we repeatedly do."

To promote the desired culture, you should define principles of action that will serve as guiding frameworks or cornerstones for all stakeholders moving forward. These cultivated behavioural patterns are observed not only in successful professional sports teams. Such principles exist in lower-tier football teams – both on and off the field. However, in many organisations worldwide, it remains surprisingly difficult to clearly define and implement these principles or performance standards. HR departments play a role in this process. Once you have defined 'who' you want to be as a company, it is time to define the 'how'. How do you intend to behave? Which attitudes should be promoted and expected? Which behavioural patterns should be supported, required and valued? Which behavioural patterns are tolerated, and, above all, which are not tolerated? Bear in mind that the worst behaviour you tolerate, determines the culture.

Once these principles of action are established, you should not rely solely on the CEO's influence and communication skills. Naturally, their behaviour will not go unnoticed and will, over time, inspire imitators at subsequent hierarchy levels. It is, however, the responsibility of HR to reinforce and accelerate this effect, generating an irreversible snowball effect, the impact of which will last, long after the CEO's departure.

HR as a Reflection Coach, Video Analyst, Groundsman and Athletic Coach

At this stage of the 'journey', it is counterproductive to continue engaging in tasks such as tidying clothes, setting up cones or enforcing rules. Instead, you should assume roles that significantly contribute to healthy and sustainable performance development.

Adopt the role of a video analyst, as established in larger clubs. These analysts assist coaching teams by compiling game footage to identify both successful behavioural patterns and actions, as well as areas with potential for improvement. Participate in meetings and reflect on your colleagues' behaviour. Analyse not only the outcomes but the manner of play. Do not hesitate to examine the dynamics at leadership level as well. Such reflection is indispensable for driving comprehensive and sustainable organisational development.

Assume the role of a reflection coach, as is already present in some clubs. To foster a learning organisation, support it in the process of reflection. It is a misconception to believe that learning occurs solely from mistakes. The true learning process occurs through reflection on all experiences, regardless of their nature. Provide opportunities for reflection in various contexts and promote it at every level.

Assume the responsibilities of a groundsman and ensure optimal conditions at the 'workplace' – wherever performance is delivered. Identify the conditions that facilitate sustainable performance enhancement and avoid those that demotivate or impede performance. It is of little benefit to the participants if the goal nets are taut and the substitute benches are covered, while the field resembles a beetroot patch and the floodlights on the training ground are not working. A fruit basket or a discount at the local gym are thoughtful gestures, but they are only truly appreciated when fundamental conditions are met. The same applies to cross-departmental cooperation: it cannot succeed if department-specific bonus systems and goal agreements work against it. Identify such limiting factors and address them with team leadership or management.

Act like a proactive athletic coach. Rather than attending to employees only when they are 'injured' (a responsibility typically assigned to physiotherapists), ensure they maintain their ability to perform at any time. Assume responsibility for performance-enhancing load management. Communicate clearly to everyone in the company what performance entails and how breaks, when properly utilised, can have a positive impact on performance. Assist your employees in managing their energy, rather than just their time. On top of investing in mental health first-aider hotlines, proactively support your employees in developing self-regulation.

HR as a Performance Coach

We have now arrived at the core of this book: applying sports psychology approaches to foster healthy and sustainable performance development within companies. Embrace the role of a performance coach by guiding employees at all levels to cultivate deeper self-awareness. This involves being aware of strengths and understanding the impact when these strengths are exaggerated. Equally crucial is the recognition of values and comprehending the potential consequences when these values are compromised.

Support your employees in identifying their thinking patterns and recognising the beliefs that enhance their performance, and those that limit it. Assist them in recognising their own strengths while avoiding potential exaggerations. Act as a protective shield for your team leaders, ensuring that well-intentioned motivational efforts do not inadvertently become demotivating.

Collaborate with the teams to sustain focus and discipline, preventing distractions from everyday matters. Rather than concentrating on colourful PowerPoint presentations featuring value pyramids, encourage the cultivation of habits that can be practised and reflected upon daily. Think ambitiously, but begin with small, concrete steps. Instead of imposing rules, remind teams of fundamental principles of action and performance standards.

Assume the role of a fitness coach as well. Ensure that your leaders and team leaders do not experience 'shortness of breath'. Many change initiatives do not fail due to a lack of willingness, but because of a premature expectation of goal attainment, or because of an impatience for results. Avoid engaging panic mode. Complete the game prudently to the end – regardless of the outcome – as Real Madrid has successfully exemplified for years, or as Bayer Leverkusen demonstrated in the 2023/2024 season. Behavioural changes require time, patience and focus to become sustainable. Ensure that everyone demonstrates the necessary patience and maintains their focus. And do not forget to occasionally take on the role of stadium announcer, to celebrate times of success and the contributors.

Ensure that the new corporate culture is not only read about in office corridors, but that it is felt and visible to all participants. In doing so, you rightfully carry the label, 'People & Culture'. Drawing on the principles of this book, I would even propose an alternative label: 'People and Performance'. However, begin with the actual work, not the new title. Titles are the outcome of work, not the ultimate goal. Titles carry responsibility.

Potential Tactical Errors in HR

Tactical error 101: We only changed our packaging, but not the content.

Tactical error 102: We act as kitmen and treasurers rather than as performance coaches.

Tactical error 103: We work within the system, not on the system.

Tactical error 104: We compensate for a lack of leadership instead of developing it.

Tactical error 105: We operate in justification mode.

Tactical error 106: We sympathise instead of coach.

Tactical error 107: We present solutions instead of posing questions.

Tactical error 108: We prioritise rules over guiding principles.

Tactical error 109: We promote compliance rather than commitment.

Tactical error 110: We accept lip service 'from above'.

Tactical error 111: We lack endurance.

Stop Managing Results, Start Developing Performance

This work attempts to explain what currently hinders companies from fostering healthy and sustainable performance development – and how, through insights from sports psychology, we can identify ways to overcome these obstacles.

Initially, we take a step back to consider the fundamental question: From where should the motivation for change originate? The long-standing formula, 'Success = Talent + Hard Work', which has yielded results for decades, appears – as outlined at the beginning of this book – to have lost its efficacy and sustainability.

Throughout this book, we have illustrated how numerous tactical errors impede healthy and sustainable performance development within organisations. Moreover, we have identified deeply ingrained limiting beliefs that contribute to these tactical errors. Do you recall them?

1. We Play Solely for the Result
We accept that only the measurable result matters. The conviction is: 'We get what we measure.' We become driven by our own target specifications. To avoid missing these, we often resort to panic mode or other short-term measures. This one-sided focus on results leads to prioritising short-term outcomes over sustainable success, and causes us to neglect the important, immeasurable success factors.

2. We Must Motivate the Players
Under the misconception that employees must be constantly motivated, we invest considerable energy in increasing willingness to perform, rather than unleashing potential and increasing self-efficacy of teams and individuals. This mindset overlooks the fact that genuine motivation arises from within and that employees perform at their best when they feel effective and can apply their strengths and abilities.

3. We Run More Than Our Competitors

We glorify going the extra mile and promote those to leadership positions who work hardest for success and prominently display their efforts. This cult of overexertion results in performance being equated with quantity rather than impact. The consequence is a dead end, where increasing amounts of work are perceived as the essential key to success.

These three limiting beliefs reinforce one another, creating a self-perpetuating vicious circle that is difficult to escape – unless these patterns are critically examined with a fresh perspective. It then becomes clear that, in many cases, we need to do less rather than more. We recognise that comprehensive organisational changes or large-scale transformation projects are not required; instead, a gradual adjustment of our attitude and behaviour to the revised definitions of performance and success are necessary. As is often the case in life, small changes can yield significant impact.

Rather than revisiting all tactical errors in detail, the key insights are summarised here. It is important to recognise that many companies deceive themselves when claiming to act in a result-focused manner. This apparent result orientation often culminates in a result-driven mindset that can rely on panic mode to achieve goals. Work is performed faster and more intensively, and processes are suboptimally adjusted, providing the executive levels with an illusion of control. In reality, this is the clearest indication of a loss of control.

Even companies that successfully liberate themselves from the fetishism of goal attainment often fail to act in a truly performance-oriented manner. Instead, they fixate on the results achieved rather than on the underlying performance. Being driven by results has a fundamental flaw: it leads us to concentrate on outcomes rather than on behaviours, attitudes, routines and habits. Such result orientation impedes our ability to achieve better outcomes. Constantly fixating on the scoreboard prevents us from entering the so-called learning zone, and from focusing on what we can truly influence – our attitude and behaviour. Consequently, this produces excellent result managers but not the success coaches we require to unlock potential and to foster a healthy and sustainable performance culture across generations.

What do those organisations do differently that do not constantly operate in a result-driven 'survival mode', but instead deliver results by fostering healthy and sustainable performance while simultaneously cultivating the foundation for success coaches?

On the path to establishing a genuine performance culture, it is essential to accept that results are merely a consequence of our daily actions. Results will follow naturally. This insight provides organisations with the opportunity to focus more on the here and now, rather than explaining past results or planning future ones.

Such organisations have moved away from the traditional definition of performance, which glorifies diligent work and delivering results at any cost. Undeserved victories are not necessarily preferable to narrow defeats for them, as they assess performance based on the quality of daily thinking and actions that contribute to their individual definition of success. This definition of success encompasses far more than outcomes. It provides a framework to distinguish what is truly important. They have internalised that we do not obtain what we measure, but rather what we focus on, what we value and what we tolerate.

This expanded definition of success enables these companies to identify the essential success factors and to direct their energy and attention accordingly. In doing so, they avoid the misconception that everything must be quantifiable, allowing themselves instead to focus on observable behaviour and to reflect on it regularly. They understand that it is not the 'stretched targets' that produce results, but rather the consistent and purposeful behaviour that underpins success. Continuity is therefore valued more highly than activity, and focus is prioritised over multitasking. These companies do not equate the frequently demanded agility with frantic activity. Rather than constantly reacting in 'survival mode', these organisations have learned to respond with intention.

It is a matter of discipline, even if this term may no longer be fashionable. It is not about visibly working harder, nor about showmanship or simply ticking off to-do lists, but about critically reflecting on the contribution each action makes to the whole. The focus is on being the best for the team, rather than on being the best in the team. This, too, is a form of discipline. Consequently, promotions are based on contribution and potential, rather than on heroic deeds or self-promotion.

These organisations have ceased to signal to the majority of their employees that they are average. Developing and unlocking potential are neither elitist nor confined to a select group of 'high performers' and 'high potentials'. Instead, these organisations endeavour to unleash the potential and increase the self-efficacy of every individual employee. In this process, they clearly differentiate between past performance and future potential. Consequently, they are less likely to make the confident more confident, and the humble more humble.

Such companies do not address the skilled labour shortage through costly employer branding campaigns or enticing offers. Rather, they act proactively by investing in their existing employees. In an interconnected world, this approach proves far more effective than any paid advertising. Instead of executing an expensive 'major transfer', they prioritise the growth of their own talents and provide them with opportunities for development.

These organisations acknowledge the uniqueness of each employee and avoid offering a one-size-fits-all training programme. They do not prescribe 'medicine' without prior diagnosis, and take potential side effects into account.

In these companies, observing is valued more highly than judging. The focus is not on knowing more, but on asking the right questions. They do not focus on speaking skills, but on listening skills. Rather than relying on feedback techniques, a culture of growth is fostered in which employees proactively seek advice to enhance their performance.

Employees in such organisations regularly spend time outside their comfort zones – specifically in the learning zone – much like successful athletes. The panic zone, characterised by chronic overload, is consistently avoided. 'Coaching on the job' is not an obscure buzz phrase, but a fundamental leadership responsibility that is just as important as achieving sustainable results. Unleashing potential and developing performance in a healthy and sustainable way is a shared responsibility between employees and managers.

These companies continuously enhance people's ability to perform, rather than expending energy on securing and increasing employees' willingness to perform. They have recognised that they neither need to nor can motivate their employees in the medium to long term. Instead, their focus is on not demotivating their employees. The focus lies on enabling healthy and sustainable performance, not on increasing employees' resilience.

This attitude enables companies to spend more time in the here and now, rather than being driven by measurable objectives and devoting most of their time to justifying past outcomes and planning future ones. They focus on what is truly influenceable and have learned to distinguish noise from signals. Consequently, there are fewer peripheral issues, and the so-called 'shit ratio' – the proportion of activities that do not directly or indirectly contribute to success – is negligible.

This is largely because these companies have recognised the importance of the right attitude. Attitude determines whether our behaviour is purposeful. While other companies often discuss the 'right mindset' without truly understanding its meaning or appearance, these companies actively support their employees in optimising both their actions and their thinking. They cultivate an attitude that fosters success and empowers every individual to contribute to their fullest potential – whether in a meeting with the executive board or on the shop floor. This self-efficacy among employees, in turn, provides the ideal foundation for their learning culture.

Employees within these organisations are conscious of themselves. They recognise their strengths and understand the consequences of exaggerating them. They are aware of their emotional triggers and deeply ingrained values, and have learned to harness their emotions rather than suppressing them or being controlled by them. This consciousness encourages employees to engage in more frequent, future-oriented reflection to facilitate learning.

In the most successful companies, continuous improvement is deeply ingrained in their DNA – not merely an empty phrase on faded posters in the lifts of corporate headquarters. Rather than succumbing to complacency, these companies commit to constantly questioning themselves and pursuing ongoing development. They recognise that there is no final 'completion'.

While many companies continue to promote unsuitable individuals and evaluate them based on a sole criterion, namely, delivering results, these companies have established alternative standards. Although results remain important, the attitude and behaviour of potential leaders have become equally critical criteria. The development of employees and teams is no longer a secondary concern but has become a central success factor. These 'success coaches' do not think in black-and-white terms; shades of grey do not unsettle them, as they are able to think and act along a continuum.

These leaders do not manage their time but their energy – in a manner that serves the whole. Like competitive athletes, they deliberately alternate between phases of performance and recovery, understanding that only through this balance can they fully realise their potential over the long term. They recognise that the former 'career accelerator' – working harder and longer – is obsolete, and identify it as a prime example of a diversity inhibitor. They also enable careers beyond the traditional and overly restrictive career windows. As a result, they possess a talent pool that is considerably more diverse – even without quotas – than that of their competitors. Furthermore, requirement profiles no longer exclude those who, alongside fulfilling work, manage other aspects of life such as hobbies, voluntary commitments or family responsibilities.

These companies are not seeking result managers but success coaches; or to use the Microsoft language, 'learn-it-alls' rather than 'know-it-alls'; the self-assured instead of the self-absorbed; the persistent rather than the activists; and energy managers instead of time managers. They value the quiet as well as the loud, and acknowledge the significance of hard-working and competent individuals who operate behind the scenes. Their leaders not only value success and performance but take pleasure in unlocking the potential of their team and every individual.

Consequently, these companies will achieve healthy and sustainable results that far exceed what is possible through a purely result-focused approach. Rather than expending energy on correcting tactical errors, they invest in value-creating and promising activities. Focus, discipline and a willingness to learn enable them to accomplish more with less effort – or achieve significantly better and more sustainable results with the same effort.

No one needs to sacrifice results and top performance when simultaneously acting in a healthy and sustainable way. These elements do not exclude one another but are interdependent. The foundation for this is an awareness of the vicious circle in which many companies find themselves, coupled with a willingness to question and adapt the underlying limiting beliefs. As in classic coaching or sports psychology, this process of reflection marks the starting point for addressing many of today's challenges – whether it be the perceived generational conflict, the skilled labour shortage, the limited talent pool, the low readiness to assume leadership responsibility, the lack of diversity, the rising rates of illness and burnout, or the absence of desired results.

SCORE – From Thinking to Action

'Simply take action' – this is a timeless piece of wisdom. As Franz Beckenbauer famously said before winning the 1990 World Cup with West Germany: "Go out and play football." The current German national team head coach Julian Nagelsmann conveyed the same wisdom in a more contemporary manner when he stated before the 2024 European Championship: "We simply have to play." In 1990, this approach secured West Germany the title of world champions. Although Germany was eliminated in the 2024 quarter-finals in a tense match against Spain, returning to the fundamentals proved more effective than merely setting a result-focused goal.

This essential point refers to our daily thinking and actions, which we have sought to illustrate in this book with 100-plus tactical errors. You may have found yourself 'caught' in one section or another – regardless of whether you are a leader, managing director, HR manager, employee, co-driver or co-thinker.

However, I am confident that in most cases you are already implementing many aspects correctly and effectively. Otherwise, you likely would not have picked up this book in the first place, nor read it through to the end.

As I stated at the beginning, my intention was not to compile another collection of generic solutions for effective leadership. My aim as a coach and author is to prompt your reflection, specifically where you sense that such reflection is warranted.

Naturally, in some instances, I found it necessary to propose potential solutions. I hope that some of these suggestions prove valuable to you. The focus, however, lies on identifying limiting beliefs that prevent you and your organisation from performing at a higher level – healthy and sustainably.

The solutions will be highly individual for each organisation and person. As a coach, I am convinced that most answers already reside within your mind – they simply need to be brought to light. Perhaps this has already happened while you were reading!

As explained throughout this book, a purely avoidance-based strategy does not usually lead to the desired success and can, in the worst case, prove counterproductive. It is not merely about avoiding tactical errors, but rather about replacing outdated limiting beliefs, attitudes, conditions or specific behavioural patterns with new, more effective approaches.

Therefore, I invite you to take a step forward. Concentrate on the limiting beliefs and tactical errors you have identified as particularly obstructive to you, your team or your organisation. This allows you to explore the underlying causes more thoroughly and develop sustainable solutions.

Below, you will find a simple coaching model that combines established concepts from executive coaching (the GROW model) with a method from sport (the WOOP concept).

As might be expected, I have named it SCORE.

SCORE is formed from the initial letters of the individual phases of the coaching process:

Success: Define your personal concept of success; that is, the
    desired behaviour.
Current State: Describe how you currently behave.
Options: Evaluate possible courses of action that can lead you
    from the current state to the desired state.
Roadblocks: Identify potential obstacles along the path to success.
Execution: Define the specific next steps.

Blanket solutions result in too wide a margin of error – to use the language of sport. This model does not replace professional coaching; however, I am confident it will assist you in fostering purposeful discussions, planning concrete steps, identifying limiting beliefs and obstacles, and avoiding detrimental tactical errors, thereby bringing you closer to your definition of success. If healthy and sustainable performance development is part of this definition, then me writing this book has certainly been justified.

I hope you enjoy putting things into practice and reflecting, because, ultimately, reflecting is like doing – only more intense.

A New Mindset

Extra Time

An Overview of Potential Tactical Errors

Tactical Errors 1–4: pages 24–30
1. We equate success with measurable results.
2. We expend too much energy on goal setting and alignment.
3. We are driven by results, rather than driving results.
4. We neglect important, non-measurable success factors.

Tactical Errors 5–6: pages 30–33
5. We attempt to motivate employees extrinsically.
6. We underestimate the unintended consequences of incentive systems.

Tactical Errors 7–10: pages 33–44

7. We prioritise 'talent scouting' over 'talent development'.
8. We underestimate the 'total costs' of new acquisitions.
9. We expect top performance from day one.
10. We are blinded by previous heroic deeds.

Tactical Errors 11–14: pages 44–51

11. We mistakenly equate increased readiness to change with higher ambition.
12. We overpay.
13. We build teams rather than develop them continuously.
14. We underestimate the importance of team cohesion.

Tactical Errors 15–20: pages 52–58

15. We judge instead of support and challenge.
16. We manage performance rather than develop it.
17. We try to measure what cannot be measured.
18. We classify 90% of our employees as average.
19. We devote too much time to the so-called 'low and high performers'.
20. We reward self-promoting heroism and compliance.

Tactical Errors 21–22: pages 58–63

21. We deduce future potential based on current performance and visibility.
22. We think in black and white. You are either a talent, or you are not.

Tactical Errors 23–24: pages 63–68

23. Our development programmes are too elitist.
24. We select our 'high potentials' too early.

Tactical Errors 25–27: pages 69–76

25. We categorise employees as either 'motivated' or 'unmotivated'.
26. We have an insufficient understanding of our employees' basic needs.
27. We unintentionally demotivate our employees.

Tactical Errors 28–32: pages 76–86

28. We look at the scoreboard too frequently.
29. We resort to panic mode to achieve results.
30. We demand going the extra mile to achieve results.
31. We engage in the blame game.
32. We change our (game) system too often.

Tactical Errors 33–37: pages 86–94

33. We do not know our true success factors.
34. We lack concrete principles of action.
35. We select inappropriate success indicators to evaluate our performance.
36. We consider success indicators in isolation.
37. We convert well-chosen success indicators into goals.

Tactical Errors 38–47: pages 94–111

38. We lack a clear definition of success.
39. We do not have a consistent definition of what is important and urgent.
40. We fail to focus on what is essential.
41. We expend too much energy on things we cannot influence.
42. We allow ourselves to be driven by impulses.
43. We react instead of respond.
44. We are unaware of our disruptive factors.
45. We spend too little time in the here and now.
46. We spend too much time justifying the past.
47. We spend too much time planning and forecasting the future.

Tactical Errors 48–53: pages 111–125

48. We confuse emotion with passion.
49. We are unaware of our emotional 'triggers'.
50. We underestimate the significance of individual values.
51. We attempt to suppress emotions instead of using them.
52. We inadequately utilise the space between emotion and behaviour.
53. We rationalise our emotional decisions.

Tactical Errors 54–59: pages 126–139

54. We lack established behavioural guidelines.

55. We interpret 'tardiness' as a sign of 'busyness'.

56. We tolerate colleagues entering the game unprepared.

57. We lack clarity on the meeting's purpose.

58. We fail to review our attitude prior to a meeting.

59. We fail to use meetings as learning opportunities.

Tactical Errors 60–63: pages 139–147

60. We allow structured employee dialogues to become an annual obligation.

61. We focus on weaknesses.

62. We attempt to make employees fit, instead of leveraging their strengths.

63. We make the self-confident more self-confident, and the humble more humble.

Tactical Errors 64–69: pages 148–161

64. We use data points for evaluation rather than for reflection and coaching.

65. We provide insufficient positive feedback (1:6 instead of 6:1).

66. We focus on feedback techniques rather than on cultivating a learning mindset.

67. We neglect the foundation of feedback – trust and self-efficacy.

68. We underestimate the triggers that cause feedback to be ineffective.

69. We fail to examine our intention before delivering feedback.

The Final Whistle

The so-called 'extra time' in football has lengthened over the years. Some teams use this additional time to remain focused on their match plan instead of acting hastily and resorting to panic mode. They are often rewarded for this and manage to turn the game in their favour at the last minute. This is precisely what I intend to do now, before you conclude and you implement your own unique game idea.

The time has come to express my gratitude to all those who have supported me in their own special way throughout this book project.

My deepest gratitude goes to my wife Svenja, who has always granted me the freedom to pursue my projects. She is both a discerning critic and a devoted supporter. Having such a person by my side is invaluable. Thanks to her, I was able to retreat on numerous weekends to conduct research and write – sometimes in the garden shed, other times with the camper along the Danish North Sea coast.

Special thanks to my daughter Nike, who patiently refrained from 'her book'. Originally, I had planned to write a very personal work for her during my one-year sabbatical. This plan is merely postponed, not abandoned – I promise. Nevertheless, I hope this book can make a modest contribution to a better future in the world of work, from which future generations – including my daughter – will benefit.

I owe my ability to write these lines to my parents, Christel and Frank Draeger. They instilled values in me, exemplified them, and granted me the freedom to find my own path. They also demonstrated that we can remain open to new experiences regardless of age, and even reinvent ourselves when the time is right.

My brother Thomas played a significant role, particularly during the periods when I travelled professionally around the world. Our conversations in his 'wild garden' were often contentious, yet always respectful, enriching and grounded. These moments reminded me of what truly matters in life.

I am grateful for all the opportunities afforded to me throughout my career. I had the chance to learn, experiment, lead and gain experience in diverse contexts. In the process, I discovered and valued various cultures and collaborated with colleagues worldwide, with whom I remain connected to this day.

None of my supervisors who entrusted me with these responsibilities were perfect – and that was appropriate. Their strengths often manifested as weaknesses when taken to the extreme. However, they all shared these common traits: appreciation and trust. They provided me with the opportunity to assume responsibility and grow, over the course of more than two decades.

I would like to extend special thanks to John Galyen, my first manager, who guided me from the United States. He recognised the strategist within me, nurtured this quality and consistently asked which of my projects I was willing to defer whenever I sought to initiate another.

I am also grateful to Jürgen Fischer, who placed his trust in me from the very first day, entrusted me with responsibility, and allowed me the space to make mistakes and learn from them. The transformation of the business unit into a client-oriented organisation was among the most exciting challenges of my career and was even incorporated into my executive master's thesis. Jürgen invested in the development of his team and supported me not only as a manager but as a mentor.

I am proud and thankful that we continue to meet regularly to exchange ideas.

Within the in-house consulting group, I encountered Bendt Joergensen, who was known as a 'hardliner'. His team consistently achieved remarkable productivity gains worldwide, year after year. However, I came to know Bendt in a different light: as a person who advocated for his employees and placed trust in them. In doing so, he exhibited a clear dislike towards a lack of focus and insufficient continuity – values that defined his leadership and the success of his team.

Christina Fuchs, my first manager in Human Resources, granted me the opportunity to establish myself in the HR field despite, or indeed because of, my unconventional professional background. The experiment proved to be both enriching and successful for us. This shift in perspective ultimately laid the groundwork for my book. In particular, the controversial discussions and challenging phases we endured together left a lasting impact on me. Although our professional paths diverged over time, our personal and professional exchanges remain vibrant and inspiring.

I extend my sincere gratitude to all employees whom I have had the privilege to lead over the past two decades. They have contributed significantly to my development and shaped my perspective on the world, particularly on the future world of work. Collaborating with global teams has been not only fascinating but groundbreaking.

I would also like to express appreciation to my clients, who were not only business partners but served as critical 'test readers' of my book. Their feedback refined my understanding and led to new insights.

A special place in my gratitude is reserved for the collaboration with athletes and coaches, who have enriched both my coaching practice and my life. These experiences provided essential impetus for this book. My close collaboration with the Flensburg Academy, the academy of the handball Bundesliga club SG Flensburg-Handewitt, facilitated the 'inside the dressing room' discussions described at the beginning of the book. This initiative, which emerged during the pandemic, connects regional companies with athletes and scientists to discuss leadership topics and foster mutual learning. Numerous ideas for my book arose from these inspiring discussions. Special thanks are extended to Jan Holpert and Johann Volquardsen.

I am also deeply grateful to all professional athletes, coaches, academy directors and experts who generously shared their insights and responded to my enquiries. These conversations revealed many enlightening insights into healthy and sustainable performance development, which have informed my work.

Two networks have significantly shaped my perspectives over recent years. First, the Meyler Campbell Community, a group of experienced executive coaches whose depth and quality of knowledge and experience are unparalleled and indispensable. I would particularly like to acknowledge Emilio Galli Zugaro, who encouraged me to write a book during my sabbatical, as well as Christian Greiser, who provided valuable advice and served as a role model with his excellent book, *Remove, Replace, Restart*[98]. Secondly, I am grateful to the group of sports psychology experts who supported me throughout my sports psychology education in Cologne and beyond, helping me to refine and strengthen my thinking.

I extend my sincere gratitude to friends, relatives, acquaintances and neighbours who generously dedicated their time to read my drafts and provided thoughtful and engaged feedback. Their support inspired me to give my very best. I am also deeply grateful to each of my friends who, over the span of three years, consistently enquired with genuine interest about the progress of the book and never lost confidence in my undertaking.

My profound thanks go to my publisher, Klaus Altepost, who offered unwavering advice and support around the clock and ensured the project remained on track through tireless commitment. I also wish to thank my editor, Carsten Tergast, who was especially supportive during the initial phase of my journey and assisted me in organising my thoughts. Additional thanks go to publisher Samantha Pearce, and editor and proofreader Craig Smith, for their significant contribution to the English version of this book.

The greatest gratitude, however, is owed to my friend Timo Görlitz, a companion from childhood. Our shared childhood ambition to become sports reporters faded before secondary school. When we met by chance during a holiday in 2023, I shared with him my book project and the fact I had been going round in circles for weeks. Without hesitation, Timo offered his assistance. His articles in the programme of our home club had already impressed me, and today Timo is established in corporate communication. Thus, the idea emerged that, forty years later, we would surprise the world with a book, rather than showcasing our talents behind the reporter's microphone. With each section, Timo became my closest companion, advisor and editor. Without you, dear Timo, my writing career would likely have ended just as our dream of becoming sports reporters did – before it even began.

It is finally done, which fills me with pride and gratitude. I look forward to implementing the ideas and concepts that have been introduced in this book.

About the Author

Markus Draeger
Executive coach, sports psychology expert, family person and author

Markus Draeger, born in 1973 in Hamburg, is an executive coach, sports psychology expert and author. He supports individuals and organisations in developing a healthy and sustainable performance culture. His expertise focuses on the development of head coaches, leaders and teams in sport and business. As a keynote speaker, he gives his audience valuable insights on their journey towards healthy and sustainable performance development.

After completing his banking apprenticeship, Markus studied business administration in Germany. He spent a semester in the English football stronghold of Liverpool. Following a brief period at a management consultancy firm, he embarked on a career spanning over 20 years with an international corporation. For 12 years, he held various global marketing positions, during which he not only honed his strategic thinking but gained valuable experience in leading global teams.

Having led and participated in various change projects, Markus completed his executive master's degree in Consulting and Coaching for Change at Oxford University / Saïd Business School between 2012 and 2014, alongside his professional commitments. His key insight: Change must be developed rather than managed. He successfully implemented his master's thesis on 'Market and Customer-centric Leadership' as a member of the leadership team within one of the business units.

Following this successful transformation, Markus was appointed to lead the sales and marketing in-house consulting group, where, as its head, he was responsible for the global digitalisation and optimisation of client experiences for nearly five years – an intense and formative period that confirmed to him that sustainable change can only be driven by the people directly involved.

His curiosity about people and his desire to unlock potential ultimately led to a step he retrospectively describes as a 'game changer'. At the end of 2018, Markus departed from the conventional corporate career path and transitioned into Human Resources. As a HR business partner, he subsequently supported executives and management teams in their personal and professional development. During this period, he also completed a one-year, part-time coaching certification in London. This new perspective transformed his understanding of leadership and collaboration, and opened new avenues for him, providing insight that helped to form the premise of this book.

In 2021, following 20 years in the corporate world, Markus took a one-year sabbatical, which he used to recalibrate his personal definition of success. He enjoyed sports psychology education in Cologne, founded his coaching company, and, ever since, has been equally at home in sport and business. Through his work in sports psychology, he realised that not only change but, above all, performance should be developed rather than merely managed.

Today, he primarily supports head coaches and leaders in defining and implementing a leadership philosophy grounded in their individual values, motives and strengths. He supports teams and organisations in cultivating a performance culture that delivers results – both healthy and sustainable. He has aptly named his company 'Beyond Results', reflecting his belief that results are not achieved by 'hunting' them, but by consistently focusing on the key success factors which often lie 'beneath the iceberg' and do not shine on the surface.

His passion for team sports is no coincidence. From an early age, Markus discovered football. Given his limited natural 'talent' and despite his small stature, he became a goalkeeper. Over the years, he succeeded in compensating for his weaknesses through other strengths. Football provided him with what his other hobby, tennis, could not – a sense of belonging and the opportunity to achieve great things in a team. To this day, he maintains close friendships with his former teammates, as well as with good friends from his youth.

At the age of 25, Markus joined the traditional football club Flensburg 08 and featured as a goalkeeper for several years for the northernmost fourth-division team in Germany. The fact that he was suddenly paid to play football was more disconcerting than motivating for him, but it helped him finance his studies. Even more importantly, friendships were formed here that endure to this day. At the age of 32, he decided to prioritise his professional career and retire from football.

His experience in football profoundly influenced his understanding of leadership. Markus became a proponent of strength-based leadership and committed himself to unlocking potential and developing performance. He firmly believes that this development must be healthy and sustainable. A pivotal experience during his sheltered childhood alongside his brother deeply reinforced this conviction. While Markus was preparing for high school, his father developed depression – a result of chronic professional overexertion. At this time, the illness was still difficult to diagnose, though it has since become more widespread.

In the ensuing years, his parents became his source of inspiration. His father overcame depression, while his mother developed remarkable abilities during this challenging period. Her life-affirming, optimistic attitude proved to be the best remedy. After recovering from illness, his father was brimming with ideas and entrepreneurial spirit, leveraging his strengths to embody his values. At the age of 82, he took part in his most recent start-up competition to date. Maintaining good health ranks very high on the priority list for both his father and mother.

These family experiences profoundly influenced Markus. Like his mother, he enjoys being 'in motion' – preferably outdoors. Alongside his daily morning yoga routine, he regularly goes running or enjoys stand-up paddleboarding with his wife, Svenja.

However, he is not an adrenaline junkie. Thus, running the Berlin Marathon represents the most extreme experience he has subjected himself to. For him, especially in times of uncertainty and complexity, clarity and continuity are the keys to success. This likely explains why he rejects sensational management concepts as well as large-scale, blueprint-style transformations. Instead, he believes in small behavioural and attitudinal changes that cumulatively and over time determine success or failure.

Consequently, he particularly values clubs, athletes and coaches who achieve sustainable success through consistent effort and a clear philosophy, and he has little appreciation for so-called 'elevator teams'.

Together with his wife Svenja and daughter Nike, Markus lives happily in what he considers the most beautiful German federal state, Schleswig-Holstein. In his free time, he enjoys watching his daughter play handball, assisting her in the stable with the care of her horse 'Delilah', cuddling the family cat 'Mucki', or exploring new places in the camper with his wife. His constant companion is his Kindle. Naturally, he also spends time on the sports fields and in the sports halls of the region to monitor the progress of 'his' athletes.

Grateful for the opportunities afforded by his corporate career, Markus does not consider himself a harsh critic of the system. Rather, he is convinced that the world of work of tomorrow can be made more engaging, motivating and healthier by challenging traditional beliefs and establishing new principles. He is convinced that health, sustainability and outstanding performance are not mutually exclusive but rather interdependent – just as in elite sport. He views the perceived generational conflict as an opportunity that CEOs and HR managers, in particular, should seize. Perhaps this is why he describes himself as an 'optimistic realist'. He embodies both the grounded nature of a family-oriented person and the positive curiosity of a coach. His ability to support individuals and teams on their journey towards sustainable success has made him a sought-after expert in sport and business.

Bibliography

Note: The author does not guarantee that the links available at the time of publication will remain accessible online in subsequent years.

1   Hammermann, A. and Stettes, O. (2024) *Verwaiste Chefsessel in deutschen Unternehmen. Einflussfaktoren auf die Karriereambitionen von Beschäftigten – Eindrücke aus dem IW-Personalpanel und der IW-Beschäftigtenbefragung 2023*, IW-Report, Nr.16.

2   Groysberg, B., Schmidt, S. and Flegr, S. (2021) *How 'Small C' Change Can Beat Large-Scale Rebuilding, Harvard Business School*: https://hbswk.hbs.edu/item/how-small-c-change-can-beat-large-scale-rebuilding

3   Walsh, B., Jamison, S. and Walsh, C. (2010) *The Score Takes Care of Itself – My Philosophy of Leadership*, Penguin Publishing Group, New York.

4   Biermann, C. (2009) *Die Fußball-Matrix: Auf der Suche nach dem perfekten Spiel*, Verlag Kiepenheuer & Witsch, Köln.

5   Küpper, J., Tacke, T., Beiderbeck, D., Frevel, N. and Krüger, H. (2020) *McKinsey: The Value Pitch: The Importance of Team Value Management*: https://www.mckinsey.com/industries/consumer-packaged-goods/our-insights/the-value-pitch-the-importance-of-team-value-management#/

6   Haufe (2023) *Zu wenig Struktur beim Onboarding*, Haufe Verlag, Freiburg, https://www.haufe.de/personal/hr-management/umfrage-zum-onboarding-in-unternehmen_80_396926.html

7   kicker.de (2024) https://www.kicker.de/la-liga/titeltraeger

8   Teßmann, L.-J. and Sen, G. (2022) *Denkfabrik Nachwuchsfussball*, Schau ma moi Verlag, Bad Driburg

9   https://www.transfermarkt.de/transfers/transfersalden/statistik/

10   Lyttleton, B. (2018) *Edge: Leadership Secrets from Football's Top Thinkers*, Harper Collins, New York.

11   Haufe (2023) *Zu wenig Struktur beim Onboarding*, Haufe Verlag, Freiburg, https://www.haufe.de/personal/hr-management/umfrage-zum-onboarding-in-unternehmen_80_396926.html

12   Swaab R.I., Schaerer M., Anicich E.M., Ronay R. and Galinsky A.D. (2014) The Too Much Talent Effect: Team Interdependence Determines When More Talent is Too Much or Not Enough. *Psychological Science*, Aug 2014, 25(8): 1581-91.

13   Swaab R.I., Schaerer M., Anicich E.M., Ronay R. and Galinsky A.D. (2014) The Too Much Talent Effect: Team Interdependence Determines When More Talent is Too Much or Not Enough. *Psychological Science*, Aug 2014, 25(8): 1581-91.

14   https://www.ted.com/talks/margaret_heffernan_forget_the_pecking_order_at_work?subtitle=en&lng=de&geo=de

15   Die Welt. (2016, 13 October) https://www.welt.de/sport/fussball/article158742659/Klopp-fuehrt-Gehaltsobergrenze-fuer-Talente-ein.html

16   Herbert, G. and Sierck, J. (2024) *Die Jungs gaben mir mein Leben zurück: Die Erfolgsgeschichte des deutschen Basketballs*, Next Level Verlag, Gräfelfink

17   Köster, P. (2008) *Setzen Sechs. Spiegel Sport*: https://www.spiegel.de/sport/fussball/noten-fuer-fussballer-setzen-sechs-a-543832.html

18   Köster, P. (2008) *Setzen Sechs. Spiegel Sport*: https://www.spiegel.de/sport/fussball/noten-fuer-fussballer-setzen-sechs-a-543832.html

19   Livingston, J. (2003) *Pygmalion in Management*. Harvard Business Manager, January 2003.

20   Düncher, C. (2020) OP-Online.de: https://www.op-online.de/sport/
kickers-offenbach/offenbach-kickers-ofc-bundesliga-u19-a-jugend-
spieler-talent-kader-90011495.html

21   https://www.youtube.com/watch?v=PXQEfVVG9bU

22   Bisselik, B. (2024) Interview 6. September 2024, Interviewer:
Markus Draeger.

23   Herbert, G. and Sierck, J. (2024) *Die Jungs gaben mir mein Leben zurück: Die
Erfolgsgeschichte des deutschen Basketballs*, Next Level Verlag, Gräfelfink

24   Lyttleton, B. (2018) *Edge: Leadership Secrets from Football's Top Thinkers*,
Harper Collins, New York.

25   Pink, D. (2010) *Drive: The Surprising Truth About What Motivates*, Penguin
Publishing Group, New York.

26   Ankersen, R. (2012) *The Gold Mine Effect: Crack the Secrets of High
Performance*, Icon Books, London.

27   Rock, D. (2024) *Neuroleadership Institute*, https://neuroleadership.com/
tools/scarf-assessment/v2

28   Honigstein, R. (2017) *Ich mag, wenn es kracht. Jürgen Klopp, Die Biographie*,
Ullstein Verlag Berlin

29   Assaiante, P. and Zug, J. (2010) *Run to the Roar: Coaching to Overcome
Fear*, Penguin Publishing Group, New York.

30   Abrahams, D. (2013) *Soccer Brain: The 4C Coaching Model for Developing
World Class Player Mindsets and a Winning Football Team*, Bennion Kearny
Limited, London.

31   Biermann, C. (2018) *Matchplan*, Verlag Kiepenheuer & Witsch, Köln.

32   Lyttleton, B. (2018) *Edge: Leadership Secrets from Football's Top Thinkers*,
Harper Collins, New York.

33   McCord, P. (2017) *Powerful – Building a Culture of Freedom and Responsibility*, Ingram Publishing, Tennessee.

34   Jürgens, T. and Gieselmann, D. (2024) *11 Freunde*. https://www.11freunde. de/international/champions-league/die-mutter-aller-niederlagen-a-4dd3 7d4c-0004-0001-0000-000000556988

35   Drandarevski, A. (2021) *Die Anwendung psychoanalytisch-interaktioneller Positionen in der fußballerischen Praxis*, Springer Verlag, Berlin.

36   Tseng, J. and Poppenk, J. (2020) *Brain Meta-state Transitions Demarcate Thoughts Across Task Contexts Exposing the Mental Noise of Trait Neuroticism*. Nature Communications.

37   O'Neil, S. M. (2021) *Be Where Your Feet Are*, St. Martins Essentials.

38   Ferriss, T. (2011) *The 4-Hour Work Week*, Vermillion Sands, California.

39   Covey, S. R. (2004) *The 7 Habits of Highly Effective People: Powerful Lessons in Personal Change*, Simon & Schuster, New York.

40   Jordet, G. (2024), *Pressure – Lessons from Psychology of the Penalty Shootout*, New River Books, London.

41   Ellis, A. (1962) *Reason and Emotion in Psychotherapy*, Lyle Stuart, New York.

42   Kahneman, D. (2011) *Thinking Fast and Slow*, Farrar, Sraus & Giroux, New York.

43   Peters, S. (2012) *The Chimp Paradox: The Acclaimed Mind Management Programme to Help You Achieve Success, Confidence and Happiness*, Vermillion Sands, California.

44   Kossak, T. (2024) Podcast 'Sport im Kopf' – Teamresilienz und Teamdynamik – erfolgreich in High-Performance-Teams. Interviewer: C. Schöpf.

45 Siegel, D. J. (2012) *The Developing Mind: How Relationships and the Brain Interact to Shape Who We Are* (2nd ed.), Guilford Press, New York.

46 Williams, C. and Penman, D. (2011) *Mindfulness: A Practical Guide to Finding Peace in a Frantic World*, Piatkus, London.

47 Rogelberg, S. (2018) *The Surprising Science of Meetings*, Oxford Universities Press, Oxford.

48 Dunning, D. and Kruger, J. (1999) Unskilled and Unaware of It: How Difficulties in Recognizing One's Own Incompetence Lead to Inflated Self-Assessments, *Journal of Personality and Social Psychology*, Vol. 77, No. 6, 1999, 1121–1134.

49 Herbert, G. and Sierck, J. (2024) *Die Jungs gaben mir mein Leben zurück: Die Erfolgsgeschichte des deutschen Basketballs*, Next Level Verlag, Gräfelfink.

50 McCarthy, P.A. (2014) John Wooden and UCLA: A Legacy of Success, *Basketball Journal*, 23 (4), 45-59.

51 Bandura, A. (1997) *Self-Efficacy: The Exercise of Control*, W.H. Freeman, New York.

52 Transfermarkt.de (2024), https://www.transfermarkt.de/yann-sommer/profil/spieler/42205

53 Gallup (2022) *The Human-Centered Workplace – Building Organizational Cultures That Thrive*, https://www.gallup.com/analytics/472658/workplace-recognition-research.aspx

54 Hattie, J. and Timperley, H. (2007). The Power of Feedback. *Review of Educational Research*, 77(1), 81-112.

55 Gino, F. (2019) Cracking the Code of Sustained Collaboration, *Harvard Business Review*.

56 Rock, D., Jones, B. and Weller, C. (2018) Using neuroscience to make feedback work and feel better, *Strategy & Business*, Issue 93.

57   Scott, K. (2019) *Radical Candor – Be a Kick-Ass Boss Without Losing Your Humanity*, St. Martin's Press.

58   Stone, D. and Heen, S. (2014) *Thanks for the Feedback*, Penguin Publishing, New York.

59   Resnick, B. (2017) Retrieved from https://www.vox.com/science-and-health/2016/12/28/14088992/brain-study-change-minds

60   Dweck, C. (2017) *Mindset: Changing The Way You Think to Fulfil Your Potential*, Robinson.

61   Gervais, M. (2023) The First Rule of Mastery: Stop Worrying About What People Think of You, *Harvard Business Review Press*, Brighton.

62   Amorose, A. (2007) Autonomy-supportive Coaching and Self-determined Motivation in High School and College Athletes: A Test of Self-Determination Theory. *Psychology of Sport and Exercise*, 654-670.

63   Amorose, A. (2007) Autonomy-supportive Coaching and Self-determined Motivation in High School and College Athletes: A Test of Self-Determination Theory. *Psychology of Sport and Exercise*, 654-670.

64   Gervais, M. (2024) How to Manage Feedback Like an Olympic Athlete. *Harvard Business Review* https://hbr.org/2024/08/how-to-manage-feedback-like-an-olympic-athlete

65   Bersin, J. (2022) *Irresistible: The Seven Secrets of the World's Most Enduring,* Employee-Focused Organizations. Ideapress.

66   Beer, M., Finnström, M. and Schrader, D. (2016) Why Leadership Training Fails – And What to Do About It, 50-57, *Harvard Business Review*, Brighton.

67   Milner, J. (2023) *The Surprising Truth in How to Be a Great Leader – TEDx Talks*. YouTube: https://www.youtube.com/watch?v=sW_PN3BDa0A

68   Telegraph. (2014) *For Sabella, the brain comes first*. Telegraph Online. https://www.telegraphindia.com/sports/for-sabella-the-brain-comes-first/cid/168124

69   Sinek, S. (2011) *Start with Why*. Penguin Publishing Group, New York.

70   Brown, B. (2015) *Daring Greatly: How the Courage to Be Vulnerable Transforms the Way We Live, Love, Parent, and Lead*, Penguin Life, München.

71   Dweck, C. (2017) *Mindset: Changing The Way You Think To Fulfil Your Potential*, Robinson.

72   Clear, J. (2024) Retrieved from https://jamesclear.com/quotes/the-reason-people-get-good-ideas-in-the-shower-is-because-its-the-only-time-during-the-day-when-most-people-are-away-from-screens-long-enough-to-think-clearly-the-lesson-is-not-to-take-more-showe

73   Groysberg, B. (2014) Headhunters Reveal What Candidates Want. *Harvard Business Review*. https://hbr.org/2014/01/headhunters-reveal-what-candidates-want

74   Sinek, S. (2021, Sept) *The Art of Listening. Medtronic Leadership Lab Cultural Circle*, YouTube: https://www.youtube.com/watch?v=qpnNsSyDw-g

75   Welbourne, T. and Schramm, D. (2017) The Pains of Employee Engagement: Lessons from Webasto to Mediate and Reverse the Pain. *Employment Relations Today*, 17-25.

76   Kline, N. (2015) *Time to Think: Listening to Ignite the Human Mind*. Cassell.

77   Ramachandran, V. (2005) *A Brief Tour of Human Consciousness, Plume*, Penguin Publishing Group, New York.

78   Stanier, M. B. (2016) *The Coaching Habit: Say Less, Ask More & Change the Way You Lead Forever*. Box of Crayons Press.

79   Beckmann, H. and Frankel, R. (1984) The Effect of Physician Behavior on the Collection of Data. *Annals of Internal Medicine*, Vol. 101, Nr 5.

80   Klein, F. (2014) Ärztezeitung, https://www.aerztezeitung.de/Medizin/Burn-out-trifft-jeden-10-Leistungssportler-241163.html

81   Hoeness, Uli. (2019) https://www.welt.de/sport/video203010986/FC-Bayern-Uli-Hoeness-Erinnerungen-an-Sebastian-Deisler-Video.html

82   Spiegel. (2023) Spiegel Sport. https://www.spiegel.de/sport/mentale-probleme-schwimm-olympiasieger-adam-peaty-verpasst-wm-a-0f270456-e8df-4909-95d8-8dce61f1076f#

83   Klopp, J. (2024) YouTube: https://www.youtube.com/watch?v=h-f4yMbvm9M

84   Hornig, M. (2013) *30 Minuten Flow*, Gabal Verlag, Offenbach.

85   Rossi, E. L. and Nimmons, D. (2007) *20 Minuten Pause: Seelischen und körperlichen Zusammenbruch verhindern: Wie Sie seelischen und körperlichen Zusammenbruch verhindern können*, Junfermann Verlag, Paderborn.

86   Hornig, M. (2013) *30 Minuten Flow*, Gabal Verlag, Offenbach.

87   Wiseman, R. (2014) *Night School: The Life-Changing Science of Sleep*, MacMillian, New York.

88   Rosekind, M., Smith, R., Miller, D., Co, E., Gregory, K., Webbon, L., Gander, P. and Lebacqz, J. (1995) Alertness Management: Strategic Naps in Operational Settings. *Journal of Sleep Research*, 62-66.

89   West, A. (2024) Interview 6. September 2024, Interviewer: Markus Draeger.

90   AOK (2022) AOK Gesundheitsmagazin: https://www.aok.de/pk/magazin/wohlbefinden/schlaf/warum-schlaf-wichtig-fuer-koerper-und-psyche-ist/

91   Altfeld, S. (2022) *Das Einmaleins der Erholung*, Lemon Media, Berlin.

92   Peter, L. J. and Hull, R. (1969) *The Peter Principle: Why Things Always Go Wrong*, William Morrow and Company.

93   Greskowiak, A. and Haubrichs, A. (2024) *Der Bessermacher: Von Spitzensportlern lernen*, Herder Verlag, Freiburg.

94   Van der Haegen, K. (2020) *The Coaching Switch*. YouTube: https://www.youtube.com/watch?v=PXQEfVVG9bU

95   Bruch, H., Lohmann, T. R. and Neu, M. (2024) PWC *Trend Barometer: People Management 2030 – Im Umbruch zwischen Technologie und Kulturtransformation*, https://www.pwc.de/de/workforce-transformation/trend-barometer-people-management-2030.html

96   Najipoor-Smith, K. and Patton, D. (2021) *It Starts With the CEO*. Egon Zehnder International: https://www.egonzehnder.com/it-starts-with-the-ceo

97   Gilbert, D. (2014) *The Psychology of Your Future Self*. www.ted.com/talk/dan_gilbert_the_psychology_of_your_future_self

98   Greiser, C. (2023) *Remove, Replace, Restart*, Gabal, Offenbach.

www.ingramcontent.com/pod-product-compliance
Ingram Content Group UK Ltd.
Pitfield, Milton Keynes, MK11 3LW, UK
UKHW021843251025
464349UK00009B/140